"Providing an overview of almost a century c
volume *Apologetics for the Twenty-first Century* m
and C. S. Lewis to postmodernism, the New
Flew's newly found belief in the existence of God. Covering the relevant authors as
well as their ideas and works, Markos writes in a popular, highly readable style that
could be viewed as a conversational journey through each of these topics. Those
interested in apologetics will find several major items of significance in this far-
reaching and fast-paced text."

    **Gary R. Habermas,** Distinguished Professor and Chair of the Department of
Philosophy and Theology, Liberty University

"This is a terrific book. I've read hundreds of books on the defense of the faith in
recent years, and this is a stand out. Professor Markos uniquely weaves together theology, literature, history, science, and philosophy to produce a work of apologetics
that is both erudite and thoroughly accessible. I enjoyed every page of it."

    **Craig J. Hazen,** Founder and Director, MA Program in Christian Apologetics,
Biola University

"It is in some ways shocking that every generation of Christians has to remind the
broader culture that we in fact have arguments and reasons for our faith. But given
the cultural hegemony and intellectual ubiquity of atheistic materialism and the way
it has shaped our understanding of the good, the true, and the beautiful, it should
not surprise us that our antagonists want to maintain that faith and reason are adver-
saries rather than, as John Paul II put it, 'like two wings on which the human spirit
rises to the contemplation of truth.' *Apologetics for the Twenty-first Century* is a readable
antidote to a conventional wisdom that is indeed conventional but not wise."

    **Francis J. Beckwith,** Professor of Philosophy and Church-State Studies,
Baylor University

"Lou Markos has joined the top rank of commentators on the work of C. S. Lewis
and is a powerful apologist for the Christian faith in his own right. His command of
the two great streams of Western thought—Christianity and classics—has enabled
him to develop a winsome, sophisticated, and convincing body of work."

    **Robert B. Sloan Jr.,** President, Houston Baptist University

"Happily, the discipline of apologetics is having something of a renaissance today.
In the mix, it would make no sense to neglect the considerable significance of C. S.
Lewis. He brought about a great resurgence of interest in the defense of the faith.
Louis Markos has done us a great service by posting Lewis's work in dialogue with
the issues of the day, some which were surely contemporaneous with the Oxford
pundit and some coming to prominence a bit later, though still issues he would have
enjoyed engaging. This volume will help readers see how Lewis would have dealt
with the issues of our day. In the end, it will remind readers of the vitality of the
claim that the Christian faith is true."

    **William Edgar,** Professor of Apologetics, Westminster Theological Seminary,
Philadelphia, PA

"Louis Markos is the Platonic form of the Christian college professor. His love of the Scriptures and his broad mastery of the Western tradition of the humanities makes him the model for a new generation of apologists rising from the universities. His lectures have been a great success with students young and old at the university and with the global audience of The Teaching Company. Readers will discover he is just as delightful in print as he is when roaming the front of a classroom."

**Hunter Baker,** Dean, College of Arts and Sciences, Union University; author, *The End of Secularism*

"Louis Markos has proved once again that he is one of today's foremost Christian apologists. Writing with the eloquence and accessibility that characterizes the work of his mentor, C. S. Lewis, he makes the rational case for faith with potency and aplomb. Mirroring the Bible in its structure, *Apologetics for the Twenty-first Century* begins with an "old testament" (part 1) in which the works of those latter-day prophets, Chesterton, Lewis, and Sayers, lay the foundation for the "new testament" (part 2) in which today's apologists defy and defeat the "new atheists" and other fashionable dragons. *Apologetics for the Twenty-first Century* shows Markos to be a twenty-first century apologist of the first and highest order."

**Joseph Pearce,** Writer in Residence and Associate Professor of Literature, Ave Maria University, Florida; author of books on leading Christian writers, including C. S. Lewis, G. K. Chesterton, Alexander Solzhenitsyn, and J. R. R. Tolkien

"Drawing on the rich resources of leading twentieth-century apologists, Louis Markos has crafted a brilliant work of Christian defense. Like Lewis and Chesterton before him, Markos uses his literary wit and scholarly precision to capture both heart and mind as he presents Christian arguments and evidences. Whether you are a skeptic, seeker, or solid believer, your faith will grow as you read this book!"

**Chad Meister,** Professor of Philosophy, Bethel College; co-editor, *God is Great, God is Good*

# APOLOGETICS FOR THE
# TWENTY-FIRST CENTURY

# APOLOGETICS FOR THE
# TWENTY-FIRST CENTURY

## LOUIS MARKOS

WHEATON, ILLINOIS

ISBN-13: 978-1-4335-1448-7
PDF ISBN: 978-1-4335-1449-4
Mobipocket ISBN: 978-1-4335-1450-0
ePub ISBN: 978-1-4335-2465-3

**Library of Congress Cataloging-in-Publication Data**
Markos, Louis.
 Apologetics for the twenty-first century / Louis Markos.
  p. cm.
 Includes bibliographical references.
 ISBN: 978-1-4335-1448-7 (tpb)
 1. Apologetics—History—21st century. 2. Apologetics—History—20th century. I. Lewis, C. S. (Clive Staples), 1898–1963. II. Title.
BT1103.M36 2010
239—dc22           2010014307

This book is dedicated to the ministry of
InterVarsity Christian Fellowship:

for instilling in me a heart for evangelism;
for giving me my first training in apologetics;
for teaching me how to lead Bible studies;
and for affording me the opportunity, at an IVCF Bible study,
to meet the most important person in my life,
my wife, Donna

# CONTENTS

## APPENDICES

# PREFACE

Since the dawn of Christianity, philosophers and theologians from Paul to Augustine to Aquinas to Luther to Pascal have sought to defend the faith from its detractors and to demonstrate that Christianity both "makes sense" and has the power to explain the nature of God, man, and the universe. People who make such a defense are known as apologists (from the Greek word for "defense"), and though no generation of believers has been without them, the twentieth century saw a vast increase in the number of working apologists, an increase that has continued unabated into the third millennium. In this book I will survey both the major apologists and the major arguments that have come to the defense of historical, orthodox Christianity over the last century. Throughout the book, my focus will remain on the more popular (as opposed to academic) strain of apologetics that finds its greatest single source in the work of C. S. Lewis, that is written in lay terms, that does not require previous training in philosophy, theology, or biblical studies, that seeks to find common ground between believers and nonbelievers and between different Christian denominations, and that maintains a pragmatic, this-worldly edge.

After an introductory chapter in which I define what apologetics both is and is not, discuss how the triumph of secular Enlightenment modernism has fueled the recent explosion of apologetics, and give reasons why C. S. Lewis remains the most successful apologist of the twentieth century, I will move swiftly into a six-chapter survey of Lewis's major apologetic works and arguments. I will begin in chapter 2 by tracing Lewis's attempt to demonstrate that both our yearnings for something that transcends the natural world and our built-in understanding of the moral code (what he calls the Tao) are observed phenomena that cannot be explained solely by recourse to natural, physical, or material processes. Having established the centrality of the Tao to Lewis's apologetics, I will go on in chapter 3 to present Lewis's argument that our inability to follow the Tao leads directly to the Christian solution. I will discuss here as well Lewis's most famous apologetic argument: Christ could have only been one of three things—liar, lunatic, or Lord. In chapters 4 and 5 I will present Lewis's answers to the problem of pain and to the modern denial of miracles. In the former, Lewis will help us understand our status as fallen creatures; in the latter, he will help us see that miracles, far from violating the laws of nature, reveal God's greater design. Just as skeptics argue that the presence of pain and suffering in our world contradicts the Christian teaching that God is a God of love, so do they argue that such a God could never confine a person to hell. Chapter 6 will be devoted to explicating Lewis's argument that, given the nature of God and his gift to us of free will, the existence of hell is not only theologically but psychologically necessary. Finally, in chapter 7 I will consider how Lewis championed the mythic elements of Christianity as arguments *in favor of* its universal truth and power. Specifically, I will analyze Lewis's belief that Christ was the myth made fact and will demonstrate, through a brief look at the Chronicles of Narnia, how Lewis was able to unite reason and imagination in his fiction.

Chapters 8 and 9 will be devoted to studying the two major apologetic works of G. K. Chesterton, a man whose witty and literate defenses of Christianity exerted a lasting influence on Lewis. First I will consider how, in *Orthodoxy*, Chesterton contrasts the gloominess and self-contradictory beliefs of modernism with the robust health and paradoxical truths of Christianity. I will then turn my attention to Chesterton's wholly unique survey of Christian history, *The Everlasting Man*. Through a close reading of this classic work, I will show how skillfully Chesterton critiques modern evolutionary thought, presents Christ as the culmination of the ancient world, and defends the church's defense of orthodoxy. Chapter 10 will shift the focus to a third British apologist who shared the wit, imagination, and wide learning of Lewis and Chesterton—Dorothy Sayers. In *The Mind of the Maker*, Sayers offers an intriguing analogy between the triune nature of God and the human creative process that both substantiates the reality of the Trinity and sheds light on the origin of evil and free will.

Chapters 11 and 12 will move the book back across the Atlantic to consider the work of two key American apologists who set the stage for most of the apologetics that would follow. An overview of the apologetics trilogy of Francis Schaeffer will help explain his argument that after the Enlightenment, science, logic, and reason became divided from religion, revelation, and faith. Josh McDowell's highly influential *More Than a Carpenter*, as well as his influential and very American apologetic style, will be the focus of chapter 12. I shall show how McDowell, in all his works, puts a heavy emphasis on biblical reliability, the claims of Christ, and the testimonies of experts and converts.

In the second half of the book, I will shift my focus from specific apologists to general apologetic themes and arguments. Rather than analyze single works, I will borrow more generally from the work of such key apologists as Lee Strobel, William Lane Craig, Ravi Zacharias, Gary Habermas, Alister McGrath, J. P. Moreland, Phillip E. Johnson, William Dembski, Francis Collins, Don Richardson, Alvin Plantinga, and N. T. Wright. Chapters 13, 14, and 15 will all offer different perspectives on the arguments for the existence of God. I will begin by focusing on more classical arguments borrowed from the worlds of philosophy and logic. Next I shall seek out arguments from the world of modern science, particularly the discovery that the universe is not eternal but was created at the big bang. Finally, I shall wrestle again and more fervently with the issue that turns the most people away from God: the problem of pain.

Chapters 16, 17, and 18 will take up one of the key concerns of apologetics: the defense of the Bible as an accurate witness to the work of the divine in the world. First, I will present arguments for the overall reliability of the scriptural record. Second, I will consider specifically the historicity of the Gospels and the claims of Christ. Third, I shall survey the many arguments that have been marshaled to the defense of the most important historical claim of Christianity—that Jesus Christ, after lying dead for three days, rose bodily from the grave on Easter morning.

In the final six chapters of the book, I will zero in on some of the recent developments in apologetics. Thus chapter 19 will contrast Christianity with other world religions and argue for the exclusivity of the gospel, while chapter 20 will expose both the errors and dangers of the growing interest in the Gnostic gospels, an interest evidenced in the success of and controversy over Dan Brown's novel, *The Da Vinci Code*. That the issues raised in chapters 19 and 20 are such pressing ones bears witness to the rapid growth of postmodern thought in America. In reaction to that growth, chapter 21 will consider new approaches that apologists have taken to reach postmoderns who yearn for spirituality but are strongly suspicious of religion, especially "institutional" religion.

Chapters 22 and 23 will enter into two of the major apologetic battlefields of the last decade—the arguments that the intelligent design movement has leveled against Darwinism and then the rise of a new and more aggressive form of atheism. Finally, in chapter 24 I will take a close look at the conversion to deism of the octogenarian atheist philosopher Antony Flew and the book he wrote to document his conversion: *There Is a God: How the World's Most Notorious Atheist Changed His Mind*.

Although this book was conceived and written as a single, unified manuscript, it does incorporate some ideas and passages from my previously published work. Several years ago I published two works (the first a lecture series, the second a book) that discuss, among other things, the apologetic arguments and approaches of C. S. Lewis: *The Life and Writings of C. S. Lewis* (The Teaching Company, 2000), and *Lewis Agonistes: How C. S. Lewis Can Train Us to Wrestle with the Modern and Postmodern World* (Broadman & Holman, 2003). There is, of necessity, some overlap between several portions of those two works and several portions of chapters 2–7 of this book. Readers who wish to explore further the apologetics of C. S. Lewis are encouraged to consult these works. Portions of chapters 11, 19, and 24 have also appeared before, in altered form, as, respectively, "Apologetics for the 20th Century: The Legacy of Francis Schaeffer," in volume 22, Number 2 of *Faith and Mission*; "An Open Letter to Lovers of *The Da Vinci Code*," in the November/December 2007 issue of *Saint Austin Review*; and "Holy Probable: A Review Essay of *There Is a God* by Antony Flew," in the May 2008 issue of *Touchstone*.

I have dedicated this book to InterVarsity Christian Fellowship, but I would like to acknowledge as well the kind support and encouragement of a number of administrators at Houston Baptist University: Robert Sloan (President), Paul Bonicelli (Provost), Diane Lovell (Dean of Arts and Humanities), Robert Stacey (Dean of Honors), and Matthew Boyleston (Chair of English). I would also like to thank HBU for awarding me the Robert H. Ray Chair in Humanities and the title of Scholar-in-Residence, awards that have given me the necessary time and opportunity to bring this book to completion.

# PART ONE

# THE LEGACY OF LEWIS AND CHESTERTON

# 1

# APOLOGETICS: WHAT IT IS AND WHY IT HAS BECOME SO POPULAR

In 399 B.C., Socrates was charged by the Athenian assembly with corrupting the youth and advocating foreign gods. In response, the seventy-year-old philosopher dragged himself before the court to answer the charges leveled against him. His speech before the indignant citizens of Athens was recorded by his star pupil, Plato, and published under the title of "Apology." Anyone who has read Socrates' witty, impassioned, and wholly unapologetic plea will realize quickly that *apologia* in Greek does not mean hanging one's head low and meekly saying, "I'm sorry." It means simply "a defense," and that is what Socrates presented to his accusers: a reasoned defense of the origin of his teaching (he was instructed to do so by the Oracle of Delphi) and of the manner of his teaching (to question all people who claimed to be in possession of the Truth).

Nearly five centuries later, Peter called on his fellow believers to be as bold as—but a bit less abrasive than—Socrates in defending their faith in Christ: "but in your hearts honor Christ the Lord as holy, always being prepared to make a defense [*apologia*] to anyone who asks you for a reason for the hope that is in you; yet do it with gentleness and respect" (1 Peter 3:15). Following in the tradition of Socrates and Peter, the modern Christian apologist neither apologizes for his beliefs nor relies solely on emotion when confronting those who consider his divine calling to be either false or fanatical, delusional or dangerous. Instead he presents—boldly but not harshly—a defense of Christianity that squares with reason, logic, and human experience. That is not to say that apologists believe they can reason themselves into Christian faith, but they do believe that faith can be a reasoned step rather than a leap into the void.

Christianity, in short, makes sense; as a system of belief it appeals to the whole person—body and soul, heart and mind.

## DEFENDING THE FAITH

Though apologists approach their defense of the faith from a number of different angles, a full apologetic must include at its core a defense of the central and defining doctrine of Christianity—namely, that Jesus of Nazareth was not just a good man or an inspired prophet but the unique Son of God. This doctrine, known as the incarnation, holds that Jesus was not half man and half God, but fully human and fully divine. Around the incarnation may be grouped the other essential doctrines of the faith: that God, though One, exists eternally as three persons—Father, Son, and Holy Spirit (the Trinity); that we are all born with a sinful nature and exist in a state of rebellion against God and his Law (original sin); that Jesus' sacrificial death on the cross brought us back into a right relationship with God the Father (the atonement); that Jesus rose bodily from the grave (the resurrection); that he will also return bodily (the second coming); and that all who are in Christ will join him in the final resurrection of the dead. To these key, nonnegotiable doctrines may be added two more: that God is the Maker of heaven and earth; that the Bible is the authoritative Word of God. Many apologists (I among them) would add more qualifications to these last two, but no orthodox apologist would reject them in this form.

These then represent the core doctrines of the Christian faith, doctrines that receive clear expression in the creeds of the church and that comprise the basic tenets of what C. S. Lewis famously dubbed "mere" Christianity. From the time of the apostles, the main task of the apologist has been to defend these doctrines from detractors both within and outside the church. More often than not, this defense has been mounted in the form of a dialogue in which the apologist answers key questions used by skeptics to cast doubt on Christianity. A list of the major questions that apologists since Paul have sought to address would include the following: 1) If God is all-loving and all-powerful, why are pain, suffering, and injustice in the world? 2) How can Christians believe in miracles when events like the parting of the Red Sea, the raising of Lazarus from the dead, the virgin birth, and Jesus' walking on water clearly violate the laws of nature? 3) How can a God of mercy condemn people to hell? 4) How do we know we can trust the accounts of Jesus' life that are recorded in the Gospels? Over the last three centuries these questions have become increasingly more bitter and strident in tone, often taking on the form of outright accusation and ridicule: 1) Isn't the story of a dying and rising God just a myth for ignorant pagans and modern children? 2) Isn't religion just a crutch and wish fulfillment for people too weak to deal with reality? 3) Hasn't science disproved Christianity and shown it to be false? 4) Hasn't the church done more evil than good and inspired more hypocrisy than any other institution in history?

The best apologist will not shy away from difficult questions like these but will address both the questions themselves and the anger, guilt, despair, and confusion that often lie behind them. And he will do something more. He will show that Christianity embodies a worldview that is coherent, consistent, and universal, one that not only answers tough questions in isolation but presents a unified vision that makes sense of all aspects of our world, ourselves, and our destinies. Indeed, one of the main tasks of the apologist is to defend Christianity from competing worldviews—whether they be religious, political, or philosophical—that claim the ability and the authority to define the nature of reality: communism, materialism, secular humanism, Islam, Hinduism, pantheism, atheism, nihilism, etc.

Of course, Christian apologetics does not treat all other belief systems as inherently false. Oftentimes apologists will begin by establishing common ground between Christianity and other monotheistic faiths (Islam, Judaism, deism, Unitarianism). Especially in our own day, many apologists find that they cannot even begin to defend the deity of Christ before mounting a defense of the existence of a single, personal God who is the Creator of the universe and the Author of morality. At other times apologists will agree about the nature of the problem—that guilt must be expiated (paganism); that modern man lives in a state of alienation (Marxism); that we must find a way to control our base instincts (Freudianism)—but disagree about the origin of the problem and its ultimate solution. At its best, the task of the apologist is a deeply humanistic one; it seeks not to abandon the physical, the human, and the ordinary for some abstract world of ideas but to redeem the physical, the human, and the ordinary so that they might be glorified.

Many today confuse apologetics with another branch of Christianity with which it bears much in common—evangelism; but the two pursuits are quite different in their focus and approach. An evangelist like Billy Graham shares the gospel message that Jesus Christ was the Son of God, that he died for our sins, and that we can only find salvation by confessing our sins and placing our faith in the risen Christ. Evangelism comes from two Greek words, *eu* (good) and *angel* (news), which, when translated into old English, become "god-spel" or "gospel." An evangelist, then, is someone who literally spreads the good news (or gospel). Good evangelists will present this good news in a way that makes sense, but they are less concerned than the apologist with presenting a reasoned defense. Evangelism sticks more to the emotional than to the rational, more to the practical than to the philosophical; it seeks a decision that will lead to a change of heart rather than an intellectual assent to a particular or universal truth. Evangelists tend not to argue for such things as the existence of God or the authority of Scripture or the possibility of miracles; they simply take them for granted, focusing instead on their message. Whereas the evangelist is first and foremost a preacher, the apologist is essentially a teacher. The latter works more like an attorney presenting a case, the former like a pastor giving comfort and counsel.

Midway between the evangelist and the apologist are a number of writers and speakers whose main concern is with winning back some portion of the American public to a true engagement with the God of the Bible. Some, like Bill Hybels, Thom Rainer, and Rick Warren, offer guidelines for sharing the gospel with unchurched people living in a secular society who yet yearn for spirituality and purpose. Others, like Chuck Colson, James Dobson, Jay Sekulow, and the late Richard John Neuhaus, are culture warriors who seek to secure a legitimate voice for the Christian worldview in the public square and to revive waning Christian ethical and sexual mores. Like these modern-day Wilberforces, apologists *do* seek to restore the intellectual integrity of the Christian worldview, especially within academia, and there are branches of apologetics that offer a reasoned defense of traditional sexual morality (see, for example, John Paul II's *Man and Woman He Created Them: A Theology of the Body*); but apologetics as such refrains from civil engagement and partisan politics. Still apologetics is essentially "conservative" in its quest to preserve the creeds of the church in the face of "liberal" attempts to strip Christianity of its supernatural elements and its universal truth claims and to replace the Christ of faith with a "historical" Jesus.

Closer to the apologetics enterprise are writers like Mark Noll, George Marsden, and Arthur Holmes who seek to reintegrate faith and learning within the academy and to convince their more skeptical colleagues that Christianity rightly understood does not stifle but enhances the pursuit of aesthetic beauty, scientific study, and scholarly research.

Close as well are writers like John MacArthur, John Piper, and Charles Ryrie who hail specifically and intentionally from within a single Christian denomination and who argue eloquently for the truth of their theological and ecclesiastical distinctives. Although some of these writers—especially those who hail from Reformed Calvinism and dispensationalism—have contributed much to the apologetic enterprise, in this book I will keep my focus firmly on the central concerns of apologetics and on those elements of Christianity that all orthodox believers share.

## WRESTLING IN THE SHADOW OF THE ENLIGHTENMENT

Since its founding, the church has been blessed by a long line of apologists who have carefully crafted philosophical and theological defenses of Christian orthodoxy. Chief among these are Paul, Irenaeus, Athanasius, Augustine, Aquinas, Luther, Calvin, Pascal, and Jonathan Edwards. In the earliest phase of the church, apologetics consisted more often than not of clarifying Christian doctrine over and against the claims of heretical sects like the Arians (who denied the deity of Christ) and Docetists (who denied his humanity). Medieval apologetics—best summed up in Aquinas's *Summa* and its aesthetic counterpart, Dante's *Divine Comedy*—sought to unify all thought under the glorious reign of the queen of the sciences—theology; for them, beauty, goodness, and truth were all one, and the theology of the Catholic Church was the glue that held them together in timeless harmony. They in turn were followed by Reformed apologists who sought to purify the doctrines of the church of later "accretions" and to present a forceful, systematic doctrine that would appeal to people who increasingly judged truth not by authority and tradition but by their own consciences.

Modern apologetics, though influenced by all three groups, is in great part a reaction to the secular Enlightenment's attempt to separate faith from reason and to refound everything, from philosophy to theology to ethics, on rational principles. Beginning in the eighteenth century and climaxing in the two centuries that followed, Western thought increasingly adopted an antisupernaturalist paradigm that insisted that everything could and should be explained solely on the basis of natural, material, physical processes. Henceforth divine revelation and miracles would remain off-limits, at least for those engaged in serious academic pursuits. Though this Enlightenment-born paradigm does not necessitate atheism, most of the major Western thinkers since Hume have treated God as an unnecessary hypothesis. He may very well exist, but we certainly do not need him to explain anything.

Let us consider briefly some of these founding fathers of the modern world. Hume restricted knowledge to empirical observation, encouraging his philosophical heirs to ignore spiritual subjects about which nothing could be known otherwise. Kant grounded morality in the categorical imperative rather than in the Ten Commandments, thus providing human ethics with a rational, as opposed to supernatural, foundation. Darwin proposed a method, natural selection, by which our body could have evolved apart from divine intervention. Freud followed, doing the same for human consciousness, which he saw as rising out of a deep, material unconsciousness rather than descending from the great I AM. Marx reduced philosophy, theology, and aesthetics to economic forces, arguing that religion, the arts, and even consciousness itself were mere products of material socioeconomic forces over which we have no control. Nietzsche did away with Plato's notion of the Forms, arguing instead that beauty, truth, and justice are not divine touchstones but man-made products that shift every time the power structure of society shifts. Saussure robbed language of its transcendent, God-given status, making it too a product of deep structural forces that control our words and our thoughts. And the list goes on and on.

Although the basic teachings of Christ continue to be respected, this post-Enlightenment paradigm has slowly displaced the Christian world-view as the foundation of modern thought and culture. As a direct result of this shift, the traditional doctrinal claims of Christianity have been removed from the realm of objective truth and deposited in that of sub-jective feeling, causing an artificial rupture to form between empirical "facts" and spiritual "values." Slowly, stealthily, systematically, the truth claims of Christianity have been edged out of the academic arena and the public square into a private, airtight compartment. Rather than persecut-ing Christianity directly, as was done in the former Soviet Union, the Western democracies rendered it irrelevant as a vehicle for discerning the truth about the human condition.

True, the majority of Europeans and Americans continued to adhere to the beliefs and practices of Christianity, but they allowed the secular elite to do the thinking for them. The faithful guarded their religious space and left the academy, the public schools, the arts, the media, and the government to fall under the sway of secular humanism. In a sense they "cut a deal": leave us our faith and we will cede reason to you. In return, the secularists cut themselves loose from their moorings in Christian morality and morphed into radically autonomous individuals accountable neither to God nor to the wider faith community.

And then an English professor at Oxford named C. S. Lewis entered the arena. Though by no means the first Christian writer to challenge the Enlightenment split of faith and reason—Cardinal Newman and G. K. Chesterton, among others, preceded him—Lewis was the spark that ignited the Christian revolt against the secular status quo. If it is true, as atheist writer Richard Dawkins once quipped, that Darwin made it possible to be an intellectually fulfilled atheist, then it is equally true that Lewis made it possible to be an intellectually fulfilled Christian while still living in a modern, post-Enlightenment world. Inspired by Lewis, a growing number of apologists over the last half century have sought to defend the intellectual integrity and consistency of Christianity. Without discounting the centrality of faith, modern apologists have set themselves the task of exploding the Enlightenment myth that Christian truth claims have no logical, objective content. Neither reactionaries nor obscurantists, they accept that we live in a secular age and that medieval Christendom is past; but their acceptance only heightens their commitment to guard the rational, universal status of these truth claims against the corrosive forces of skepticism, rationalism, and relativism.

I have already laid out, in the preface, the organizational scheme that I will be following in this book. Rather than repeat that scheme, I will end this introductory chapter by defending my choice to devote six of my twenty-four chapters to the arguments of a single apologist, C. S. Lewis. Here are my "top ten" reasons for doing so:

1) It is no exaggeration to say that every modern apologist has been influenced in some way by Lewis. Whether they were brought to faith by reading *Mere Christianity*, emboldened by his witness, or influenced by his key arguments, the last two generations of apologists owe a strong and enduring debt to Lewis.

2) Lewis was an atheist for half his life and therefore knew the kinds of arguments that modern skeptics most need to hear. Indeed, he once said of his apologetic works that he had tried to write the kinds of books he wished he could have read during his atheist years.

3) Rather than base all of his proofs on the Scriptures, Lewis sought proofs outside the Bible by which he could establish common ground with nonbelievers.

4) He argued both for Christianity and for theism, and he understood

clearly the difference between the two. Though the last two sections of *Mere Christianity* defend specifically Christian doctrines, the first two argue for theistic beliefs that most Jews and Muslims share.

5) Rather than reject the systematic logic he was taught during his atheist years, he took that logic and put it in the service of Christian apologetics.

6) With the courage and tenacity of a modern-day Galileo, Lewis boldly questioned the key tenets of modernism. Rather than confine himself to surface arguments, he dug down deep to uncover and critique the foundational assumptions of naturalism and secular humanism.

7) Lewis, who was an English professor rather than a theologian or clergyman, was always careful to balance reason and emotion. In the apologetic works of C. S. Lewis, the reader encounters arguments from both the head and the heart.

8) Unlike most of his contemporaries in the academy, Lewis wrote in personal, lay terms that spoke directly to his readers. Though one of the most learned men of his age, Lewis actually wanted to be understood. His commitment to clarity has helped inspire dozens of apologists to imitate his crisp, highly readable style.

9) Rather than come up with exotic new theories about Jesus or the Scriptures or the doctrines of the church, Lewis contented himself to repackage the traditional claims of Christianity in a fresh, nonjudgmental way.

10) Though himself a committed Anglican, Lewis the apologist remained doggedly nondenominational and kept his focus on mere Christianity. For this reason, his books are read and distributed by Catholics, Baptists, Methodists, Orthodox, Lutherans, and Pentecostals alike.

# 2

# THE THINGS THAT COULD NOT HAVE EVOLVED: C. S. LEWIS ARGUES FOR THE EXISTENCE OF GOD

Whether you consider him a great world leader or an opportunistic dictator, a reformer, or a tyrant, Napoleon was a man who understood well the consequences not only of actions but also of ideas. Perhaps that is why when Pierre Laplace explained to his emperor the nebular hypothesis, Napoleon responded with a philosophical, rather than a scientific, question: "Where is there room in all this for God?" Laplace's reply ("I have no need for that hypothesis") has proven prophetic in its assertion that the post-Enlightenment thinker can explain all things without recourse to a divine creator or regulator of the universe. As we saw in chapter 1, those who embrace the modernist paradigm feel confident that all things can be explained solely on the basis of natural, physical, material processes.

In the middle decades of the twentieth century, few European academics questioned, at least out loud, the ability of the modernist paradigm to provide evolutionary explanations for all natural and human phenomena. During his atheist years, Lewis acquiesced wholeheartedly with this paradigm, considering academics who brought God or religion into the discussion to be sloppy medieval thinkers. After his conversion to theism (at age thirty) and Christianity (at age thirty-two), however, he began to question the all-sufficiency of the modernist paradigm and the naturalistic worldview that supported it. In such books as *Mere Christianity*, *Miracles*, and *The Problem of Pain*, he identified a number of phenomena in our world that could not have evolved by natural processes alone and that therefore demanded a supernatural source.

## THE ARGUMENT BY DESIRE

"O Lord, you have made us for yourselves," muses Augustine in the opening lines of his *Confessions*, "and our hearts are restless until they rest in
you." Though we are, by nature of our physical bodies, members of the
animal kingdom, there is that within us that which is not and cannot be
satisfied by the natural world alone. Our desires and yearnings transcend
the physical confines of our world and of our bodies, leaving us restless
in a way that no animal has been or ever could be. According to Lewis,
the reason for this strange perpetual restlessness is that we all possess an
inbuilt sense of joy that drives us toward God.

Lewis's own long journey to faith, documented powerfully in his
spiritual autobiography, *Surprised by Joy*, began in early childhood through
a series of seemingly mundane and yet spiritually intense moments of
supernatural insight. When he was only a small child, his elder brother,
Warren, showed him a makeshift toy garden that he had just fashioned
inside a biscuit tin. It was a quick and unlovely affair, but when Lewis
gazed upon it, he was suddenly filled with a sense of moist green places,
an intimation, the elder Lewis felt, of Eden. Sometime later, while reading Beatrix Potter's *Squirrel Nutkin*, Lewis was troubled by what he called
the Idea of Autumn. A third experience occurred when he gazed by
chance upon some words from a book of Norse mythology. As the words
from *Squirrel Nutkin* opened his eyes to the fullness of the autumnal
season, so the words from this book transported him to cold northern
places. In all three cases, the experience itself was swift, but it left the
young Lewis with a sense of longing for something beyond himself and
beyond the limits of his world.

At times Lewis used the German word *sehnsucht* (longing) to refer
to these moments, but he more often referred to them simply as joy.
By sharing with his readers these moments of joy, Lewis the apologist invites us to explore our own moments of joy and to question the
source of our deepest longings. As citizens of the modern world, we have
been taught—consciously or unconsciously—by Freud and his heirs to
interpret our spiritual longings as either a sublimation of more primitive emotions or a product of wish fulfillment. But why and how could
unconscious nature produce in us a conscious desire for something that
transcends the natural world? On the foundation of our *shared* experience of joy, Lewis rests one of his most appealing and original apologetics
for the existence of God: the argument by desire.

Just as the fact that we experience thirst is proof that we are creatures for whom the drinking of water is natural, so the fact that we desire an object that our natural world cannot supply suggests the existence of another, supernatural one. The desire does not guarantee that we will achieve that other world—if stranded in the desert, we will die of thirst—but it does suggest that we are creatures who are capable of achieving it and who were in some sense made to achieve it. We would certainly think it strange if a woman who had lived all of her life in Kansas and had never seen or heard about the ocean or the mountains were suddenly to be possessed by a desire to walk on a beach or scale the side of an ice-capped peak. And yet we do not think it strange that creatures purportedly fashioned by material processes alone should yearn for something outside those processes. Water cannot rise above its source, and if we were indeed the products of nature alone, then we should not be able to rise, in body or "soul," beyond the limits of our earthbound mother.

In the conclusion of his *Reflections on the Psalms*, Lewis, expanding on his argument by desire, offers what I consider the finest apologetic for the immortality of the soul. Is it not odd, Lewis asks, that we are continually surprised by the passage of time? We see someone we have not seen for years and are surprised to see that he has grown; we find it impossible to believe that the children we bore have "suddenly" matured into adults and left us to start their own families. It is not vanity or a fear of growing old that triggers these moments of temporal vertigo. We simply do not know where the time "went" or how it could have escaped us without our noticing it. Given the fact that we have never known anything but past, present, and future and that time is the element in which we live, it is strange indeed that its passage should come to us as a perpetual surprise. Our continual shock at its passage, Lewis suggests, is tantamount to a fish being surprised by the wetness of water. That, of course, would be a strange thing, since water is the element in which a fish lives out its existence. But it would not be a strange thing if that fish were destined someday to be a land animal. If our surprise at the passage of time teaches us one thing, it is this: we were not made for time but for eternity, for another mode of existence in which all abides in a perpetual present.

I would add to Lewis's profound insight that not only time but space itself is finally an alien thing to us. Our mind constantly struggles with the spatial limits of our world, yearning to shatter the physical constraints that hem us in. Why, our mind wonders, can we not move things toward or away from us by the power of our wills? I have often joked, half seriously, that the greatest intimation of heaven that our modern world affords is the remote control—for with it we suddenly possess a ten-foot arm that can magically alter the world around us while we sit motionless in our chairs. If the modernist paradigm is right and we are products of natural processes that "know" only the time-space continuum, then we simply cannot explain our deep and unshakable sense that the twin tyrannies of time and space should have no dominion over us.

Apologists today, following the lead of Lewis's argument by desire, often take a slightly different approach. Borrowing a phrase from Pascal, they speak of all people as having a God-shaped vacuum in their hearts. We try to fill that vacuum with all manner of earthly things, but nothing can quite fill it. Whether we try to fill it with "bad" things like drugs and promiscuity or "good" things like patriotism and mother love, we inevitably find that the aching within persists. Only when we come to understand, as Augustine did, that we were made by and for God and that the emptiness we feel inside comes from a lack of intimacy with the divine do we realize that only Christ—the God who became man—can fill the hole in our hearts.

## ETHICS, RELIGION, AND REASON

Lewis begins his central apologetic work, *Mere Christianity*, by asking a seemingly random question: When two people disagree about something, why is it that they argue about it? Lewis's question may seem innocuous enough, but behind it lurks another observed phenomenon that cannot be accounted for by natural evolutionary forces alone—one that not only suggests but demands a supernatural source.

The only way two people can argue about something, Lewis explains, is if they accept a common standard from which to make their argument; in the absence of this standard, they can only fight. Modernists can hem and haw all they want, but the fact of the matter is that we are, by nature, ethical animals. We know that real ethical standards exist and that we are obliged—not by the law but by our own inner consciences—to live by them. Yes, we break the standards on a daily basis, but the fact that we nevertheless expect other people to treat us in accordance with those standards is proof of their reality and their binding nature. We do not live in a morally relative universe but in a world of shoulds and oughts. Even a self-professed relativist will get angry if someone cuts in front of him in line. And if that other person were to counter that he came from a culture where cutting in line is acceptable, the relativist would surely reject the argument as fallacious.

If real moral and ethical standards did not exist, there could have been no Nuremberg trials after the fall of the Third Reich. The only reason that the court was able to convict Nazi war criminals was because of the existence of two indisputable facts: 1) moral standards exist that transcend nations and cultures; 2) the Nazis were aware of those standards and broke them anyway. We do not put a pit bull on trial if it kills a child, for the pit bull is not a moral agent. But human beings are moral agents living in a moral universe and can thus be punished for making wrong decisions and acting on them. Sometimes, of course, a criminal will be exonerated by reason of insanity, but that is the exception that proves the rule. Our obligation to adhere to ethical standards is primary, and though the moral centers of our brains can be temporarily impaired by mental illness or an overwhelming moment of passion, we as a species are defined not by relativism but by commonly held moral standards.

Lewis insists that these standards are universal and cross-cultural, and to make his point linguistically, he chooses to refer to this universal law code by an Eastern rather than Western word: the Tao. All societies, Lewis argues in *The Abolition of Man*, have a basic understanding of the Tao, and to back up his bold assertion he offers an appendix in which he lines up the law codes of over a dozen ancient peoples from the Greeks and Romans to the Babylonians and Egyptians to the Norsemen and the Native American Indians. When he does so, it quickly becomes clear that all ancient cultures have a basic understanding of what Jews and Christians call the Ten Commandments.

Those who first hear Lewis's assertion of the universality of the Tao will often balk, for modern anthropology has been very effective at convincing us that morality varies wildly from tribe to tribe. But it doesn't. The supposed upside-down morality of isolated tribes in Africa or New Guinea turns out, in the end, either to be largely invented by overzealous anthropologists or to be the result of a fact about our fallen world that is often overlooked. For whatever reason, our world is populated by a small but significant number of psychopaths and sociopaths. Well, what is true for individuals is often true for tribes as well. Yes, there are a few tribes out there who seem to dwell outside the circle of ethical norms, but the aberrant behavior of these sociopathic groups no more disproves the universality of the Tao than the existence of paraplegics disproves the fact that legs were made for walking. Since Freud, our society has suffered from a sort of mental and moral amnesia. We really have come to believe that normalcy no longer exists and that everyone has a phobia or a neurosis. It is not so.

What might be called the argument by exception embodies the strongest rebuttal to Lewis's claim that the Tao is universal and cross-cultural. But there are others. Some moderns dispute Lewis's claim by arguing that the Tao is not a transcendent code implanted in us by our Creator but the invention of charismatic prophets and teachers. In response, Lewis reminds his critics that the true role of prophets and teachers is not to invent the Tao but to remind us of the Tao that we already know but fail to heed. Indeed, those who do attempt to make up their own moral codes are generally false prophets and cult leaders. Even Jesus himself did not "invent" the Law but fulfilled and perfected it.

Other critics of Lewis claim that the Tao is not a gift of divine revelation but a product of natural instincts. Lewis concedes that we have natural instincts for survival, procreation, and so forth, but then asks what we do when two such natural instincts come into conflict. To solve this conflict we must appeal to a third thing (*tertium quid* in Latin) that *transcends* both instincts; that third thing is the Tao. Finally, in response to the critique that the Tao cannot be divinely given since we must teach it to children, Lewis reminds us that we also must teach children the mathematical tables. The analogy is an important one, for math and morality share something in common: the Tao, like the Pythagorean theorem, is not something that we make up but something that we discover.

In *The Problem of Pain* and *Miracles*, Lewis discusses two further phenomenas that not only could not have evolved but that come to us through discovery rather than invention. The first, interestingly enough, is religion. Although anthropologists and other modernists argue that religion finds its true source in an uncanny fear of the unknown that evolved from our natural, primitive fear of physical danger, Lewis says this is unlikely. To equate fear of physical danger with fear of the unknown is to play fast and loose with the word *fear*. Our fear of a tiger is not quantitatively but qualitatively different from our fear of a ghost; the one could not simply have evolved into the other. To put it another way, the difference between the two fears is not one of degree but of kind. And to try to fudge by saying that our fear of the unknown evolved from our reverence for the tribal chief is to put the cart before the horse. The real question is not whether reverence can evolve into a sense of the sacred, but where the reverence came from in the first place.

No, says Lewis, the true origin of religion is to be located in a numinous fear of the supernatural, a fear that is unique to humans—the only animals on our planet who are afraid of their own dead. But that is not the whole story. To move from primitive religions based on fear to more sophisticated monotheistic religions like Judaism, Christianity, and Islam, a second qualitative leap must occur for which there is no evolutionary mandate. True theism does not arrive until the God who inspires in us numinous fear is united with the God who created and directs the Tao. There have been and continue to be both nonmoral religions and nonreligious morality. We encounter the first in pagan cults that mix human sacrifice or ritual prostitution with a deep sense of the holy and the sacred. We encounter the second in Stoics and Buddhists who seek to live a life of rigorous moral discipline but do not worship a God outside of themselves. According to Exodus, however, there was a climactic moment in the history of religion when the God who thundered on Mount Sinai, provoking abject fear in the people of Israel, revealed himself to be the same God who gave to Moses the tablets of the Law.

Religion then, Lewis argues, demands a supernatural source, but then so do science and the rational principles upon which science rests. For the modern naturalist who considers evolution to be an all-sufficient explanation, nature is the whole show, a total system that can account for everything that is; no other explanation is needed. But if that is true, Lewis reminds us, then naturalism, which expresses itself through laws and principles that transcend nature, is itself self-refuting. Just as no one can say absolutely that everything is relative, so the scientific and philosophical statements of the naturalists are rendered meaningless by the naturalist claim that our minds are the mere products of a random movement of atoms.

Human reason rests not on empirical observations but on abstract principles that lie outside the system of nature in a supernatural realm of eternal oughts and givens. Indeed, our reason so transcends nature that, by use of our reason, we can alter nature herself. True, animals can make simple cause-effect (inductive) connections ("when the bell rings, I will be fed"), but they can go no further. Only humans can make logical (deductive) leaps based on the existence of preexisting (*a priori*) principles that lie outside of nature. Indeed, the seemingly empirical statement, "if I study nature, I will discern her laws," rests upon our prior knowledge that nature is real and ordered and that we can trust our senses and our reason.

Within each one of us, Lewis concludes, there must exist a super-natural entity called reason. Yet that supernatural reason must itself have a greater supernatural source since our reason often sleeps and can be impaired by such physical substances as alcohol. Lewis's answer to this logical conundrum is that behind and above our limited, individual self-consciousness ("I") there must lie a greater, eternal Self-consciousness (I AM). Remove the I AM—the name by which God revealed himself to Moses at Sinai—and the human "I" loses both its origin and its ability to sustain itself. For consciousness, like joy, morality, and religion, is ulti-mately a gift from above. The modernist evolutionary paradigm cannot account for it.

# 3

# FROM THEISM TO CHRISTIANITY: C. S. LEWIS'S CASE FOR CHRIST

In the previous chapter, we saw that Lewis's argument by desire, his claim that the Tao is universal and cross-cultural, and his contention that religion and reason could not have evolved by natural processes alone all point to a supernatural Being or Force who dwells outside the confines of our space-time continuum. But what kind of a God *is* this Being/Force? What proof do we have that the divine Source of joy, morality, religion, and reason is equivalent to the God of the Bible?

In *Mere Christianity* Lewis argues that once we accept the existence of god(s), we are left with two competing versions of what god is like: either he transcends nature (theism proper) or he is immanent in nature (pantheism). In the former scenario, God dwells above and apart from his creation; in the latter, he lives in and through his creation and has no separate existence apart from it. Though both options may seem at first to be equally valid, only the former is compatible with our experience of the Tao. Only a God who is separate from his creation can function as the Guide and Embodiment of pure moral goodness. If pantheism is correct and God is indistinguishable from his creation, then he can be neither good nor evil—he can only be an amoral spiritual force. In pantheistic religions, the gods do not live outside time and space but are themselves born out of the primal (material) chaos; they do not embody either a holy or universal standard and thus cannot serve as the source of our idea of the good.

But what if, Lewis suggests, the dualists are right and there are not one but two gods: a good god who is perpetually at war with an equal and opposite bad god. This option also sounds reasonable until we realize that it runs into the same problem as the argument that the Tao is a product of natural instincts—namely, the problem of the third thing (the *tertium quid*). If the two powers are equally strong, then how can we say which *is* the good one? In the absence of a higher standard (a *tertium quid*) by which to judge the two competing powers, we cannot determine which is good and which is evil. In that case, the Tao is lost, and we are left to rely on might makes right—on fighting rather than quarreling.

No, concludes Lewis, the most rational option is that the Source of the Tao is a single good transcendent God who created the world but is not himself a part of it—precisely the God who is described in the Bible.

But if that is the case, we must ask, then why is there evil in the world? Oddly enough, the short answer to that question provides yet another proof for the existence of the God of the Bible. Moderns complain that there is so much evil and injustice in the world, but they forget that the only way we can call something "evil" or "unjust" is if we have some "good" or "just" standard against which to measure it. If we were not created by a good God but were merely the product of an amoral process of natural selection (survival of the fittest), then we would not know the world is filled with evil and injustice. How could primitive man, gazing daily on the suffering around him, have ever invented a good God? We cannot call a line crooked, Lewis reminds us, unless we know what a straight line is.

That is the short response to the presence of evil in our world. The long response, as Lewis develops it in *Mere Christianity* and his other apologetic works, provides the map that can lead us from theism to Christianity.

## PROBLEM AND SOLUTION

According to the Bible and to Christian theology, evil is not a positive entity but a parasite, a cancer, a perversion of goodness. St. Augustine calls evil a negation or privation of goodness. Evil is like a tear in a shirt; apart from the shirt itself, the tear has no existence. Even Satan is not a figure of "pure" evil; rather, he is a fallen angel who was created good but chose to disobey and rebel against his Maker. Indeed, Lewis explains, while good can grow toward perfection, evil can never succeed in becoming perfectly evil; if Satan ever were to become "pure" evil, he would cease to exist.

It is for this reason that Christianity ultimately rejects the popular Asian concept of yin/yang: dark with a seed of light in it, combined with light with a seed of dark in it. Yes, evil/darkness does have a seed of goodness/light within it—otherwise it could not exist at all—but God's light is pure and uncorrupted. If we confine our vision only to our fallen world, where all goodness has been corrupted by sin, then perhaps we can ascribe some truth to yin/yang; however, once we raise our vision beyond our world, we must circumscribe yin/yang within the perfect goodness and light of God—apart from which yin and yang, goodness and evil, light and dark become ultimately meaningless terms. It is, incidentally, significant that Chinese philosophy itself recognizes something higher than yin and yang: the ineffable, primordial Way or Tao. Lewis, it seems, chose his terms well! If even the pantheistic proponents of yin/yang can recognize a supernatural force that transcends our amoral world, then truly the word *Tao* is a fit designation for the universal, cross-cultural moral code.

No matter when or where we were born, no matter the culture or religion in which we were raised, there are two truths of which we are all conscious: 1) we should live in a certain way; 2) we fail to live as we should. Genesis tells us that man was created in God's image and at first dwelled in a state of innocence, but that we disobeyed our Creator and fell into sin. Is it really necessary to "prove" this key theological doctrine? Are we not all aware both of the evil in our world and of our own failure to keep the Tao? And the same holds true for those who reject the binding nature of the Tao. If we cannot even follow our own man-made laws—and no honest person can claim even to have followed his own personal moral code—then how can we follow the higher Law that transcends individuals and cultures and whose Director is God?

In one sense, Lewis argues, all religions are conscious of the fact that we not only live in violation of the Tao, but also are ultimately incapable of fulfilling it. And yet, though all religions, and all people, know that we can't fulfill the Tao, only Christianity really takes this problem seriously. Whereas all other religions, in one way or another, say that we can't follow the Tao but then instruct us to try anyway, Christianity accepts fully our human inability and seeks instead a divine remedy. By accepting, *really* accepting, the problem—that we exist in a state of rebellion against and separation from the Director of the Tao and that we cannot return to a right relationship with God by adherence to the Tao—Christianity alone leads us to the necessary and inevitable solution.

Nearly all religions, and nearly all people, accept and hail Jesus as a good moral teacher who, in his Sermon on the Mount and other teachings, laid down the fullest and most perfect expression of the Tao. But if that is all that Jesus was (and is), then we don't really need him; he is superfluous. Since no one, apart from Jesus, has ever kept or will ever keep the Tao, Jesus' presentation of the Tao, no matter how perfect, cannot bring us back into a right relationship with the Director of the Tao. Our world has provided us with any number of good moral teachers—Moses, Buddha, Muhammad, Confucius, Gandhi, the Dalai Lama. Our problem is not that we are ignorant of the Tao but that, knowing the Tao, we break it nonetheless.

Christianity, says Lewis, has *nothing* to say to us until we realize our true status vis-à-vis God and the Tao. "We are not merely imperfect creatures who must be improved," writes Lewis in chapter 6 of *The Problem of Pain*; "we are rebels . . . who must lay down our arms." Only once we accept that Jesus as merely a moral teacher is incapable of saving us from our inability to follow the Tao will we realize the greater purpose that brought Jesus to our fallen earth. Christ's main mission, explains Lewis in *Mere Christianity*, was not to teach but to invade. Our earth is enemy-occupied territory, and the story of Christianity is the story of how the good King has landed in disguise and is calling followers to his side. Christianity begins not with moral effort but with a humble confession that we cannot satisfy the requirements of the Tao and with a surrender of our whole selves to Christ. Christ is God in human form; through his suffering and death on the cross, he brought us back into a right relationship with God (the atonement). Though he resists defining the exact nature of the atonement, Lewis explains that Christ, by truly dying and rising, empowered us to participate vicariously in his death and resurrection.

Christianity means far more than acquiring a get-out-of-hell-free card. True, it begins by saving us from the spiritual consequences of our sin, but its final goal is to draw us into the very presence of God. Salvation, explains Lewis, means nothing less than participating in the eternal life of God—not in some generic spiritual force or One Soul, but in the dynamic life and joy that exists within the Trinity: Father, Son, and Holy Spirit. When the Bible says that God is love, it does not mean that he is the Platonic form of love—Love with a capital L—but that God is love in action. For all eternity, Lewis (after Augustine) explains in *Mere Christianity*, the Father has loved the Son, and the Son has loved the Father; and that Love is so real, so dynamic that the Love is *also* a person: the Holy Spirit. To enable us to participate in that Love, Christ did not think it an ignoble thing to be rejected, beaten, and crucified on a cross.

For only by defeating death and sin in the flesh of a man was God able to redeem humanity and draw it upward into glory.

To help make this most wondrous and sublime aspect of Christian theology more clear, Lewis distinguishes between two kinds of life: the animal life that all living things possess but that will one day run out (*bios* in Greek) and the eternal, indestructible life that only exists within the loving dance of the Trinity (*zoe* in Greek). Salvation does not mean gaining more *bios* but having our *bios* killed and replaced by *zoe*. The promise of Christ is not that we will be resuscitated from the dead (as was Lazarus) but that we will triumph *through* death to share in the resurrection life of Christ. Or, to put it another way, salvation is less like a good man becoming a saintly man than it is like a statue coming to life.

Lewis also describes this process as a change in status from made creatures to begotten sons. Whereas an artist might make (or create) a statue that resembles her in some way but is still qualitatively distinct from her, she begets a child who shares in her essential nature. In a similar way, whereas we are creatures made in God's image, Jesus, the only-begotten Son of God, shares fully in the divine nature. When, through the mediation of Christ's life, death, and resurrection, we are brought back into a right relationship with God, he literally adopts us into his family and allows us to share in the life of his only-begotten Son. Though we will not be God, this powerful doctrine, known to Orthodox Christians as *theosis*, promises us a final glorification that will lift us higher than we were in our prefallen, Edenic state. As Athanasius explains in *On the Incarnation*, God became like us so that we could become like him.

## THE TRILEMMA

The full Christian doctrine of salvation is truly a glorious thing, but it rests squarely on a single, central belief—that Jesus of Nazareth was not just a good teacher or prophet but the incarnate Son of God. Of all the apologetic arguments that Lewis makes in *Mere Christianity*, his most essential, most famous, and most enduring seeks precisely to substantiate this central, nonnegotiable belief. Lewis knew that for a growing number of twentieth-century Christians the doctrine of the incarnation was no longer viewed as tenable or even necessary. Many modern critics who approached the Bible from a naturalistic, antimiracle point of view dismissed the incarnation as a superstitious relic of a credulous, unscientific age. It was later theologians, they claimed, who formulated the doctrine of the incarnation and then imposed it backward upon Jesus and the Gospels.

But that, Lewis argues, is the one claim that we cannot logically make. Again and again, throughout the Gospels, Jesus makes claims about himself that he could only have made if he was the Son of God: to have the power to forgive sins, to be one with the Father, to be the resurrection and the life as well as the way, the truth, and the life, and to be himself the proper object of our worship and service. If Jesus was only a man and not what he claimed to be (the Son of God), then he was either a raving lunatic or the greatest deceiver who ever lived. The asylums are filled with people who think they are God or Jesus, just as our world continues to be plagued by cult leaders who claim for themselves divine status. But almost no one today who has read the Gospels believes that Jesus was either insane or a charlatan. To the contrary, Jesus is universally heralded as a man of great wisdom and goodness. What the modern skeptic fails to see is that if Jesus was not who he claimed to be, then he was either bereft of all wisdom or bereft of all goodness. Indeed, I would go further than Lewis to add that if he was not the Son of God, then he was the worst blasphemer who ever lived, and the Pharisees were right to condemn him to death and turn him over to the Romans.

To use the oft-quoted wording of Josh McDowell, Christ could only have been one of three things: a liar, a lunatic, or the Lord. The one thing we *cannot* say about him is that he was a good man but not the Son of God. Jesus did not leave us that option.

Now, let me hasten to add that Lewis's trilemma only works because Jesus was a Jew. Had he been a Hindu monist—had he believed that all is one and that we are all part of the same universal spirit—then the trilemma would not work. The historical Jesus, we must remember, was a strict monotheist; his claim that he was the Son of God—a claim that would be far less shocking if it were made, say, by the Dalai Lama—would have been considered high blasphemy by the Jews of his day. Though modern theologians who deny the incarnation often claim they are being true to the historical context of the Gospels, the fact of the matter is that the more we understand Jesus' Jewishness, the more we should be staggered by the audacity of his claims.

Indeed, perhaps the best way to understand Lewis's trilemma is to place it in the context of other world religions. Were one to ask a Jew, a Muslim, or a Deist if he believes that Jesus was the Son of God, his reply would be a resounding "No," followed by the indignant insistence that

God has no Son. If one were to ask a Hindu, a Buddhist, or a New Ager if he believed that Jesus was the Son of God, his answer would most likely be "Yes." However, after agreeing that Jesus was the Son of God, he would likely add, "and so was Buddha, and so was Confucius, and so was Gandhi, and so are we all—if we only knew it." In contrast to both sets of believers, the Christian would answer that Jesus was the only-begotten Son of God.

Finally, it must be noted that the trilemma cannot be extended to all holy men and prophets. Prophets like Moses and Muhammad and holy men like Buddha and Gandhi only claimed to have heard from God and to have been a conduit for his word. Jesus, in contrast, claimed to be God himself in the flesh. Whereas prophets promise to show us the way, to teach us the truth, and to lead us to the life, Jesus claimed to *be* the way, the truth, and the life (John 14:6). Most, if not all of us, at one time or another have believed that we heard God speak to us. We might even have been inspired to write down those words in a book and share them with others. Those who then read our books might agree or disagree with what we wrote, but they would not be forced to tag us as a liar, lunatic, or Lord (prophet). God might indeed have spoken to us, but we might not have heard him fully or correctly. Or, more likely, God did speak to us, but he meant the revelation for us personally, not for all people at all times.

There is a qualitative difference between Christ's claim to be God and Moses' and Muhammad's claim to have heard from God. Let us suppose that the president of the United States were to speak at my university and then return immediately to Washington before anyone had the chance to question him. If I were to take the podium after he left and give my interpretation of the president's words, I might be right or wrong or partly right or partly wrong, but I would not be a liar, lunatic, or Lord. But if I were to stand boldly behind the podium and say, "I *am* the president, and therefore my interpretation is infallible," then I would either be lying to the audience, seriously deluded, or the president himself. In that case, there would be no fourth option.

# 4

# THE ONLY POSSIBLE WORLD:
# C. S. LEWIS ON THE PROBLEM OF PAIN

Though published in 1952, *Mere Christianity* began its life a decade earlier during those dark days when London was being bombed from the air by the German Luftwaffe. In 1941 the BBC, hoping to strengthen the faith and resilience of its citizens, asked Lewis to give a series of "Broadcast Talks" over the radio to explain to the British public the key tenets of Christianity. One of the reasons that Lewis was chosen to perform this service was the success he had recently achieved in explaining why the widespread presence of pain in our world was not incompatible with an all-powerful, all-loving God.

Written in a straightforward, jargon-free style rich with wit, wisdom, and compassion, Lewis's *The Problem of Pain* (1940) had succeeded in conveying abstract philosophical and theological concepts in a way that spoke with equal force to the man in the pew, the man in the pub, and the man on the street. In this, his first major apologetic work, Lewis demonstrated that Christianity, far from demanding blind faith from its followers, embodied a worldview that could be defended rationally and that could provide answers for life's most difficult questions. Given that the problem of pain has long proved to be the greatest stumbling block to Christian faith, it is hardly surprising that Lewis, the budding young apologist, chose to tackle it in the early stages of his apologetic career. Lewis seems to have understood intuitively that if an apologist living in a modern, pain-aversive society could not offer some explanation for pain and suffering, he could hardly hope to gain a fair hearing from seekers and skeptics. This has particularly been the case since David Hume, one of the intellectual gatekeepers of our post-Enlightenment world, held up the problem of pain as *the* chief argument against the God of the Bible.

## WE'RE NOT HERE TO HAVE FUN

Though he does not mention Hume directly, and though Hume did not technically invent the argument, when Lewis begins his second chapter with a capsule definition of the problem of pain, he seems to have the skeptical ghost of Hume in the back of his mind. Hume's knock-out punch against biblical theism may be stated in a single sentence: The Bible claims that God is all-powerful and all-loving; yet, the presence of pain suggests that he either lacks the power to eliminate our suffering or the loving desire to do so. In answer to this supposed contradiction between God's nature and our actual experience of the world, Lewis offers the traditional Christian response: that human pain and suffering find their origin not in some lack of divine power or love but in man's misuse of the free will granted to him by his Creator.

Well, that at least is Lewis's short answer to the problem of pain. His long answer is far more complex and original and calls on us to wrestle with the fuller implications of free will. Though Christian philosophers and theologians continue to debate the exact nature and extent of human free will, all acknowledge that God created us as volitional beings and that our choices are therefore real. Indeed, if we did not possess some degree of choice, then we could hardly be what Genesis insists that we are—creatures made in the image of God. God created us not as parts of himself but as separate creatures with our own unique identities; to us alone of all the animals he granted reason, consciousness, and will.

So far so good, writes Lewis, but what does all this *mean*? Too often those who ponder such issues grant with one breath that God gave us free will and then, with the other, act as if he didn't *really* give it to us. This is untenable, Lewis insists. God cannot give us free will and take it away from us at the same time. A logical contradiction is a logical contradiction even if we preface it by saying, "God said." If God chose, for whatever reason, to give us free will, then he must have been willing to accept the ramifications of such a decision. Lewis even goes so far as to describe God as conducting a free-will experiment. By this phrase Lewis did not intend to suggest that God amuses himself by playing frivolous games with his creatures, but to remind us that there was some divine purpose behind God's choice to create us as we are. It was and is a matter of great import to God to see what we will do with what he has given us: will we use his gifts—the gift of choice in particular—to love, serve, and glorify him or to lift up ourselves into the place of God?

Once we grant the reality of this free-will experiment, Lewis argues, we will quickly realize that for such an experiment to be conducted, there needs to be some kind of arena. If we were all bodiless souls flitting around in space, we could hardly participate in God's "game." In order for true choice to be exercised in a communal way, God needed to provide us with a neutral playing field—something, that is, like our natural world. And that field must, like our earth, be relatively fixed, stable, and unchangeable. Had I the power to shift the playing field in accordance with my every whim and desire, I would be robbing my neighbor of his free will. Likewise, were God to shift nature every minute to prevent the pain and discomfort of each of his creatures, his whole free-will experiment would fall apart.

All that is to say that even before the fall the possibility of pain must have existed in the garden of Eden. Otherwise, the game would have been unplayable from the start. No, concludes Lewis, this may not be the best of all possible worlds, but it may be the only possible *kind* of world for the experiment God chose to carry out.

To this intractability of nature Lewis adds a second condition that is essential to the carrying out of God's free-will experiment. Many moderns who balk at pain often do so out of a sense that they are being treated unfairly, that God is a spoilsport who refuses to let them just have fun. But those who make such complaints misunderstand God's greater purpose for humanity. Although God is by no means opposed to happiness, he did not put us on this earth simply to have fun. God put us here that we might grow and develop into the creatures he created us to be. We Christians, says Lewis, claim to worship a heavenly Father, but what we really want is a grandfather in heaven who will indulge our every whim and who will be satisfied if everyone has a good time.

Thankfully, the Bible presents us with a God whose desires for us transcend the mere having of fun. Far from revealing an impassive, uncaring, or contemptuous God, human pain reveals an involved God who pays "us the intolerable compliment of loving us, in the deepest, most tragic, most inexorable sense" (chapter 3). Like most parents, my wife and I will be *satisfied* if our children don't do drugs and stay out of jail, but that is not what we *desire* for them; it is certainly not the reason we gave birth to them. Indeed, we would be willing, though not happy, to see them experience some pain and suffering if it meant that they would grow into their full potential.

To help us better understand the relationship between God and man,

Lewis presents us with a series of four earthly relationships of increasing intimacy. In the first, God is a sculptor who strives patiently and lovingly to make us into a masterpiece, even though he knows that the process will necessitate deep and painful cutting. In the second, God is a pet owner who uses strict training and discipline to make us better than we are in nature. In the third, Lewis, following a persistent biblical metaphor, presents God as a wise and loving father who would rather see his son good but unhappy than triumphant but evil. Finally, borrowing an even more persistent biblical metaphor, Lewis presents God as a passionate, devoted husband who responds with righteous jealousy when his wife strays from her covenant, but who nevertheless labors to make her pure and worthy of love. In all four scenarios, growth and perfection cannot be achieved without at least the possibility of pain and suffering.

## GOD'S MEGAPHONE

Even in our prefallen state, Lewis suggests, pain and suffering were real possibilities. Since the fall, however, they have greatly intensified and have become necessary tools in God's salvage operation. In fact, until we fully grasp our status as fallen creatures, we cannot begin to appreciate the central role that suffering now plays in leading us back to God.

To help us understand better the nature and effects of the fall, Lewis devotes the fifth chapter of *The Problem of Pain* to a mythic retelling of Genesis 1–3. Taking the six days of creation in a figurative rather than literal sense, Lewis spins a tale in which God uses natural forces to slowly shape our physical body. After millions of years, we reach human form, but we are still nothing more than irrational hominids. Only when God directly breathes into us our souls do we become conscious, rational, volitional creatures able to know God, to judge and enjoy beauty, and to obey or disobey our Creator. In that original state of innocence, Lewis rhapsodizes, we were a wonder to behold. Unfallen man effortlessly controlled nature, the animals, and his own will, yet relied fully on God and obeyed him completely. True, this obedience called for some surrender, but it was a surrender of a pleasant kind, like the thousand little yieldings that newlyweds make to one another on their honeymoon.

Three years after publishing *The Problem of Pain*, Lewis would publish a strange and haunting sci-fi novel (*Perelandra*) in which he would retell the garden of Eden story as it might have played out on Venus. As Lewis describes it, most of Venus is covered by oceans, and skimming the surface of its pristine waters, floating islands move and fluctuate and dance on the waves. It is a paradise indeed, but like our own paradise, it comes with a divine restriction. God tells his Venusian Adam and Eve that though they may walk during the day on dry ground, they must sleep at night on the floating islands. Lewis's point here is that God's forbidding of the fruit of the knowledge of good and evil in Genesis 3 had less to do with diet regulations than with God's desire that we should obey him and rely fully on his will and his provision. Alas, despite God's goodness to the terrestrial Adam and Eve, we chose to forsake his lordship and to call our souls our own. Or to use Lewis's clever metaphor, we insisted on being a noun when God had intended us to be an adjective.

The moment we asserted our own direct lordship over God, nature, and ourselves, we fell, sacrificing our original status and plunging ourselves and our world into a state of brokenness and futility. Whereas the soul of prefallen Adam had controlled his body, after the fall his body seized control of his soul and itself fell sway to natural laws. His mind, too, fell sway to natural (psychological) laws, leading to repression, neurosis, and the birth of the dark subconscious mind. Worst of all, the obedience that we still owed to our Creator ceased to be an easy, pleasant surrender and became a hard and bitter struggle.

Man's proper good was, and still is, to surrender to God and glorify his name, but that is the one thing fallen man refuses to do. Just as we find it impossible to follow the Tao, so we find it equally impossible to yield our wills to God's will and to trust him completely. Since the Enlightenment, Western man has increasingly claimed that the real problem with the human race is ignorance and poverty; if we could only eliminate those two "sins," then we could perfect humanity and build a utopia. But the problem is, that is not the problem. It is sin, pride, and disobedience that lie at the root of war and poverty and injustice, and at the root of sin, pride, and disobedience lies our refusal to yield ourselves to God. Lewis compares fallen man not to some great rebel or fiery revolutionary but to a spoiled and willful child. Since the fall, all of us—men, women, and children—are guilty of harboring "the black, Satanic wish to kill or die rather than to give in" (chapter 6).

The only way to escape that wish is through self-surrender, but our rebellious will makes us deaf to God's call. As a result, God must use pain to, quite literally, get our attention. "God," writes Lewis, "whispers to us in our pleasures, speaks in our conscience, but shouts in our pains: it is His megaphone to rouse a deaf world" (chapter 6). We spend most of our lives building our own little towers of Babel, unaware that our supposed fortress is nothing but a house of cards. Pain is one of the weapons God uses to topple our house of cards, and it is a weapon that he must use over and over—for no sooner do our houses of cards topple than our desires for self-sufficiency apart from God set us to work rebuilding them again. Pain demolishes our self-sufficiency and our illusions of earthly security; it makes us drop what we are holding so that we might embrace the love of God.

Throughout *The Problem of Pain*, Lewis adds a number of caveats to his apologetic that round out his analysis. Four of these caveats are worth mentioning in brief for their ability to poke holes in some of our faulty thinking about the nature and purpose of pain. First, in the face of endless outcries against the mind-boggling, soul-numbing sum of human misery, Lewis boldly asserts that there is no such thing as a "sum" of human misery. The concept is a wholly abstract one, for no one on the earth actually feels that sum of misery (though one could argue that God in Jesus felt and bore that dreadful sum of misery). Once we reach the most pain that a single individual can feel, we have reached the limit of pain. Second, pain, unlike sin, is disinfected; once it is over, it is over. Third, suffering, like poverty, is not good in itself, but God uses it for good. Christianity does not instruct its followers to seek pain or to relish it; we are called only to bear the pain that we must so that God might be glorified through it. Finally, pain reminds us of something that our post-Enlightenment world has almost completely forgotten—that this world is not our final home but is only a rest station along the way.

Almost two decades after writing *The Problem of Pain*, Lewis, a lifelong bachelor, married Joy Gresham, only to lose her to cancer three years later. As a way of dealing with his intense grief, Lewis began to keep a private journal. Though he did not originally intend to publish his journal, Lewis decided in the end that his personal musings might help others who were suffering grief over the loss of a loved one. Accordingly, he published (anonymously) his musings as *A Grief Observed* (1961). I consider this book to be one of the finest ever written on grieving, not so much because of the answers it gives as because of the uncompromising honesty with which Lewis presents his initial doubts and struggles. Sadly, the very honesty with which he presents these doubts has led some (unfair) critics of Lewis to use *A Grief Observed* as a weapon for attacking his earlier apologetic works.

Indeed, many Christians who read *A Grief Observed* are at first confused by the despairing tone of its opening two sections. "Can this be

Lewis the great apologist?" they wonder. "How can a man like that suffer from such terrible doubts?" But suffer he does, and his initial suffering is increased, not decreased, by his faith in the Christian God. As a Christian, Lewis knows that this is not the way it was meant to be, and for several weeks his faith is tested as gold is tested in the fire. Though he never doubts the existence of God, he wonders, for a brief, terrifying moment, whether God might not be a Cosmic Sadist or an Eternal Vivisectionist playing with his human rats. "Why," he cries out to God, "did you pull me out of my bachelor's shell only to take Joy away? And why, when I most need you, do I hear only the sound of a door slammed in my face?"

In the end, after intense emotional and spiritual struggle, Lewis's faith does return, but not via the cool logic of *The Problem of Pain*. Instead the answers—or, better, resolutions—come in a more personal, anecdotal, even childlike way:

- To a sick animal, a vet would appear like a Vivisectionist; perhaps God must hurt to heal.
- Was it not in truth I who slammed the door in God's face; am I not like a drowning man who, because he clutches in fear at his rescuer, cannot be rescued?
- Am I not guilty of seeking God as a means of getting Joy back? God must be loved for himself, not as a means to an end. Only by seeking God for himself can we receive back what we lost.
- Did I even really love Joy or just my image of her? Perhaps God had to shatter that image, that house of cards, lest I make it into an idol.

And finally, he offers a simple but profound parable to help him (and us) understand the true nature of his (and our) situation and place his grief in the proper perspective. Picture a man, he writes, in total darkness. Because it is dark, he believes that he is locked in a dungeon from which he cannot escape. Then, far off in the distance, he hears a sound—the sound perhaps of birds singing or trees swaying in the wind or water falling over stones. And suddenly he realizes that he is not in a dungeon but is outside in the open air. In one sense his situation has not changed; he still waits in darkness. But now he knows that he is not a prisoner, that he has not been forsaken, that there is a reality and a life greater than he can comprehend.

# 5

# THE GREATER WEAVE:
# C. S. LEWIS DEFENDS MIRACLES

In part 1, question 2, article 3 of his *Summa*, Thomas Aquinas takes up the question of whether or not God actually exists. In keeping with his organizational scheme, he begins by listing the reasons *against* the proposition that God exists. Significantly, Aquinas can think of only two reasons why a rational person would deny God's existence: 1) because of the problem of pain; 2) because everything can be explained by natural processes. Lewis seems to have agreed with Aquinas on this point, for he devoted two of the three books in his apologetics trilogy (*Mere Christianity*, *The Problem of Pain*, *Miracles*) to addressing Aquinas's two reasons for atheism.

On the one hand, Lewis's answers to the problem of pain and the all-sufficiency of nature are consistent with those presented by such traditional apologists as Augustine and Aquinas. On the other hand, he infuses his apologetic arguments with a freshness and a vitality that compel skeptics and believers alike to question their assumptions about the true nature of God, man, and the universe. We already saw in chapter 4 how Lewis, in *The Problem of Pain*, forces us to explore the full ramifications of God's free-will experiment. In this chapter we will see how Lewis, in *Miracles*, forces us to rethink what a miracle is and is not. Far from violating the laws of nature or God's divine dignity, Lewis boldly asserts, miracles reveal God's greater design.

## BELIEVING IS SEEING

Lewis begins his defense of miracles with a statement that should be obvious but that two centuries of Enlightenment indoctrination have rendered shocking: a belief in miracles is not synonymous with ignorance. Whether consciously or unconsciously, we have all been taught that the less enlightened people of the past believed in miracles because they did not understand the laws of nature. Just as "primitives" cower before eclipses and comets, so ancient and medieval Christians, awed by a universe they could not comprehend, labeled everything they could not explain as a miracle. Now, I will concede that superstition was (somewhat) more prevalent in the days before modern science, but there is a qualitative difference between a belief in good luck charms or voodoo spells and the miracles recorded in the Bible.

Though they would likely not state it this baldly, a considerable number of highly educated academics think that the only reason the early Christians believed in the virgin birth was because they did not understand the science of reproduction. If we can put aside for a moment our Enlightenment prejudices, simple common sense will show this argument to be fallacious. Although Joseph never saw a sperm or an egg and although he was ignorant of embryology, he did know where babies came from. He did not need a modern science textbook to tell him that a woman can only have a child if she has sex with a man. It is precisely *because* of his knowledge of this scientific fact that he was prepared to divorce Mary. It is, further, only *because* of this knowledge that Joseph and the early church recognized the virgin birth *as* a miracle. Indeed, the only way anyone can recognize a miracle *as* a miracle is if he knows how nature normally works. Throw out the laws of nature, and you throw out miracles as well.

The difference between medievals and moderns lies not so much in their knowledge of the universe as in their *interpretation* of that knowledge. Modern man gazes on the immensity of the universe and concludes that our world must be too insignificant for God to intervene in history or in our lives. But the miracle-believing ancients and medievals also knew the universe was vast. Boethius and Dante both describe it as nothing but a dot in space. It was not their ignorance that allowed them to believe in miracles, but their refusal to interpret the smallness of our planet or of ourselves as an indication of insignificance. During his atheist years at Oxford, Lewis accepted without question the modernist dismissal of the Middle Ages as a time of darkness, ignorance, and superstition—until his friend Owen Barfield challenged him to look again at the evidence. What Lewis discovered was that the real reason the medieval belief in miracles has been abandoned by post-Enlightenment thinkers is not because the belief has been disproved but because people have simply stopped believing it. From Barfield as well, Lewis learned to refer to this modern prejudice as "chronological snobbery."

Because of our chronological snobbery, we who live in the modern world are too quick to assume that because we have "moved beyond" a belief in miracles the issue is settled and does not need to be debated or even acknowledged. Rather than investigate evidence or wrestle with assumptions, many moderns, including many in the clergy, simply *take for granted* that miracles don't occur. Of course, most of these miracle debunkers will claim to have arrived at their conclusion through a scientific analysis of the facts, but the truth is generally the exact opposite. Their disbelief is not arrived at as a result of rigorous investigation; on the contrary, their disbelief is *forced* upon them by their prior (*a priori*) rejection of the miraculous.

It is precisely *because* of their *a priori* rejection of miracles that modern readers of the Bible are *impelled* to come up with a "natural" explanation for such miraculous events as the parting of the Red Sea. Once they have come up with this "natural" explanation, however, they use that explanation as "proof" that miracles don't happen. The same is true when it comes to dating the Gospels or the prophetic books: if such a book contains an accurate prophecy of the future—Jesus' prediction of the destruction of the Temple, for example—then it *must* have been written (or reached its final form) after the predicted event took place. Modernism's *a priori* rejection of prophecy—which demands the existence of a supernatural intelligence outside time and space—*forces* such a conclusion. To put this in terms of logic, though modernists claim to be working through an inductive proof based solely on the collection of objective, empirical data, they are really engaging in what I call "deduction in disguise," for their interpretation of the facts is guided, if not predetermined, by a previous unproven assumption (that miracles don't happen).

Moderns, writes Lewis, will often resort to the most improbable "rational" explanation rather than accept a far more probable miracle. Although most scientists and philosophers, following the principle known as Ockham's razor, favor simple solutions that don't necessitate the multiplication of causes, when it comes to miracles, they quickly change their standards. This inconsistency is driven home by a famous (if possibly apocryphal) story about a modernist teacher who, after reading to her students the story of the parting of the Red Sea, informs them that the event was not really miraculous, for "we now know" that the Red

Sea was only a few inches deep at that time of year. Immediately a boy in the back of the room cries out that if that is true, then the miracle was an even greater one. When the teacher asks him what he means, the boy responds with a smile, "Imagine that! God drowned the entire Egyptian army, chariots and all, in a few inches of water!" One of the modernist creeds that is especially popular in America is "seeing is believing." As a matter of fact, argues Lewis, it is more often the case that believing is seeing. If we refuse to accept the validity or even possibility of miracles, then we will reject even the miracles that occur before our eyes.

Once we take into account the combined force of chronological snobbery and the *a priori* rejection of all miraculous explanations, it should come as no surprise that the modern world has all but outlawed miracles. But the situation, alas, is even worse. Today even those who *do* manage to rise above these two post-Enlightenment prejudices are liable to reject miracles out of hand because they have been falsely led to believe that miracles violate the laws of nature. Lewis, keenly aware of how deeply ingrained is this misunderstanding of miracles and the laws of nature, takes pains to instruct us in the true nature of both.

Whereas most modern people take for granted that the laws of nature define events, they really define a sequence or process. If I pick up a vase with my right hand, lift it over my head, and let it go, the vase will fall to the ground and shatter. I know that is so because I am aware of the downward force exerted by the law of gravity. What would happen, however, if, one second after letting go of the vase, my left hand were to reach out and catch the vase? The vase would neither hit the ground nor shatter. Have I broken the law of gravity? Of course not! I have merely added a new factor (my left hand) into the equation, a new factor that *suspends*—but does not break or destroy—the natural sequence of events. Indeed, if my left hand were to let go of the vase, the natural course of gravity would take over again, and the vase would continue falling until it hit the ground.

Or, to offer a second scenario, suppose I open the top drawer of my dresser and place five pennies in it. Five hours later, at midnight, I open the drawer again and place in five more pennies. When I open the drawer in the morning, the law of addition demands that there be ten pennies in the drawer . . . unless, of course, a thief broke into my house in the middle of the night and stole four of the pennies. If that happened, there would only be six pennies in the drawer when I opened it. Has the law of addition been broken? No, a new factor (the thief) has been added, causing the Law to be temporarily suspended. Or, to offer one final scenario, imagine that I am playing a game of billiards. If I hit a billiard ball at a certain speed and at a certain angle, and if the table is perfectly flat and smooth, the laws of physics determine the course or trajectory that my ball will follow . . . unless, one second after I hit the ball, two mysterious hands reach out and shake the table!

Miracles are like the hand that grabs the vase or the thief that steals the pennies or the hands that shake the table. They document a moment of supernatural intervention into the fixed affairs of our world. But it is a fleeting moment, for once the miracle changes the situation, nature quickly domesticates the change, and the laws of nature go on as before. Jesus healed many people during his three-year ministry, but all of those he healed eventually died. No, concludes Lewis, miracles do not violate the laws of nature. To the contrary, it is only the believer in miracles who really *sees* nature at all. For only the supernaturalist can get the proper perspective, can appreciate nature for the strange and beautiful creature that she is.

## MIRACLES OF THE OLD AND NEW CREATION

Thus far I have surveyed reasons for the modern rejection of miracles that are most likely to influence secular humanists and others who are deeply skeptical, or at least apathetic, about the existence of God and the supernatural. But they are not the only people in our modern world whose initial reaction to miraculous claims is one of suspicion and disbelief. Just as the modern "man of science" dismisses miracles because they seem to violate the uniformity of nature, so the modern "man of faith" will often dismiss miracles because they seem to violate the dignity of God. Indeed, many Christians today who are quite orthodox in their beliefs and who accept the historicity of the miracles recorded in the Bible will often balk or even jeer when they hear someone claim to have witnessed a miracle. "Our God," they reply indignantly and with a touch of condescension, "does not do parlor tricks!" "Modern people," writes Lewis in an essay titled "Miracles" (anthologized in *God in the Dock*), "have an almost aesthetic dislike of miracles. Admitting that God can, they doubt if He would. To violate the laws He Himself has imposed on His creation seems to them arbitrary, clumsy, a theatrical device only fit to impress savages—a solecism against the grammar of the universe."

As a Protestant with a high regard for order, system, and rationality, I can understand this reaction. We modern people, regardless of our religious beliefs, tend to be suspicious of events that don't conform to expected patterns. Though we may enjoy the occasional surprise, we would much rather that nature—and God—keep with the program and follow the rules. Lewis too, himself a product of the modern world, understood this desire for predictability and precision; nevertheless, he challenges us, in *Miracles*, to consider the matter again from a higher perspective. Perhaps, he suggests, the reason that we view miracles as artificial and disruptive is that we lack eyes to see and ears to hear.

My students often stare at me with disbelief when I inform them that eighteenth-century critics of Shakespeare generally considered his plays to be great in parts but inconsistent and poorly executed on the whole. From the point of view of neoclassical writers like Samuel Johnson, Shakespeare was perennially guilty of breaking dramatic decorum, of not following the rules for tragedy and comedy that were set down by Aristotle, Horace, and other classical critics. Starting with nineteenth-century writers like Samuel Taylor Coleridge, however, critical estimation of Shakespeare began to change. Rather than censure him for his frequent breaches of decorum, more recent critics have learned to praise Shakespeare's so-called inconsistencies as intentional devices that reveal the greater, organic harmony of his plays. Just so, while the naturalist and the Christian skeptic see in miracles a break in that artificial decorum that they have imposed on the universe and on God himself, the true supernaturalist sees the fuller design, the deeper unity of what God is doing in our world.

As I, following Lewis, like to put it, a miracle is not a violation of the laws of nature or the dignity of God but a sublime act during which the Creator, for a brief, glorious moment, restores the truly natural—that is, original—order of his creation. For Lewis, all God's miracles coalesce around one grand miracle: the incarnation. All the greatest themes of mankind—the dying and rising god of pagan myth, the seed that must be buried to grow, the child born out of the dark womb, the two-into-one nature of marriage, the need to reconcile body and soul—find their fullest expression in the incarnate Christ, the God-Man. In a beautiful metaphor, Lewis compares the incarnate Christ to a diver who must descend to the murky depths of the sea before he can recover the hidden pearl. To effect our salvation, God did not just appear in human form but entered fully into the physical, material confines of our world. God *became* a man in Jesus, and as such, he became also a fetus, a zygote, and a sperm! That God should rend his heaven and come down, that he should "dirty" himself with matter that he might redeem and sanctify it is not a violation of his creation. Rather, it is a historical enactment of what that very creation has longed for. God, the true divine playwright, first writes the pattern into nature and then enters and enacts that pattern in himself.

To help develop further this deeper, richer view of miracles, Lewis considers closely the miracles of Jesus that are recorded in the Gospels. Though they all point to a God whose "artistry" transcends artificial rules of decorum, Lewis discerns a subtle difference between two types or categories of miracles.

In the former—what he calls Miracles of the Old Creation—we see Christ do quickly and on a small scale what God does every day on the large scale. Through a long and involved series of "natural" processes, God continually transforms water into wine, but the miracle is so slow that we miss it. When, however, at a wedding at Cana of Galilee, Jesus suddenly and instantaneously transforms water into wine, the truth that was always before us but that we were too blind to see—namely, that God is the True Bacchus, the true maker of wine—is revealed. Every day, because of the "miraculous" properties with which God has invested soil and water and sun and grain, some wheat becomes much wheat. And the same is true for the ichthyic fecundity that we see in every lake and stream. When, however, Christ feeds five thousand men with five loaves and two fish, we see the miracle that we missed and understand, in a flash of insight, that Jesus' miracles reveal a God who does not violate nature but who created and fashioned it in the first place. And the same holds true for Jesus' miracles of healing. As Lewis reminds us, doctors rarely "heal" our bodies. Our bodies heal themselves; the real role of the doctor is to immobilize the broken limb and fight infection. The miraculous power manifested by Jesus of Nazareth is written into the very cells of our bodies. Though our sin-diseased bodies will eventually run down, the boast (and praise) of the psalmist that we are fearfully and wonderfully made is manifestly plain to any doctor who has eyes to see.

Miracles of the Old Creation attest to the fact that the God of the Bible is also the God of nature. Christ is not some usurping impostor but the true King come to his kingdom. There is a qualitative difference between the miracles recorded in the Bible and those that appear in the work of such pagan writers as Homer, Hesiod, Virgil, and Ovid. If the miracles of Christ are true, then we have much cause for rejoicing, but we only enjoy reading Ovid's *Metamorphoses* because we know its "miracles" are *not* true. If I were to discover that the stories of Daphne and Callisto (lovely maidens who were transformed into a tree and a bear respectively) were true, I would run for my life in terror, convinced that the universe was run not by a God of love and order but by an arbitrary monster. In contrast, when I came to believe in the historical truth of Jesus' miracles, it confirmed what I had always felt in my heart was true—that this is, truly, our Father's world and that all of nature bears the mark and yearns for the touch of its Creator.

Though most of the miracles recorded in the Gospels fit in Lewis's category of Miracles of the Old Creation, there are a few that seem to speak a different message. In these miracles—Lewis calls them Miracles of the New Creation—Christ does not so much remind us of what God is *doing* in nature as what he will *one day* do in a redeemed and perfected nature. We catch a glimpse of that perfection in Jesus' walking on the water, an event that transcends rather than speeds up the normal processes of nature. We see it supremely in the resurrection of Christ. In this, the greatest miracle recorded in the Bible, Jesus does not merely return from the dead (like Lazarus) but rises in a new spiritual body no longer bound to the tyrannies of time, space, and decay.

With perhaps a backward nod to his *The Problem of Pain*, Lewis reminds us of the vision that the Bible holds out for us of the New Jerusalem that will be our final home. When the last trumpet sounds and we are clothed in resurrection bodies like that of Christ, we will regain that effortless control over nature that would have been ours in Eden. Christ is our Savior, but he is also something more: the firstfruits of a new and higher mode of being. In the face of our modern tendency to speak of God and heaven in negative terms, Lewis triumphantly asserts that our resurrection bodies will be greater than, not less than, our earthly ones. Even so, the eternal God who spoke our world and us into being is neither incorporeal nor impersonal: he is transcorporeal and transpersonal!

# 6

# THE PSYCHOLOGY OF SIN:
# WHY C. S. LEWIS BELIEVED IN HELL

If there is one doctrine of the church that is least likely to be preached from the modern pulpit, it must surely be the traditional teaching of hell. Angels are OK and are often believed in by people who don't necessarily believe in God, but any talk of devils is liable to inspire bemused laughter and haughty scorn. Ironically, the types of preachers who are most likely to exorcise hell and devils from their sermons are the ones who boast that "their" Christianity is not based on later church councils but on the words of Christ himself—on the words in red. I say that this is ironic because of all the figures in the Bible, the one who speaks the most about the devil and who gives us the most information about hell is none other than Jesus. If I may be forgiven the pun, the words in red tell us more about hellfire than any other verses in the Bible!

Why, we must ask, has the modern age felt the need to expunge hell and devils from Christianity when Christ himself clearly taught both and when both teachings have always played a central role in church doctrine? Though I could devote an entire chapter to this puzzling cultural and spiritual phenomenon, I will instead quickly survey seven of the major reasons for the modern dislike and dismissal of hell. By so doing, I hope to lay a groundwork for Lewis's powerful and still relevant defense of hell.

First, in sharp contrast to past ages, our age seems unable to reconcile God's love and compassion with his justice and judgment. When we read the Old and New Testaments, we see only a God of unmitigated anger and all-consuming wrath in the former and only a God of pure forgiveness and boundless tolerance in the latter. We seem unable to conceive that God might be capable of "tough love" or that his mercy might be inseparable from his holiness.

Second, we have reduced hell to a primitive superstition that no educated modern could possibly take seriously. The way we have accomplished this is by presenting ourselves with what logicians call a false dichotomy: *either* we must accept literally the colorful (and unbiblical) imagery of devils with red tights and pitchforks *or* reject altogether the existence of devils.

Third, following the Romantic misreading of Milton's *Paradise Lost*, we reason that if the devil exists, he must be a tragic hero or noble rebel. Modernism is, in great part, a child of the French Revolution, and we are therefore very likely to sympathize with, rather than despise, an angelic being who refused to obey his "oppressive" Creator and left his heavenly home to form his own separate "entrepreneurial" kingdom.

Fourth, also being children of Sigmund Freud, our natural tendency is to dismiss hell (and heaven) as forms of wish fulfillment—with the former embodying our desires for our enemies and the latter embodying our desires for ourselves and our friends.

Fifth, as children also of Karl Marx, whose utopianism we have absorbed even if we have rejected his socialism, our natural tendency is to dismiss hell (and heaven) as impediments to our building of utopia. By holding out the promise of some otherworldly "pie in the sky"—either for our enemies or our friends—hell and heaven take our focus off of the world and cause modernism's utopian mandate to come grinding to a halt.

Sixth, hell violates our modern belief in the absolute sanctity of equality, even as it threatens our postmodern allegiance to moral relativism. If there really is a place of eternal punishment, then our cherished belief that all people are the same and that no one can, or should, judge our individual choices is, if you will excuse the expression, shot to hell.

Seventh, following the lead of William Blake's Gnostic epic *The Marriage of Heaven and Hell*, we tend to reduce hell (and heaven) to states of mind. Good and evil, right and wrong, black and white, virtue and vice—none of these things represent essential, transcendent values placed into the universe and our consciences by a divine Creator. It is we and our perceptions that label things as good or bad, right or wrong. Heaven and hell exist, if they exist at all, only in our minds.

## HELL IS A PROCESS

In the face of modernism's rejection of hell, Lewis, in works like *The Screwtape Letters* and *The Great Divorce*, argues forcefully and repeatedly for its theological and psychological necessity. Indeed, according to Lewis, not only is hell consistent with the nature of a loving God and a fallen humanity, it is always something that *we choose*. The divide of heaven and hell is not an attack on equality or on the intrinsic worth of every human being. Our modern, egalitarian-loving age rejects heaven and hell, for they seem to smack of an unequal world of winners and losers. What we do not understand is that all souls, whatever their final destination, consider themselves to be winners. Those who end up in heaven are those whose greatest desire is to be in God's presence for eternity; those who end up in hell are those who cling eternally to themselves and their sins. The damned, writes Lewis in *The Great Divorce*, are, like Milton's Satan, *successful* rebels. In contrast to human prisons, the doors of hell are locked on the *inside* by those who refuse to let go of themselves and embrace God's love, mercy, and forgiveness.

If God's gift of free will is a real one, Lewis reasons, then he must allow us to reject his love. But if God is omnipresent, then where can souls go that have lost all desire to be in his presence? The tragic but logical answer to this conundrum is that God set aside hell as the one place in the universe from which his direct presence has been withdrawn. If we desire to be left alone, God *will* ignore us; if we choose ourselves and our sin over God and heaven, he *will* leave us to our terrible, self-enslaving freedom. It is simply irrational both to hate God and to blame him for sending you to hell. If you truly hate God and do not desire to spend eternity praising and fellowshiping with him, then where else are you going to go? There is only one place in the universe where God's presence does not dominate all, and that place is hell.

But how, Lewis asks, can one *not* desire heaven? Or, to put it the other way round, how can one *choose* hell? To answer this question, Lewis encourages us to think of hell not as a destination but as a process. Though most people envision hell as a pit that we are thrown into on account of some heinous, mortal sin, Lewis in *The Screwtape Letters* depicts hell as a marsh or a swamp that we slide into one little sin at a time. Each time we choose ourselves or our sins over God and others, we surrender another spark of our humanity. If pursued consistently and single-mindedly, without that saving backward turn to God that theologians call repentance, a life of sin will cause us, in the end, to dehumanize ourselves.

In the at once comforting and terrifying Parable of the Sheep and the Goats (Matthew 25:31–46), Jesus speaks the following words to the souls of the damned: "Depart from me, you cursed, into the eternal fire prepared for the devil and his angels" (v. 41). Remarkably, this verse strongly suggests that hell was never intended to house human beings; to the contrary, hell's original purpose was to house only the fallen angels who followed Satan in his rebellion against God. If I (and Lewis) am reading this verse properly, then there is reason to hope that anyone who is still "human" when he dies will have at least a chance at heaven. But that, sadly, is the whole problem with the damned; there is no human being, no *person* left to save.

In *The Screwtape Letters*, Lewis allows us to read over the shoulder of a senior devil named Screwtape as he writes a series of letters to his nephew Wormwood, educating him in the fine art of temptation. Being a young and enthusiastic tempter, Wormwood is eager to catch his human prey in a big, messy, scandalous sin, but the wiser Screwtape patiently explains to him that the size of the sin doesn't matter, only its effect on the human soul: "It does not matter how small the sins are, provided that their cumulative effect is to edge the man away from the Light and out into the Nothing. Murder is no better than cards if cards can do the trick. Indeed, the safest road to Hell is the gradual one—the gentle slope, soft underfoot, without sudden turnings, without milestones, without signposts" (letter 12). Sin does its most effective work on our souls when we don't even notice that it is working. While we justify our thousand little white lies and peccadilloes, our humanity drips out of us bit by bit, leaving us stranded in darkness, cut off from the light, from God, from life, from joy, from our own true selves.

## HELL AS NARCISSISM

For those who remain unconvinced that we can willingly and knowingly choose a course of life that will cause us to lose our humanity, I would suggest a close reading of Lewis's *The Great Divorce*. In this uniquely entertaining and powerfully convicting work, Lewis takes us on a fanciful bus ride from hell to heaven, allowing us to eavesdrop as saved souls try to convince damned souls *even now* to forsake their sin, receive the love and mercy of Christ, and enter heaven. Throughout the book, Lewis adopts a case-study approach to sin that uncovers the insidious psychological process by which human souls are reduced to shades of their former selves—pale, greasy, diaphanous ghosts whose insubstantial feet cannot even bend the strong grass of heaven.

At one point Lewis listens in as the damned soul of a garrulous, grumbling old woman has a dialogue with a bright and joyous saint—or better, monologue, since the woman won't cease her "pity party" long enough to listen to the saint sent to help her. To Lewis, she does not seem an "evil" woman, only a grumbler; but that, his guide (George Macdonald) tells him, is the whole point: is she a "grumbler or only a grumble"? If there's even an ember of humanity left inside of her, the angels can nurse the flame till it blazes again, but if all that is left is ashes, nothing can be done. To reiterate a point made earlier, the trouble with this woman is not that she is beyond salvation—God's grace is a powerful thing—but that there is nothing left to save.

Christ instructs us in the Gospels to love the sinner and hate the sin, a teaching that may at first seem inconsistent with the existence of hell. "Certainly," we complain to God with a note of indignation in our voices, "you cannot claim yourself to love sinners when you allow people to be punished in hell for eternity." It is my hope that Lewis's case study of the grumbling old woman will absolve God of this charge of hypocrisy. Hell does not violate Christ's call to love sinners, for there are, ultimately, no "sinners" in hell—all that there are in hell are sins going on forever and ever. Perhaps the greatest tragedy of hell is that in that terrible place the sinner is swallowed by his sin and ceases to exist. What is cast into hell, Lewis warns us, is not a sinner but the remains of what once *was* a sinner.

In a second case study that expands on the dehumanizing aspects of sin, the damned soul of a landscape painter (the Ghost) meets up with the blessed soul of another landscape painter (the Spirit). When the Ghost sees how beautiful heaven is, he kicks himself for not having brought his painting gear, but the Spirit tells him not to worry. He has not been brought here to paint heaven but to take it in directly and innocently as a child basks in the sun. Then, to help the Ghost understand why his paintbrushes are unnecessary, he begs him to look backward to that magical moment when he first decided to devote his life to landscape painting. His real reason for painting was not to capture the landscape itself, but to use his art to reach the light *behind* the landscape. Scornful of the Spirit's "naiveté," the Ghost replies that he has moved beyond such childish desires: he has come instead to appreciate art for its own sake, not as a means to reach some shadowy light source. In the end he chooses, of his own free will, to leave heaven and return to hell, oblivious to the fact that he has been standing in the very place that is the *source* of that golden light that was his first love. Lewis's hell, like that of Dante's, is a sad place of wasted dreams and shattered illusions. There is nothing grand or honest or realistic about it; it is like a rusted fountain after the plug has been pulled and all the water drained away.

A third case study features a mother whose son had died while still very young. After his untimely death, the mother devoted the rest of her life to preserving his memory, ignoring in the process her husband and other children. Now that she herself has died, she has taken the long bus ride from hell to heaven for the express purpose of seeing her son. Accordingly, the very moment she arrives in heaven, she insists on seeing her boy. In response, the saint sent to greet her explains that before she can have her boy back, she must first learn to love and desire God. But the woman will have nothing to do with such "inhuman" nonsense. God *is* Love, she insists, and any God who will not let her see her son must be a false one: what, after all, can be more holy than mother love? Her son or, more precisely, her smothering, manipulative love for her son *is* her god: if God gets in the way of that, he must go; if God won't step aside, then she's ready to drag her son down with her to hell where she can really care for him.

The theological and psychological problem with the mother is that she worships a virtue (love) that she has made into an idol, not the God who is the source of that love. She claims that God is Love, but what she really means is Love is God. Here, as in many of his other works, Lewis drives home a point that may seem at first counterintuitive but that is played out again and again in the Gospels. More often than not it is the good things (mother love, patriotism, religion, good works) rather than the bad things (drugs, alcoholism, promiscuity) that keep us away from God. The reason for this is that good things make better substitutes. Few people who are caught in a life of drug abuse or serial promiscuity can convince themselves that they have found the meaning of life and need search no further, but those who practice good and godly things like mother love and good works can easily turn those good things into idols that take the place of God. That is why when God came to earth in Christ, the Pharisees rejected him while the sinners, prostitutes, and tax collectors crowded to hear his words. Modern readers of the Bible may smile condescendingly when they read about God's anger over the idolatry of ancient Israel, but I believe that if we search ourselves honestly, we will find ourselves guilty of taking things from this world—sex, power, money, philanthropy, volunteerism, politics, the arts—and turning them into surrogate gods.

In one way or another, that is what all the damned souls in *The Great*

*Divorce* have done. They are, one and all, idolaters, and because they have persisted to the end in their idolatry, they are all utterly narcissistic. Capable only of loving themselves, their sins, and their idols, they have lost the ability to move out of themselves toward God or even toward other people. In hell they have no fellowship but live secluded in their own private prisons of narcissism. According to Lewis, "There are only two kinds of people in the end: those who say to God, 'Thy will be done,' and those to whom God says, in the end, '*Thy* will be done'" (chapter 9). But there is a great irony here: those who choose the former will find themselves growing more and more real, more and more substantial, while those who choose the latter will slowly deteriorate into insubstantial, personless ghosts.

I have found that many Americans consider hell "unfair" because they imagine that going to heaven or hell is like getting an A or an F in a college class—a concept that violates our modern egalitarian belief that all people should be treated the same. Thankfully, the analogy is a false one. There is not one college but *two* colleges: those majoring in the true external God enroll in the College of Heaven; those majoring in their own internal idol-god go to the College of Hell. The alma mater of the first school is "Thy Will Be Done"; the alma mater of the second is "I Did It My Way." There is no third option.

Hell then is a necessity if God is to honor the free will that he bestowed upon us from the beginning. Besides, as Lewis's case studies demonstrate so convincingly, those who choose to cling to themselves, their sins, and their idols have no desire to dwell in heaven, where the presence of God searches the hearts of all and illumines all with its light. Hell must exist, if only to give people who reject God a place to go. But that is not the whole story. Hell is not only a necessity for sinners; it is a necessity for saints as well.

Like petty-minded adolescents who insist that all siblings get exactly the same-size piece of pie for dessert, modern people have made a pseudo virtue (or idol) out of absolute equality. We refuse to believe that anyone in heaven can be happy while there are miserable people stuck in hell. To this piece of modern logic chopping, Lewis gives the lie. Beware, he warns us, lest we fall into that fine-sounding liberal plea that none should be happy until all are; that kind of logic only spreads misery. It would taint heaven itself if God were foolish enough to allow it. On earth, a willful child, by refusing to enjoy his trip to the park, has the power to spoil the day for his entire family; in heaven that power is denied him.

The manipulation that parades as unselfishness, the pity that binds, the love that smothers are all strictly confined to hell; heaven is free of such petty blackmail. God, insists Lewis, will not allow a miserable dog in a manger to tyrannize all heaven.

Blake was half right when, in *The Marriage of Heaven and Hell*, he claimed that heaven and hell are states of mind rather than objective realities. Hell is indeed a state of mind—a surrender to eternal misery, a final closing of the heart to love and joy, a shrinking of the human personality and its God-given potential. But heaven is the very opposite—an embrace of true reality that is more real and tangible and substantial than anything we have ever encountered on earth. The reason why Lewis gave his Dantean study of heaven and hell such a strange title was that he wanted to proclaim not the marriage of heaven and hell, but their great divorce. For between the joy of heaven and the narcissism of hell there can be no union, no trespass, no echo.

In closing, let me add that Lewis was not only an apologist for hell but a great defender of heaven. In the face of modern detractors who dismiss heaven as wish fulfillment or "pie in the sky" or, worse yet, a mercenary payoff, Lewis championed the higher vision of heaven that is presented to us in Scripture. Heaven marks the consummation both of our yearnings and desires and of our spiritual and emotional growth. Our *final* goal, as I explained in chapter 3, is not salvation but *theosis*: becoming like God. And as for the charge that Christians are mercenaries because they seek heaven as a reward for services rendered, Lewis responds that no one is mercenary who seeks an *appropriate* reward. The true lover is not a mercenary because he seeks marriage; neither is the noble general a mercenary because he seeks a victory in battle. Marriage and victory are the proper, fitting rewards of love and battle; just so, heaven is our true home, the natural, logical end to all our earthly longings.

# 7

# MORE THAN BALDER, NOT LESS: C. S. LEWIS AND THE APOLOGETICS OF MYTH

Most readers of C. S. Lewis are aware that the greatest Christian apologist of the twentieth century spent the first half of his life as a confirmed atheist and naturalist. Fewer are aware that Lewis's conversion did not occur in a single leap from atheism to Christianity but in a series of two distinct leaps (or steps) of faith. Lewis spent two years as a theist—as a believer in the existence of God but not in the deity of Christ—before embracing Jesus of Nazareth as the Incarnate Son of God. Significantly, the impetus behind his "second conversion" came not from the rational arguments surveyed in the previous chapters but from a more imaginative and intuitive rethinking of myth. I say this is significant because it is one of the reasons that Lewis the apologist continues to speak not only to modernists who seek a logical reason for believing in the supernatural but to postmodernists who seek a religion that will not rob them of their sense of wonder, magic, and mystery.

## MYTH MADE FACT

Like many educated men of his age, Lewis, guided by his reading of Sir James Frazer's *The Golden Bough*, considered the gospel story to be a myth. Even after accepting the existence of God, Lewis's reading of Frazer convinced him that no modern, rational man could accept as historical fact the virgin birth or the atonement or the resurrection. True, Lewis's lifelong love of mythology allowed him to enjoy the gospel as a cracking good tale, but Frazer seemed to have "proven" that it couldn't be thought of as anything more.

Frazer, like the later Joseph Campbell, was a comparative anthropologist who cataloged such persistent mythic patterns as the god or demigod who dies and rises again. Nearly every ancient and/or primitive culture possesses some version of the Corn King archetype—of a divine or semidivine hero whose death and rebirth follow the seasonal cycle of the sowing and reaping of the grain (what we call wheat, the British call corn) or of the planting and harvesting of the grape. In Egypt the hero's name is Osiris; in Greece he appears as Adonis or Bacchus. The Babylonians and Persians call him Tammuz and Mithras respectively, and among the Norsemen he bears the name of Balder. In all cases, his dying and rising bring new life and fecundity to those who worship him and an expiation of taboo guilt to those who celebrate his rites.

Few who study such Corn King myths fail to make the connection between Osiris or Adonis and Jesus. Don't the Gospels present Christ as just such a demigod who was slain as a ritual scapegoat to pay for our sins and who subsequently rose to new life? And doesn't the connection between Osiris-Adonis and Christ prove that Christianity should, indeed *must*, be read in purely mythic terms? For the pre-Christian Lewis it seemed clear that the modern "science" of anthropology had demonstrated beyond a shadow of a doubt that the Nativity and Passion plays celebrated by Christians represented nothing more than the Jewish version of the same old mythic archetype, that is, until his friend J. R. R. Tolkien, author of The Lord of the Rings trilogy and a committed Catholic, suggested to Lewis another way to interpret the evidence.

On one fateful evening in 1931, Lewis and Tolkien took a long walk around the lovely grounds of Oxford's Magdalen College. As they walked, they discussed the mythic aspects of the gospel story, and Lewis confessed his inability to believe in the historical truth of Christmas, Good Friday, and Easter. Tolkien granted the difficulty but then suggested to Lewis that perhaps the reason Christ resembled so closely the myths of the pagans was that Christ was the myth that came true. Perhaps the stories recorded in the Gospels represented God's historical enactment of a divine plan and truth that the pagans yearned for in their myths.

Indeed, inspired by Tolkien's suggestion, Lewis the apologist came to view myths not merely as ancient tales or communal dreams but as glimpses, road signs, pointers to a greater truth that would be revealed literally and historically in Christ. "The heart of Christianity," explains Lewis in an essay titled "Myth Became Fact" (anthologized in *God in the*

*Dock*), "is a myth which is also a fact. The old myth of the Dying God, *without ceasing to be myth*, comes down from the heaven of legend and imagination to the earth of history. . . . We pass from a Balder or an Osiris, dying nobody knows when or where, to a historical Person crucified (it is all in order) *under Pontius Pilate*." What makes the Christian story unique is that it happened at a specific time in a specific place—not in mythic time but in datable, historical time. The ancient Egyptians and Greeks who celebrated the rites of Osiris and Adonis felt no more need to fix their Corn Kings on a chronological timetable than Hindus today feel the need to date the many incarnations (avatars) of Vishnu. What "saves" such religious followers is not the actual historical enactment of incarnation/resurrection but the idea, the story, the myth. The case is exactly the opposite for Christianity. If it could be shown that Christ's miraculous birth, death, and resurrection were only stories and not physical, historical realities, then Christianity would be exposed as a hoax.

Christianity is first and foremost a historical religion, and yet it is also, at the same time, a mythic religion. In fact, one of the apologetic insights that Lewis took away from his night walk with Tolkien was that the pervasive, cross-cultural presence of Corn King myths does not weaken but strengthens the case for Christ! Far from undercutting the claims of Christ, the Corn King myths show that Christianity is not a foreign thing "imposed" on the world by a small Middle Eastern tribe but is the answer to a universal human need. Until the coming of Christ, writes Lewis in book 2, chapter 3, of *Mere Christianity*, God spoke to us in three ways: through our consciences, through a historical people group (the Jews), and through the "good dreams" of the pagans: "I mean those queer stories scattered all through the heathen religions about a god who dies and comes to life again and, by his death, has somehow given new life to men."

From the very foundation of the faith, Christians have believed that Jesus Christ fulfilled all the messianic prophecies recorded in the Old Testament. To this central tenet of biblical Christianity, Lewis adds a second level: in addition to fulfilling the Law and the Prophets, Christ fulfilled as well the highest yearnings of the pre-Christian pagan world. What makes the gospel of Christ so compelling is that it appeals not only to our reason but to our imagination. Since it is true, Lewis explains in "Myth Became Fact," that Christ is more than Balder and his fellow Corn Kings, he is not therefore less. Without sacrificing historical truth, Christ sums up within himself the perennial mythic longing for a bridge between the human and the divine. He is the True Myth, able to satisfy our twin desire, and need, for earthly reality and heavenly mystery.

Building on Lewis's apologetic, and conscious of our postmodern unease with absolutist truth claims, I would argue that believing Christians need not insist that Christianity is the only truth. Though fallen, we were all made in the image of God, and therefore we should expect to find bits and pieces of truth in every culture and religion—whether in the teachings of sages like Buddha or Confucius or in the myths of poets like Homer and Virgil. Rather than claim that Christianity is the only truth, I would argue instead that it is the only *complete* truth. Yes, truth is at the top of the hill, and there are many ways around that hill, but the Truth that lies at the top is Christ himself—he who is the Way, the Truth, and the Life. To my mind, the Magi offer a powerful symbol of pre-Christian pagans who trusted to their limited knowledge of the stars and followed it until it led them to the full revelation of Christ. When they arrived at Bethlehem, they accepted the Christ-child not as a contradiction to their search for wisdom but as the fulfillment, the consummation of what they—and, behind them, their culture and religion—had yearned for all their lives. Just so, Christians throughout the Middle Ages recognized Plato and Virgil as proto-Christians used by God to prepare the pagan world for the coming of Christ. The Renaissance artist Michelangelo even included the pagan oracles and sibyls on the Sistine Chapel, interspersing them with the prophets of the Old Testament. The apostle Paul himself quoted pagan poets as pointers to Christ in his great apologetic address before the Stoic and Epicurean philosophers of Athens (Acts 17:28).

A parallel to Lewis's argument that Christ is the myth made fact may be found in the way moderns have interpreted the flood story recorded in the Epic of Gilgamesh. Many social studies teachers—sharing the modernist presuppositions of Frazer and Campbell—have taught their students that because all ancient cultures tell stories of a universal flood, the biblical account of Noah must clearly be dismissed as a myth. There is, however, as there is with the Corn King myths, another way to read the factual data: if every culture has a flood story, that suggests there was an actual flood that was the *origin* of all these stories. And if that is true, then perhaps the memory of this flood, while retaining only mythic value in the various cultures of the world, retained some historical value in the sacred book of the Jews.

Though the claims of Christianity do not rest on the historicity of the Genesis flood, I use this example to show how modernism is driven as much by assumptions as by facts. Jung would tell us that such mythic archetypes as the flood or the dying god rise up from our "collective unconscious," but what is the origin of this universal memory bank? The fact that we all share a universal feeling that the world should be better than it is suggests either mass delusion or that we all share an antenatal memory of Eden. Why is there in mankind a universal feeling of guilt that necessitates not just human but divine expiation and a universal longing for God to dwell with man? The fact that these feelings and longings cut across all times and cultures suggests that they were put in us not by a purposeless and unconscious "collective unconscious" but by a purposeful and personal Creator who desires communion with his creatures. And if that is the case, it stands to reason that when that Creator enacts our salvation literally and historically, he will do it in a way that squares with our deepest mythic desires. Once again, the fact that the gospel story resembles so strongly the myths of the pagans should draw us closer, not further, from the One who claimed to be, in real historical time, the only-begotten Son of God.

## FACT MADE MYTH

When Lewis's work came to America, it impacted two distinct groups: those who feared Christianity was only about feeling and emotion and had little rational content and those who tried to guard Christian doctrine by keeping it free from the "taint" of myth, fiction, and imagination. In contrast to the second group, Lewis's conversion allowed him to re-access his love of fairy tales, a love of which his embrace of modernism/materialism had partly robbed him. One of the milestones on his way to faith occurred a full fifteen years before his conversion, while he was studying under a tutor who was both a strict logician and an atheist. By chance he read George Macdonald's *Phantastes* and found that the experience had baptized his imagination and reintroduced him to a sense of the sacred and the holy. Only in Christ, Lewis came to believe, does one encounter a doctrine and a story that inspires joy *and* terror, beauty *and* fear—an emotion Lewis would call, after Rudolf Otto's *The Idea of the Holy*, the numinous.

In search of an apologetic that would open the eyes of cynical and worldly moderns to the numinous aspects of Christianity, Lewis turned not to traditional nonfiction works like *Mere Christianity* but to fantasy. In his beloved Chronicles of Narnia, Lewis infused his greatest fictional creation, Aslan, the Lion King of Narnia, with just this sense of numinous awe, thus fashioning a unique apologetic that has proven able to speak not only to moderns but to postmoderns as well. Lewis asked himself what the Second Person of the Trinity might have been like had he been incarnated in a magical land of talking animals. His answer was Aslan, and most readers, whether they be moderns or post-moderns, who encounter Aslan in the Chronicles are drawn to his sacrificial goodness (he willingly bears humiliation and death for a traitor) and his awesome power (he rises from the dead and restores Narnia). With Aslan at their center, the Chronicles embody a world where all the eternal, invisible truths I have discussed in the last six chapters exist in real, tangible form. Indeed, as the Chronicles not only illustrate but incarnate and bring alive to the emotions the more rational arguments I have been making in this book, I shall end this chapter by sketching a number of scenes that give, as it were, flesh and blood to Lewis's more abstract apologetic proofs.

*The supernatural origin of joy and the Tao*: In *The Silver Chair* two children and a Narnian Marsh-wiggle named Puddleglum journey into the underground lair of the Emerald Witch and rescue Prince Rilian from a powerful enchantment. Unfortunately, before they can escape, the Witch catches them and locks the doors (chapter 12). We expect that she will use violence to stop them, but instead she throws magic dust into the fire and begins to strum on a mandolin. Slowly, seductively she convinces them that the world of Narnia that they *know* exists does not really exist, that it is nothing but a childish dream they have made up for themselves. Neither the sun nor Aslan really exists; they are just illusions they made up, mythic copies of real, mundane torches and cats. They almost give in, when Puddleglum, in an act of desperation, shoves his foot in the fire; the pain brings him back to his senses, and he boldly proclaims that even if Narnia and Aslan are myths, he prefers them to the Witch's dark world. Contra the teachings of Freud, Marx, and the secular academic world, material things are not the source of our religious yearnings. What we know in our hearts to be true really is true: heaven is the true original; the things of our world are but pale copies.

*The Trilemma*: In *The Lion, the Witch and the Wardrobe*, a young girl (Lucy) tries to convince her siblings that she has been to the land of Narnia, but they reject her story. Again and again she insists on the reality of Narnia, but the other children simply refuse to accept the possibility that a world like Narnia could actually exist. Not knowing what else to do, the two older siblings consult a Lewis-like professor on the matter (chapter 5). To their great surprise, the professor explains to them that, logically speaking, Lucy must be either mad, telling a lie, or telling the truth. Since it is clear to everyone that she is not crazy, and since her siblings have always known her to be truthful—and since, the professor adds, a charge of lying against someone who has always been truthful is a serious charge indeed!—they *must* consider the possibility that she is telling the truth about Narnia. Faith in Christ, the episode helps us to see, is based on logical arguments and should not be dismissed merely because it doesn't fit into our modernist worldview.

*The Problem of Pain*: In *The Magician's Nephew*, a boy (Digory), whose mother is dying of cancer, is commanded by Aslan to pluck a magic apple with which he will heal Narnia. Digory finds the apple but is tempted by a Witch to steal it, return to the earth, and use it to heal his mother. Digory stays faithful, and Aslan tells him (chapter 14) that had he stolen the apple it would have healed his mother, but both boy and mother would have lived to regret the choice. In a moment of shocked and painful insight, we and Digory learn "that there might be things more terrible even than losing someone you love by death."

*Miracles*: In *The Voyage of the Dawn Treader* (chapter 14), an imagination-less boy (Eustace), trained to think only in material terms, learns that in Narnia stars are people. Surprised by this revelation, Eustace tells a star-man (Ramandu) that in our world a star is nothing but a flaming ball of gas, but Ramandu corrects him: "Even in your world, my son, that is not what a star is but only what it is made of." The modern world has reduced all things, from the beauty of the cosmos to the soul of man, to material principles: our self-satisfied arrogance has blinded us to the unseen.

*Hell*: In *The Magician's Nephew*, Digory and the evil Queen Jadis—who will eventually become the White Witch—witness the creation of Narnia, which is literally sung into being by Aslan. However, while Digory and the other good characters take joy in the music and are uplifted by it, the Witch has a very different reaction: "Her mouth was shut, her lips were pressed together, and her fists were clenched. Ever since the song began she had felt that this whole world was filled with a Magic different from hers and stronger. She hated it. She would have smashed that whole world, or all worlds, to pieces, if it would only stop the singing" (chapter 8). Unable to appreciate or understand the music, the Witch even tries, unsuccessfully, to kill Aslan with an iron bar. Like the damned souls in

*The Great Divorce*, she lacks ears to hear and is trapped in her own self-imposed hell of ugliness and cacophony.

*Myth made fact*: In *The Last Battle* (chapter 15), a noble pagan, Emeth (Hebrew for "truth"), dies and expects to meet his god (Tash). Instead he meets Aslan, who tells him that the good he did for Tash was actually done for him and that his search for truth has led him to Aslan. Interestingly, this episode has caused many Christian fans of Lewis's work to feel uneasy. "Is Lewis the orthodox apologist advocating universal salvation?" they wonder. But that is not Lewis's point at all. If Aslan had invited Emeth to enter and dwell in the Tash part of heaven, then Lewis's critics would be justified, but something very different happens. As Emeth stands before Aslan, he realizes that Tash and Aslan are not two different names for the same God but that they are complete opposites. Rather than learning that all religions are the same, Emeth learns that Aslan alone is the true end of his "pagan" longings and desire. "Beloved," Aslan explains, "unless thy desire had been for me thou wouldst not have sought so long and so truly. For all find what they truly seek." Like the Magi, faith and salvation in Aslan mark for Emeth the end of a long spiritual pilgrimage.

# 8

# THE JOURNEY BACK HOME:
# HOW G. K. CHESTERTON "DISCOVERED"
# ORTHODOXY

Though most of Lewis's philosophical and theological arguments can be traced back to such classic apologists as Athanasius, Augustine, and Aquinas, his unique style, approach, and tone can be traced back to a writer who was far closer to him in time: G. K. Chesterton. Born twenty-four years before Lewis, Chesterton was the twentieth century's first great apostle of common sense—a man of prodigious talent and energy who took Christianity to the masses in a way that few had done before. Able to comment intelligently and entertainingly on almost any topic, Chesterton challenged Englishmen of all classes and backgrounds to wrestle seriously with the doctrinal claims of Christianity. He even showed himself courageous enough to debate publicly the late Victorian age's most eloquent and charismatic skeptic, George Bernard Shaw.

Like Lewis, the key to Chesterton's lasting appeal is that he speaks both to the head and to the heart, transforming Christianity from a collection of dry, dusty doctrines into a vital and passionate love affair with God and with orthodoxy. Though Chesterton's apologetics is ever backed by reason, he writes with imaginative force and a generous helping of wit and paradox. Lewis himself was unashamed to acknowledge the debt that he owed to Chesterton and strove to inject the same kind of wit and paradox into his own writing. Indeed, as one who loves both Chesterton and Lewis, I would argue that one of Lewis's greatest achievements as a popular apologist was his ability to enshrine Chestertonian paradox in his work while simultaneously trimming back its rough edges. As anyone who has read Chesterton can attest, his prose, while delightful and invigorating, can also be a bit exhausting—for his love of paradox often gets the best of him, taking both author and reader down wonderful, if distracting, tangents. In this chapter and the next, I will, in the spirit of Lewis, attempt to present Chesterton's apologetics in a somewhat more linear fashion.

Still, those unaccustomed to Chesterton's style may wish to pause for a moment to put on their mental seat belts!

## ORIGINAL SIN

A sort of sui generis mixture of Lewis's *Mere Christianity* and *Surprised by Joy*, Chesterton's *Orthodoxy* presents its reader with a defense of traditional creedal Christianity in the guise of an autobiographical account of Chesterton's personal journey to faith. As we accompany Chesterton on his journey, our eyes are successively opened to the philosophical and theological weaknesses of Western-inspired materialism, with its attempt to remove God from the universe, and Eastern-inspired pantheism, with its attempt to make God and the universe the same. In the face of these flawed systems, Chesterton struggles to create a system of his own that can account for the downright strangeness of man and his world. Bit by bit he constructs his system only to find, when the last piece is put in place, that what he has invented is that very Christian orthodoxy passed down to us by the apostles and the fathers of the Church. Like Lewis after him, Chesterton discovers that only Christianity really makes sense of everything—that it, and it alone, possesses just the right twist of truth.

The core problem with the modern world, Chesterton reveals to us in a burst of insight, is that it has taught us to "humbly" doubt the truth and believe in ourselves. Rather than recognize our own intellectual and moral limits and seek to conform ourselves to higher truths that transcend our own personal and cultural narcissism, we insist on debunking the truths of our forefathers and "thinking for ourselves." Alas, writes Chesterton, our mad pursuit of this upside-down ethic has not led us upward toward joy, fullness, and wisdom but downward into despair, emptiness, and mental suicide.

As exhibit A in his case against the modern world, Chesterton argues that our misplaced self-confidence has led us to deny the one Christian doctrine that does not need to be proven: original sin. According to the Bible, we were made good and perfect in the image of God, but we rebelled against our Creator and fell into sin, separation, and decay. Does the history of human thought know of any other explanation that can adequately account for both the goodness and the evil, the glory and the baseness of humanity? The great riddle of man is not merely that the same human race can produce both a Hitler and a Mother Theresa, but that every one of us contains *within himself* both a Hitler and a Mother Theresa. To paraphrase the great Russian Orthodox writer Solzhenitsyn, the dividing line between good and evil does not run through this or that party or this or that nation but through every human heart. Our human potential for love, courage, and altruism is matched only by our equally human potential for hatred, cowardice, and greed.

The presence of evil in our world and in ourselves, reasons Chesterton, suggests one of two scenarios: either God does not exist (atheism and its functional equivalent, materialism) or God and man are in a broken relationship (original sin). But take care, warns Chesterton. If we embrace the first option, we will find ourselves stranded in a dead, cramped, fatalistic universe without any set standards. Materialism may seem, on the surface, to provide an all-sufficient answer, but it is ultimately a philosophical dead end.

Chesterton, in chapter 2 of *Orthodoxy*, compares the materialist to the madman, for both come up with a simple system that they think can explain everything, but that in fact explains almost nothing. Both are trapped "in the clean and well-lit prison of one idea," and that is why we encounter in their systems "the combination of an expansive and exhaustive reason with a contracted common sense." What they leave out of their system far exceeds what they put into it. In the face of the apparent triumph of atheism and materialism, Chesterton reminds us of what such a triumph really means: "If the cosmos of the materialist is the real cosmos, it is not much of a cosmos. The thing has shrunk . . . the whole of life is something much more grey, narrow, and trivial than many separate aspects of it. The parts seem greater than the whole." In the end, the cosmos of the materialist is not all that different from the padded, if well-illuminated cell of the madman—neither offers true liberation or true engagement with that double marvel that is man and his world.

But the cramped nature of its cosmos is not the only flaw that Chesterton finds in the materialist worldview. It is flawed at a much deeper and more foundational level. In constructing his worldview, the materialist thinks that he can simply separate reason from faith, but no such divorce is possible. Reason, as it is celebrated and utilized by the materialist heirs of the Enlightenment, rests firmly upon a *religious* faith that our thoughts are meaningful and linked to reality. Therefore, to doubt faith is to doubt reason itself. The triumph of materialism marks the destruction of rationalism. In chapter 3 of *Miracles*, Lewis, perhaps influenced by Chesterton, makes the same observation about the materialistic theories of the naturalists: "A theory which explained everything else in the whole universe but which made it impossible to believe that our thinking was valid, would be utterly out of court. For that theory would itself have been reached by thinking, and if thinking is not valid that theory would, of course, be itself demolished. It would have destroyed its own credentials."

## BUILDING UTOPIA

Central to the apologetic arguments of both Lewis and Chesterton is the commonsense observation that the systems of the materialists and naturalists are, as systems, self-refuting. They cannot account for the very thing that allows them to account for everything else—that is, the reality and validity of human reason. Worse yet, adds Chesterton, materialism renders the modernist mission to build utopia null and void. True, a materialist society like our own *can* strive to be progressive, but without any fixed, transcendent standard of good and evil, right and wrong, how can we know that we *have* progressed? Apart from such a standard, we can never reach utopia, for we will be forever redefining it!

Indeed, in seeking after utopia we may discover that we have built a dystopia instead. With great sadness, Chesterton exposes a paradox that lies at the heart of post-Enlightenment materialism and skepticism: though most modern materialists think of themselves as liberal, their teachings do not liberate humanity. To the contrary, such teachings enslave us to materialist dogma, leaving us *un-free* to find real purpose in the universe or to conform ourselves and our society to absolute, transcendent standards or to believe in a miracle-working God who intervenes lovingly in the affairs of his cosmos. For if materialism is true, then we are all trapped in a deterministic universe in which free will is ultimately meaningless. This loss of all human volition, dignity, and purpose marks Chesterton's strongest critique of materialism, a critique that he boldly extends to any form of Christian hyper-Calvinism that would ascribe to a doctrine of total predestination. Any system, whether religious or secular, that cannot account adequately for the mystery of human choice is a partial system at best and must be rejected by those who would truly seek after the Truth about man and his world. It is also a system that cannot really change the world for the better—and

Chesterton, for all the "conservatism" of his orthodoxy, was very much a "liberal" in his desire to see justice done in our fallen world.

Chesterton's was not the only voice in his day, or in our own, that spoke out against the philosophical flaws of materialism and its inability to foster true justice. Many thinkers over the last century have sought to escape from the disenchanted, fatalistic world of the materialists by turning to the more mysterious, pantheistic religions of the East. Unwilling to embrace the transcendent view of God taught by the Bible (God created the world), such thinkers find solace in the more immanent view of God held by Hindus and Buddhists (God *is* the world). But here, too, Chesterton identifies serious flaws. If the materialism of Europe cannot change the world because it has no standard, the Buddhism of Tibet is even less able to change the world because it is too isolated and indifferent. The excessive introspection of Buddhism is finally just as fatalistic as materialism. In its Western incarnation, this stoical, inward-focused Buddhism often looks to the "inner light" for guidance. Unfortunately, Chesterton reminds us, those who worship the inner light, whether they be Eastern Buddhists or Western Transcendentalists, inevitably end up worshiping not God but themselves.

Buddhism is finally centripetal, turning the self back upon itself in an endless circle without change or growth. Christianity, in contrast, is centrifugal and breaks out of the circle.

The Buddhist worldview, Chesterton explains, is not just pantheistic but monistic; it believes not only that God is in everything and is everything but that all things, if we only knew it, are actually one—that is to say, there is no final distinction between God and man. Not only does this worldview collapse all standards of good and evil, it makes it impossible for us to praise God, to discern any real magic in nature, or to desire truly to reform the world around us. "By insisting specially on the immanence of God," writes Chesterton in chapter 8, "we get introspection, self-isolation, quietism, social indifference—Tibet. By insisting specially on the transcendence of God we get wonder, curiosity, moral and political adventure, righteous indignation—Christendom. Insisting that God is inside man, man is always inside himself. By insisting that God transcends man, man has transcended himself."

Like the materialist, the Buddhist fails to understand the true nature of creation and the fall. Whereas Christianity posits that God created us as separate beings in hopes that we would grow to be like him, but we fell into disobedience, Buddhism posits that individual personality *is* the fall of man. Once again, only the Christian doctrine of original sin can preserve the dignity and integrity of man while accounting for the evil within him. Nietzsche, writes Chesterton, seemed at first to have found a way to break us out of the Buddhist circle of indifference and the materialist box of fatalism by calling for a group of over-men (or supermen) with the charisma to shake off religious and cultural paralysis and assert their will to power. But Nietzsche, too, leads us to a dead end, for if *everything* we will is correct, then choice and will are meaningless.

In contrast to Nietzsche's vigorous call to move society beyond all bourgeois notions of good and evil, the last century has more often produced passive, "wishy-washy" voices that lull us into believing that all religions are ultimately the same, differing only in their external practices. But such a "compromise" cannot provide the answer to the riddle of man and his world, for the truth about religion is exactly the opposite. *All* religious people fast, pray, give alms, and attend worship services; it is not in the periphery but at the center, in their cores, in their nonnegotiable theological doctrines, that religions differ widely. Besides, argues Chesterton, most moderns will *say* all religions are equally true, but then go on to show either that their materialistic principles have superseded all religions or that all religions are somehow contained in a generic pantheism.

It was this insincere stance and, behind it, the final inability of materialism and pantheism to account for the true nature of man and his world that pushed Chesterton, at first unwillingly, to consider seriously the doctrines of Christianity. And one more thing. Why, Chesterton began to ask himself, do the critics of Christianity persist in accusing it of contradictory sins and weaknesses? No sooner does one group of critics accuse Christianity of being too optimistic, with its "fairy-tale" belief that man was a special creation of God, than another accuses it of being too pessimistic, with its "dark" doctrine of the fall and its "obsession" with sin and guilt. One group says Christianity is too weak and unmanly, the other that it is too warlike. One says its focus on celibacy is antifamily, the other that it overemphasizes procreation. "What was this Christianity," Chesterton asks himself in chapter 6, "which always forbade war and always produced wars? What could be the nature of the thing which one could abuse first because it would not fight, and second because it was always fighting? In what world of riddles was born this monstrous murder and this monstrous meekness? The shape of Christianity grew a queerer shape every instant."

## FAIRY-TALE ETHICS

As we have already seen, Chesterton was forced in the end to acknowledge that this queer-shaped Christianity, with its strange doctrines of original sin, the incarnation, and the Trinity, was the only system of belief that could make sense of us and our world and inspire true growth and progress. In contrast to the gloominess and self-contradictory beliefs of materialism and pantheism, Chesterton found in Christianity a robust health that appealed to his heart and an inexhaustible supply of paradoxical truths that appealed to his head. And he found, too, a kind of wonder and magic that spoke to the perennial child within.

Like Lewis after him, Chesterton was a great lover of and advocate for fairy tales; indeed he believed that fairy tales, far from being frivolous tales for immature children, embodied the collective wisdom of mankind. Long before the adult Chesterton took up the Bible as God's authoritative Word, the child Chesterton had learned from fairy tales to discern the true magic in nature and her Creator. Materialism tries to systematize everything in the universe, but fairy tales know better; like the Gospels, they open our eyes to the mystery inherent in every tree, every frog, and every man.

In chapter 4 of *Orthodoxy*, Chesterton, the apologist for fairy tales *and* the Gospels, answers the critique of materialists who claim that the clockwork nature of our universe precludes the existence of a personal Creator. What if, he suggests, the fact that the sun has risen and set in a fixed pattern since time began does not indicate an empty, mechanical lifelessness but a dynamic divine activity. When we play a game with our children, and they enjoy it, they will ask us to repeat it again and again until we are bored, exhausted, or both. For you see, counsels Chesterton, we grown-ups "are not strong enough to exult in monotony."

> But perhaps God is strong enough to exult in monotony. It is possible that God says every morning, "Do it again" to the sun; and every evening, "Do it again" to the moon. It may not be automatic necessity that makes all daisies alike; it may be that God makes every daisy separately, but has never got tired of making them. It may be that He has the eternal appetite of infancy; for we have sinned and grown old, and our Father is younger than we. The repetition in Nature may not be a mere recurrence; it may be a theatrical *encore*.

There is something of that "eternal appetite of infancy" in many of those moderns who have rejected materialism in favor of pantheism.

Chesterton, like Lewis, would use his apologetics to direct them back to the wonders of a fully realized Christian universe in which God is both the Creator of and a Participant in that sacred story that stretches from the fall of man to the death and resurrection of Christ to the final redemption of man and his world.

It was the fairy tales that first spoke to Chesterton of God's eternal appetite, and it was the fairy tales as well that first revealed to him why we live in a state of estrangement from that divine exaltation and joy. From fairy tales Chesterton learned that though we are all meant to dwell in the garden of Eden, our residence in that most beautiful of fairy-tale kingdoms is always, always conditional. Moderns dismiss the fall of man as *only* a myth, but Genesis discerns the truth behind the myth: we can have anything we want as long as we don't pluck a flower or open a box or speak a forbidden word. Experience, fairy tales, and orthodoxy tell us that we are involved in a drama in which our choices are real and have consequences; we can win all, but we can also lose all.

And that brings us back to where we began—original sin. Only that much-maligned doctrine can make sense of our status as castaways adrift from some great ruin; it alone explains why we feel at home in the world and yet strangers in the world. In a nice twist, Chesterton argues that original sin is the great bulwark of democracy, for it alone puts prince and pauper on the same footing. Christian Europe never really believed that aristocrats were superior people, but the Hindu caste system believed it. The Christian doctrines of creation and fall exalt *and* humble man, providing a firm, unshakable foundation both for realism (we can't build utopia) and revolution (but let us seek to restore Eden).

Only the paradoxes of Christianity—particularly the incarnation and the Trinity—can achieve a higher equilibrium between pessimism and optimism, resignation and willfulness. Christ, who was fully man and fully God, reconciles in himself all the furious opposites of our world: he was both the great King come to earth and the great Rebel. In Christ, and in Christ alone, does God demonstrate courage, joy, and a romantic spirit of adventure. The doctrine of the incarnation is humanity's one great metaphysical-historical proof that matter and personality are inherently good and that they can and must be redeemed. The incarnation tells us that our world was made good while simultaneously teaching us that our destiny lies beyond this world.

It has been the two thousand-year mission of the church to guard the orthodoxy of the incarnation, lest it fall into Arianism (denying the divinity of Christ) and thus seek only worldly power or into Gnosticism (denying the manhood of Christ) and thus dismiss both flesh and matter as evil. It has guarded as well the Trinity, for only the Trinity teaches us that God is a community, that he is more like a parliament in session than an absolute autocrat. When Muhammad denied the Trinity, he started a religion that, in the name of its lonely, radically unitarian God, ever seeks to destroy Western democracy: "Out of the desert, from the dry places and the dreadful suns, come the cruel children of the lonely God; the real Unitarians who with scimitar in hand have laid waste the world" (chapter 8).

So warned Gilbert Keith Chesterton a full century before 9/11.

# 9

# FROM CAVEMEN TO CHRISTIANS: G. K. CHESTERTON'S PRÉCIS OF HISTORY

In *Orthodoxy*, Chesterton pauses often to list the many paradoxes that lie at the heart of Christianity. Here are five of them: 1) Christianity hails her martyrs as heroes but completely condemns suicide; 2) Christianity praises and exalts both virginity and marriage; 3) Christianity teaches us how we can both love the sinner and hate the sin; 4) Christianity teaches us how to be severe in judgment and rich in mercy; 5) Christianity holds the lion and the lamb in tension, ever preventing one from devouring the other.

In *The Everlasting Man*, written seventeen years after *Orthodoxy*—during which time the Anglican Chesterton converted to Catholicism—he moves beyond these scattered paradoxes to view as from a great height the crazy-wonderful, chaotically meaningful pageant of human history. With wit, audacity, and great bravura, Chesterton, in the space of some 250 pages, offers a remarkably detailed Christian overview of history that critiques modern evolutionary thought, presents Christ as the culmination of the ancient world, and defends the church's defense of orthodoxy.

## OF PRIMITIVE ART AND PRIMITIVE MEN

Chesterton begins his précis of history by both inviting and challenging his reader to view Christianity and the central role it has played in the parade of human history, either from the inside (as a believer) or from the outside (as, say, a Hindu might). This may sound like an odd request until we realize that most of the scientists, anthropologists, and biblical critics of Chesterton's day—and our own—studied Christianity from the point of view of antagonists or rebels against the church. True, modern academics *claim* impartiality, but they more often than not view Christianity with the nonobjective eyes of the iconoclast, of the Oedipal son who rises up against the authority and identity of his father. They neither afford it the love paid it by full believers nor the disinterested detachment paid it by curious outsiders. Indeed, they never really *see* Christianity at all, for they are both too close to it (as the outsider never is) and too far away from it (as the believer never is). By empowering us to see from just the right perspective, Chesterton helps restore to us a proper vision not only of Christianity but of the historical forces that led up to it and that culminated in the creeds of the church.

Moderns begin human history with the caveman, from whom they claim we evolved along Darwin's branching tree. But what, asks Chesterton, do we really know about these so-called cavemen? On the basis of what evidence can we claim to know what they thought and felt and believed? Regarding Chesterton's question, the evolutionists of his day had a ready answer: the cave drawings we have found of reindeer and other animals provide us with a window into the primitive mind of the caveman. But the very evidence they use to prove the existence of the caveman is the evidence that refutes their claim. For the one thing that is clear about those famous drawings is that they were painted by *men*—not half men or glorified apes but men! Yes, the art is primitive, but that is only because the tools and methods used—*and not the artists themselves*—were primitive.

Art is a *fully human medium*; it gives evidence of a soul that does not exist *at all* in the animal kingdom. Art, writes Chesterton in part 1, chapter 2 of *The Everlasting Man*, "belongs to man and to nothing else except man; [it marks] a difference of kind and not a difference of degree. A monkey does not draw clumsily and a man cleverly; a monkey does not begin the art of representation and a man carry it to perfection. A monkey does not do it at all; . . . he does not begin to begin to do it at all. A line of some kind is crossed before the first faint line can begin." The difference between bird nests and human homes, between the scratch marks of a cat and the cave drawings of a man is not quantitative but qualitative. The leap from beast to man is not a matter of evolution but of revolution; as soul-possessing, art-creating animals we are truly freaks of nature.

People in Chesterton's day—and in our own—pointed to the "missing link" as proof of the evolution from ape to man, but Chesterton reminds us of what should be obvious—it is called the missing link precisely because it is *missing*. To speak positively or to reason scientifically about such a hypothetical creature is like trying to marry the girl you dreamed of last night or to purchase a live unicorn for your daughter's tenth birthday. Now Chesterton, like Lewis after him, did concede that evolutionary forces might have played a part in fashioning our bodies, but he excluded the soul from such naturalistic processes. The leap from beast to man, from animal to artist, takes place outside of time and has nothing to do with the evolutionary forces of time and chance.

Chesterton devotes much space to exploding the myth of the caveman as a warm-up to the greater purpose of his book: to expose how modern thinkers' obsession with evolution as the grand explanatory tool causes them to misread human history and to accept illogical conclusions. Victorian author H. G. Wells, in his influential *Outline of History*, argued that tribal man's fear of the chief combined with his mystical dreams and his awe at the seasonal cycle to form the "primitive" foundation of early religion. But the evolutionary Wells puts the cart before the horse: the only reason early man forged a link between these three things is because he *already possessed* a religious sense. To this day, evolutionary-minded anthropologists continue to posit a gradual progress from barbarism to civilization, from the Dark Ages to the Renaissance to the Enlightenment, from ritual to myth to religion to science, from animism to polytheism to pantheism to monotheism to rationalism. Anyone who has attended a public school in America or Europe should be familiar with this standard "social studies" spiel. It makes for a handy pedagogical tool, and it squares nicely with the evolutionary paradigm of the biologists, chemists, botanists, and geologists. The only trouble with it is that it is not true.

The fact is that the oldest cultures we have written records of (Babylon and Egypt) *already* show themselves to be highly civilized and to be living alongside more barbaric, nomadic tribes. The most ancient myths and legends we have tell of the *loss* of a golden age, not of some heroic struggle out of barbarism. Indeed, barbarism is more often than not something man has devolved into rather than evolved from. A close study of pagan cultures, argues Chesterton, suggests a "fall" (*not* an evolution) from an earlier monotheism into myths and rituals. The one God is never fully forgotten; rather, he slowly passes out of the religious life of the community until all that remains of his Presence are whispers in the dark.

Of the ancient peoples of the world, Israel alone retained in its purity the worship of the one true God. Only Israel resisted the pagan tendency toward syncretism that would form a pantheon out of innumerable competing gods. In the literature of the ancient world one encounters Athena-Isis or Zeus-Jupiter or Osiris-Adonis or Demeter-Cybele, but never a Jehovah-Jupiter or a Jehovah-Osiris. Moderns accuse the Jews of ethnocentrism and ethnic cleansing, but if Jehovah had not been a jealous God of war, the purity of Jewish monotheism would have been lost—not only to the Jews but to the world. While the pagan nations melted "into a mass of confused mythology, this Deity who is called tribal and narrow, precisely because he was what is called tribal and narrow, preserved the primary religion of all mankind. He was tribal enough to be universal. He was as narrow as the universe" (part 1, chapter 4).

## OF GOOD PAGANS AND BAD PAGANS

Though all the Gentile nations fell away from this primitive, original monotheism, they were not all equal in their falls. Chesterton distinguishes carefully between the good pagans who practiced the white magic of myth (what Lewis calls the good dreams of the pagans) and the bad pagans who practiced the black magic of witchcraft (whose single-minded pursuit is for power). Good paganism reached its culmination in Rome, where devotion to one's family and to one's household gods was expected and honored. The Roman people at their best sought to inculcate virtue and to rein in the excesses and perversions of surrounding nations, especially Greece. In the great soldiers and statesmen and poets of the Roman Republic, the four classical virtues defined by Plato and Aristotle—wisdom, courage, temperance, and justice—approached their zenith. Here were men who lived by a code, who sacrificed themselves for honor, who refused all bribes, who did not overindulge the flesh but beat their bodies into submission.

In direct opposition to Rome, bad paganism reached its culmination in Phoenicia, where human sacrifice was practiced and where innocent children were "fed" to the god Baal. Like the Aztecs and Mayans, the Phoenicians worshiped pitiless deities who shared their lust for power, blood, and conquest. Phoenicia controlled a mercantile empire run on greed, realpolitik, and the bottom line, and they set up outposts all over the Mediterranean world to ensure their control of the sea. The richest of those outposts was Carthage in North Africa, and it was only a matter of time before the Carthaginians sought to wrest control of the

Mediterranean from the young but virile Roman Republic. The result was the Punic Wars, a three-part series of battles between Rome and Carthage that stretched out over a century (from 264 B.C. to 146 B.C.) and that pushed Rome to the very brink of ruin.

According to Chesterton, the Punic Wars are the "good pagan" equivalent of the wars fought by Israel to acquire the Promised Land. Though Israel and Rome were poles apart, they both hated the evils of Phoenicia and were commissioned alike by the one true God to wipe these child-killers from the face of the earth. What Israel began under Joshua and David was brought to completion by the good pagans of Rome. The Punic Wars, argues Chesterton, were but the physical manifestation of a greater spiritual war between gods and demons, divine virtue and soulless power. During the Second Punic War, the brilliant Carthaginian general Hannibal (whose name means "the grace of Baal") swept through Italy like a storm and defeated every army that Rome sent against him; yet Rome did not fall. By the grace of a God whom she did not know, Rome rose again miraculously to defeat her enemy—and by defeating her enemy, she defeated as well the true enemy of man.

Once Carthage was defeated, Rome grew and matured and reached her perfection . . . and then stopped. She could, by the power of human wisdom and virtue alone, progress no further. It was at this very moment in history, Chesterton reminds us, that a long-awaited child was born who would lead the good pagans of Rome to their final glory. Whereas Rome had defeated the evil of Carthage and her allies, it would be left to Jesus Christ to defeat the evil itself that fueled the fires of Baal. When we view the birth of Christ through Chesterton's eyes, we see that his coming fulfilled not only the prophecies of the Jews but the pagan struggle for virtue, justice, and order. In Christ, the righteous Jew and the good pagan were reconciled—and something more, something that the pre-Christian world could not reconcile on its own.

Until the coming of Christ, writes Chesterton, none of the pagan nations could bring together myth and philosophy. On the one hand, the people and their priests sought, through myth, to reach god with their imaginations. On the other, the philosophers, both the neo-Platonists of the West and the Confucians of the East, sought truth through an appeal to reason. Whereas the religion of the former was based on tales, rituals, and images rather than on a systematic creed, the meditations of the latter either dismissed myths altogether or so allegorized them that they ceased to exert any hold on the imagination. Only with the birth of

Christianity did philosophic thought ally itself with the yearning for god and redemption that had always resonated behind the myths. The result of this marriage was something new in the history of man: a *true story*.

This miraculous alliance of myth and philosophy is best illustrated by the Christmas story itself, which presents us with simple shepherds and learned Magi who both kneel in wonder and reverence before the Christ child. And in that same Christmas story we catch sight as well of Phoenicia's last bid for power. For when Herod, threatened by the messianic child, murders the innocent babies of Bethlehem, we hear the last gasp of the demonic kings who would sacrifice innocent children to the Baal of their own lust for wealth and power.

Truly, the hopes and fears of all the years met in Bethlehem that night.

## OF DOCTRINE AND HERESY

If we study fairly and objectively the history of the world, Chesterton maintains, we will see that all the yearnings of man, from the artist in the cave to the astronomers of Babylon to the prophets of Israel to the good pagans of Rome, found their consummation in the One who reconciled in himself philosophy and myth and who, like Rome during the Second Punic War, died and rose again. But what of the church herself, she who has preserved the truths revealed and enacted by Christ? Does she represent the consummation of the consummation, or is she an unnatural growth that must be cut down by Enlightenment gardeners who study the church not as intimate insiders or detached outsiders but as rebels and iconoclasts?

In the face of modern critics who claimed—and who continue to claim—that Christian doctrine was invented by powerful political and religious leaders and then imposed upon the people, Chesterton asserts that the true origin of Christian doctrine is none other than the Incarnate Christ himself. Although all the higher myths longed for it, no human philosophy could have constructed the revolutionary and paradoxical truth that was revealed to the world on the first Christmas morning: the omnipotent Creator was also a defenseless child. "A mass of legends and literature, which increases and will never end, has repeated and rung the changes of that single paradox; that the hands that had made the sun and stars were too small to reach the huge heads of the cattle. Upon this paradox, we might almost say upon this jest, all the literature of our faith is founded" (part 2, chapter 1). The modern scientific mind dislikes jests and distrusts paradoxes, but the fact remains that it is upon this paradox—the God in the manger—that the entire foundation of the Christian church and its theology rests.

The doctrine of the incarnation embodies an eternal truth, not one unique to the Jewish people or to the culture of first-century Palestine. Indeed, the same may be said of all that Jesus says and does in the Gospels: none of it can be reduced to a cultural product, for all of it transcends that culture. Neither Jesus' exaltation of children nor his sacramental view of marriage, argues Chesterton, was held by people of his day. Jesus spoke not in platitudes but in timeless and prophetic truths. Most vital of all, no Jew of Jesus' day, whether Pharisee, Sadducee, Zionist, or Essene, would have made the claim that Jesus was God, unless Jesus himself made it. It would have been simply unthinkable. In fact, if there is one thing a study of Jesus' culture *can* teach us, it is how radically shocking his teachings would have sounded to contemporary ears.

Paving the way for Lewis's famous argument that Jesus was either liar, lunatic, or Lord, Chesterton boldly states that Jesus' humility and his grand claims are inconsistent unless he was God. Maybe if he were a Greek or a Roman his claims to divinity could have been accepted in the same way that Alexander the Great's or Julius Caesar's were; but he was neither. Modern critics of the Bible prefer simply to overlook this dilemma by placing all their focus on the moral and ethical teachings of Jesus and ignoring his claims about himself and his mission on earth. Such an approach, however, does violence to the Gospels. The Gospels, Chesterton reminds us, are not just records of sayings, like those of Buddha or Confucius, but dramatic accounts of Jesus' intentional and purposeful journey toward his sacrificial death. Remove the incarnation, the atonement, and the resurrection and you remove the very point of the gospel; indeed, apart from these three, there is no gospel, no "god-spel," no "good news."

The early church understood this well, and they fought as bravely and as persistently as their Jewish ancestors to preserve the truth revealed in Christ from the heretical forces of syncretism that would water it down and turn it to mush. The truth of this is evident to anyone who reads carefully and objectively the book of Acts and the letters of Paul and John, but the modern world has succeeded in obscuring this obvious and elemental truth. Just as paleontologists partly ignore and partly hide the fact that the fossil record shows not a slow evolution but an abrupt appearance of plant and animal species, so critics of Christianity partly ignore and partly hide the fact that the dogmatic witness of the church does not develop slowly but is already in full form at Pentecost. At an extremely early date, writes Chesterton in book 2, chapter 4, the Church "had a doctrine; it had a discipline; it had sacraments; it had degrees of initiation; it admitted people and expelled people; it affirmed one dogma with authority and repudiated another with anathemas." It fought the heretics with all its force, even when it was weak and persecuted itself.

Ironically, modern critics attack the church for its early heresy hunting, forgetting that the early church could only have engaged in such activities if it knew from the beginning what it believed and what it had been commissioned by God to preserve. But the irony does not stop here. As unlikely as it may seem, the critics who attack the church most fiercely for its heresy hunting will, in the next breath, accuse the Church for advocating and spreading those very heresies it fought to destroy. Critics accuse the church—the Catholic Church in particular—of denying the flesh, hating the world, and rejecting sex and marriage, but that is what the Gnostics taught, and the church condemned Gnosticism. Yet again, critics accuse the church of holding to the status quo, but the real default religion of man is not Trinitarianism but Unitarianism, and the church condemned the Unitarians just as it condemned the Arians and the Deists. Had the church been only a force for simple theism and morality rather than an upholder of the Trinity and the incarnation, writes Chesterton in part 2, chapter 4, "there is no reason why Christendom should not have been swept into Islam. The truth is that Islam itself was a barbaric reaction against that very humane complexity that is really a Christian character; that idea of balance in the deity, as of balance in the family, that makes that creed [the Trinity] a sort of sanity, and that sanity the soul of civilization." The church speaks not of a distant, lonely, inaccessible God but of a liberal, loving, adventurous God who embarks on a quest, who performs miracles, who answers prayer.

# 10

# THE MIND OF THE MAKER:
# DOROTHY SAYERS MAKES THE TRINITY
# MAKE SENSE

Though best known for her Lord Peter Wimsey detective novels, Dorothy Sayers was, together with Lewis and Chesterton, one of the foremost popular apologists of the twentieth century. Indeed, the three writers constitute a sort of unofficial British school of apologetics, a school that is often expanded to include five more writers who, though not technically apologists, share a similar outlook on faith and art: George Macdonald, J. R. R. Tolkien, Charles Williams, Owen Barfield, and J. B. Phillips. In contrast to the American school of apologetics, which flourished in the second half of the twentieth century and which tends to take a practical, evangelical Protestant approach, the British school, which flourished in the first half, is distinctly Anglo-Catholic in sensibility and takes a far more literary approach. Just as Lewis wrote science fiction and fantasy and Chesterton wrote detective stories (Father Brown) and poetry, Sayers supplemented her Lord Peter Wimsey novels with an acclaimed translation of Dante's *Divine Comedy* and a series of radio plays based on the life of Christ.

Born five years before Lewis, Sayers shared Lewis's love of Chestertonian wit and paradox and was strongly influenced by Chesterton's ability to fuse, in his apologetics, reason and imagination, logical force and emotional resonance, praise for the majesty of God and admiration for the creativity of man. Balancing perfectly literary playfulness with a firm defense of Christian doctrine, the apologetic writings of Dorothy Sayers bear witness to a fact that modern Europe has forgotten—namely, for over a millennium the church was a friend, not a foe, of great literature, art, and music. From early church fathers like Athanasius to the medieval Dante to the Renaissance Donne, theological orthodoxy, aesthetic sophistication, and philosophical profundity went hand in hand. Hailing from that estimable tradition, Sayers refuses to surrender either the arts or the creeds of the church to modern cynicism and materialism. Rather, she blends the two in a fresh, genial way that brings the tenets of the Nicene Creed to shimmering life. And nowhere does she do this more effectively than in *The Mind of the Maker*, a wholly original work that develops an intriguing analogy between the triune nature of God and the human creative process that both substantiates the reality of the Trinity and sheds light on the origin of evil and free will.

## IDEA, ENERGY, AND POWER

According to the orthodox doctrine of the Trinity, God is one God yet exists as three distinct persons (Father, Son, and Holy Spirit) who are coeternal and coequal. Our solar system revolves around a single sun, but that which we call the sun is in fact a triune reality that consists of the sun itself (the source), the light *from* the sun (which is the only part of the sun that we see), and the heat from the sun (which brings life and warmth to our planet and ourselves). Just so, while God the Father is the source of the Godhead, God the Son is the Light who reveals the Father to us, and God the Holy Spirit is the power of God that sustains not only the believer and the church but the universe itself. Or, to switch analogies, though I am myself a single person, I exist and function in a number of different relationships: as a father to my son, a son to my father, a husband to my wife, a brother to my brother, and so forth.

Intimately related to the doctrine of the Trinity is the doctrine of the incarnation: Jesus of Nazareth was not just an inspired prophet or a man with a strong God-consciousness, but God himself in human flesh. The incarnate Christ was not half man and half God but fully man and fully God; he shared fully in the Godhead and entered fully into time, space, and matter. It is no exaggeration to say that nearly all heresies, past and present, have sought to alter these two central doctrines in some way. While deniers of the incarnation have tended either to reject Christ's divine nature or his human nature, deniers of the Trinity have tended either to collapse or tear apart God's triune nature.

In our own, more skeptical age, deniers of the Trinity and incarnation tend to take a different approach. Rather than line themselves up "doctrinally" with one of the age-old heresies, they simply dismiss all the creeds of the church as man-made inventions. In the preface to *The Mind of the Maker*, Dorothy Sayers quickly lays to rest this oft-repeated charge:

> In the creeds of Christendom, we are confronted with a set of documents which purport to be, not expressions of opinion but statements of fact. . . . They were originally drawn up as defenses against heresy—that is, specifically to safeguard the facts against opinions which were felt to be distortions of fact. It will not do to regard them as the product of irresponsible speculation, spinning fancies for itself in a vacuum. That is the reverse of the historical fact about them. They would never have been drawn up at all but for the urgent practical necessity of finding a formula to define experienced truth under pressure of misapprehension and criticism.

The purpose of the early church councils was not to create but to confirm and preserve long-standing orthodox teaching in the face of a historical crisis. When a family or university is threatened by increased crime or a sexual harassment charge, they respond not by making up laws out of thin air but by codifying heretofore unwritten, tacitly accepted rules. Just so, when the church was threatened from without and within by heretical groups indulging in fanciful speculations that contradicted several centuries of church teaching, she put into philosophical language doctrines she had always believed.

Sayers's goal in *The Mind of the Maker* is not to provide a historical survey of the formation of church doctrine but to demonstrate that the orthodox doctrine of the Trinity makes sense—that it squares with something of which we all have some knowledge: the God-given mystery of human creativity. Now Sayers is fully aware that such an argument by analogy cannot logically "prove" the Trinity, but it does demonstrate that the Trinity is neither a logical contradiction nor a totally foreign concept. She is also aware that her argument could be construed to suggest that the church fathers might have projected upward from the artist to God—as Freud claimed that divine Fatherhood was a projection upward of human fatherhood; but if that is the case, then the chief modern criticism of the Trinity—that it is obscure, artificial, and antihuman—is shown to be false. Still, though it is theoretically possible—though highly improbable—that the church fathers argued upward from human creativity, the reverse makes far more sense of the data. Thus, as Lewis argues that joy and the Tao can only be fully explained via a divine origin, so Sayers argues that human creativity is best explained as reflecting a divine pattern.

According to Sayers, every work of art consists *simultaneously* of Idea, Energy, and Power. The Idea (which she also calls the Book as Thought) is the invisible conception of the entire work that resides outside of time and space in the mind of the artist. The Energy (the Book as Written) takes the invisible Idea and embodies it in the material, space/time reality of our world; it proceeds from the Idea while still being one with it. The Power (the Book as Read) proceeds from both Idea and Energy; it allows a reader to experience the Idea through its embodiment and the artist to really *see* his work. Ideally, Sayers adds, the Power is fruitful and will inspire the reader to proceed through his own creative trinity. Although the fullness of the book exists in the Idea that exists only in the head of the artist, the world would have no knowledge of that Idea if it did not proceed from Idea to Energy and from Energy to Power.

The triune nature of human creativity, argues Sayers, is a direct reflection of the triune God in whose image we were made. God the Father is the Idea of the Trinity; he exists outside of time and space and cannot be seen. God the Son is the Energy that Incarnates the Idea and makes it visible. God the Spirit is the Power that enables the Incarnate Idea to be experienced directly by believers. The Spirit indwells the church, we might say, as the Power of the Book indwells all who partake of it. It is no wonder, writes Sayers, that theologians have always had a hard time defining the Holy Spirit; the Power is not so much something we see as something that empowers us *to* see. We do not look *at* it but *by* it, and therefore it is difficult to define.

In the same way that the threefold process of human creativity helps mortals bound within the confines of time and space to conceive of the eternal and boundless Trinity, so does it provide us with a window into the related mystery of the incarnation. Sayers delves into this mystery by highlighting the human art of autobiography. When an artist writes an autobiography, she explains, he is at once the Idea (for he conceived the work) and the Energy (for he himself is the main character of the work). In his persona as author (Idea) he is not bound by any constraints, but in his persona as character (Energy) he is bound by the limits of language and the form of the work. Just so, Christ, while fully one with the Father (Idea) was, while incarnate on the earth, a character (Energy) bound by the constraints of time/space and the human body. Though equal in *essence* with the Father, Christ was limited in *expression* to that which can be revealed through the human form; in that sense, he was lower than the angels.

In working out this thrilling analogy, Sayers registers her agreement with Chesterton: Christ showed *courage* in entering our world. He could have remained in the pure, boundless world of the Idea, but he chose to leave the "safety" of heaven to venture into a dangerous world of corruption, death, sin, and decay. That God could or would make such a descent was inconceivable to the Gnostics and Neoplatonists, but it forms the central part of the divine autobiography of the triune God. In a similar vein, Lewis once suggested that the only way Shakespeare could truly communicate with his characters would be to write himself into one of his plays. Rather than manipulate his characters from above, God the divine Playwright chose the difficult path of entering into the restricted world of the play where he would become subjected to the exigencies of his own sacred narrative of salvation by atonement, a narrative that made necessary the sufferings of the cross.

Sayers further develops her analogy to demonstrate why heretical teachings that deconstruct the Trinity or incarnation are so destructive. A Book that lacks Idea will be formless and incoherent; without Energy, it will be dry and cerebral; without Power, it will lack feeling and have no impact. By dividing or collapsing either the three persons of the Trinity or the two natures of the Incarnate Christ, heresy distorts and perverts the mind of the Maker and his divine work. A God, or work of art, that is all Idea and no Energy is distant, elitist, and inaccessible; it is powerless to truly change the world or the heart. If, in contrast, it is all Energy and no Idea then, no matter how beautiful or supple it may be, it is rootless, empty, and incoherent. Passion without Idea or Energy wastes itself in an expense of feeling. The church fathers were right to insist that the three natures can neither be confused nor separated, and their wisdom is echoed in the human realm of the arts.

Significantly, behind Sayers's God/artist analogy lies a deeper analogy that challenges us to open our eyes to the greater truth about ourselves and our world. God's Idea about the universe, writes Sayers, takes shape in the structure of the universe (Energy), but the Power of the Idea is made manifest in us who embody and propagate the triune nature of the mind of the Maker. Or, to put it another way, God is the Book as Thought, and nature is the Book as Written, but we are the Book as Read. According to J. R. R. Tolkien, man is a subcreator—he makes because he was made in the image of a Maker. What Sayers adds to this trenchant observation is that we were made not only in the image of God the Father but of the whole Trinity. What Lewis liked to refer to as the dance of the

Trinity is played out not only in the production of every great work of art but in the human race itself.

## HAMLET, NOT-HAMLET, AND ANTI-HAMLET

Having used her analogy to sound the depths of the Trinity and incarnation, Sayers ventures yet further to explore one of the greatest of theological conundrums—the origin of evil. In one way or another, all apologists worth their salt must attempt to solve—or better, resolve—the following riddle: if God created everything, then he must have created evil; if God created evil, then he is to blame for evil in the world; if God is to blame for evil in the world, then he must not be a good God. To find an answer to this perennial puzzle, Sayers turns once again to the realm of human creativity.

When Shakespeare created Hamlet, explains Sayers, he also created, by default, a not-Hamlet. Though the not-Hamlet exists, at least in potential, from the moment of Hamlet's creation, the not-Hamlet is inert and can neither disrupt nor pervert *Hamlet* the play. If an actor playing Hamlet, however, chose to forsake the Hamlet created by Shakespeare and bend it to his own will, he would, by his action, transform the not-Hamlet into an anti-Hamlet. Only when that happens—when a human actor chooses to transform not-Hamlet into anti-Hamlet—does not-Hamlet cease to be inert and begin to cause aesthetic evil.

Now one *could* lay the blame for this evil at the feet of Shakespeare—for there could be no not-Hamlet apart from his creation of Hamlet. But the true *moral* guilt lies not with the playwright who created not-Hamlet but with the actor who perverted not-Hamlet into anti-Hamlet. In creating a physical universe populated by enfleshed souls, God did not bring evil into actual being (anti-Hamlet) but left open the *potential* for evil (not-Hamlet). God-created matter is good in itself, but in being good it creates, by default, the potential for not-good. Again, the matter God made was not evil in itself, but it provides a medium *through which* not-good can be chosen—and not-good chosen yields anti-good (evil).

God (as Idea) lies outside time and space. As such, he can have a *knowledge* of not-good without becoming himself evil. We, on the other hand, who live within time and space could only have learned about not-good by choosing it, as we did when we ate the forbidden fruit (the fruit, that is, of the knowledge of good and evil). When we made that fatal choice, we not only became *aware* of not-good but fell headlong into anti-good (evil). God, then, is "responsible" for the fall in the sense that he created the not-good, but he is not morally guilty, for the not-good was inert until our choice converted it to active evil (anti-good).

But there is still, insists Sayers, good news. The tragedy of our world may yet prove to be a comedy: in the late romances of Shakespeare (*Cymbeline*, *Pericles*, *The Winter's Tale*, and *The Tempest*), the death that reigns in act 3 may yet yield a marriage in act 4. The ill consequences of anti-Hamlet (or of evil) *can* be undone if we can get ourselves back in touch with the original Idea in the mind of Shakespeare (or of God). If we could do that, we could transform anti-Hamlet/evil into a new form of good. This redemption, however, though empowered by Idea, must be worked out in the material world (Energy). For the redemption to be effective, the playwright must enter the world of the play. Redemption, argues Sayers, is a profoundly creative act carried out through the vehicle of the incarnation: as the fall was enacted in time and space, so did Christ's birth, death, and resurrection take place not in the fairy world of myth and legend but in the real, historical world of first-century Palestine.

But what role, we must ask, does human free will play in this at once cosmic (Idea) and human (Energy) drama? Are we just puppets in the hands of an arbitrary puppet master, or do our choices make a difference? In answering this equally perennial question of theology, Sayers once again makes use of her analogy to help explain why God granted us free will, what the nature of that free will is, and how our free will does not violate the sovereignty of the Maker.

We have all read poorly constructed novels, writes Sayers, in which the author so manipulates his characters as to make some die who should not die and others find a happiness inconsistent with their natures. Such novels are contrived and dismissive of the integrity of their characters; their authors are like bad parents who force their children into a mold that is alien to them. God, Sayers insists, is not such an author. The divine Playwright allows his characters to develop naturally. Though God *is* a miracle-worker, he does not perform them indiscriminately or in violation of plot and character: his miracles rise up naturally and are—as Lewis notes in *Miracles*—part of the greater weave.

Since God's Idea of our universe (and our role in it) exists fully in his mind and lies outside time and space, God has full knowledge of our past, present, and future choices. We, in contrast, who live in the Energy of the universe must make our choices within the limits of time and space. We are, that is to say, part of a play *in motion*, and we therefore lack God's vision of the whole. Still, as a true playwright God respects the autonomy of our characters and allows our choices to unfold naturally in accordance with the contingencies of the play.

So *says* Sayers the apologist, but so also *did* Sayers the artist. When asked once whether Lord Peter Wimsey would ever become a Christian, Sayers the novelist, true to the convictions of Sayers the theologian, responded that she highly doubted it. Though as a Christian she would have rejoiced at Lord Peter's conversion, she knew as an artist that it would be inconsistent with his character. She would not force it on him!

# 11

# THE PREAPOLOGETICS OF FRANCIS SCHAEFFER

In chapter 12, I will shift the focus from the British school of apologetics, best summed up in the work of Lewis, Chesterton, and Sayers, to the American school initiated by Josh McDowell. Before doing so, however, I would like to pause in this chapter to consider an apologist who may be viewed as a transitional figure between the two schools. Although he was an American and although he boasted a firm Reformed-evangelical, rather than Anglo-Catholic, pedigree, Francis Schaeffer maintained throughout his life and career a distinctly European air. His love for philosophy, art, literature, music, and film not only added color to his apologetic arguments but gave his work a literary flavor that smacks more of Europe than North America.

Indeed, though Schaeffer lectured often throughout America, he did much of his best work leading informal discussions at L'Abri, a Swiss chalet where Francis and his wife, Edith, lived and to which they invited seekers from around the world. Run as a cross between a hostel and a commune, L'Abri opened its doors to a host of young people (mostly "university types") disaffected with modern materialism but unable to accept a Christian faith that they saw as backward, exclusivist, and anti-intellectual. While they stayed at L'Abri, they were empowered to ask whatever questions they liked and to challenge Schaeffer's informal lectures on the history of Western metaphysics. No matter their hostility to the gospel, Schaeffer treated his guests as sincere seekers after the truth; he even immersed himself in their countercultural, even anti-Christian, music, art, and cinema so as to be able to speak more effectively in their language. Rather than attack or belittle the agnostics, atheists, skeptics, nihilists, and socialists who congregated at his home, Schaeffer treated them with great compassion and empathy. He worked hard not only to understand but to sympathize with their internal struggles. To him, they were never statistics, never people he could pigeonhole into this or that "ism"; they were individuals made in the image of God who were trapped in a modern despair from which only Christ could free them.

Though Schaeffer was a prolific writer, most of his best work is contained in what has come to be known as his apologetics trilogy: *The God Who Is There*, *Escape from Reason*, and *He Is There and He Is Not Silent*. In these three works, Schaeffer surveys the historical process by which science, logic, and reason became divided from religion, revelation, and faith and demonstrates how that divide has made it difficult for modern (post-Enlightenment) Christian apologists to make rational (or propositional) truth claims about their faith.

## THE DIVIDED FIELD

In his apologetics trilogy, Schaeffer warns the would-be evangelist that when he presents the gospel of Jesus Christ to an unbeliever, he may very well be speaking a foreign language. We may think that all we have to do to convince the modern seeker that Christ is the only way to God is to explain the gospel in simple terms and then back it up with appropriate verses from the Bible; but that, asserts Schaeffer, is no longer true. Modern skeptics are liable to dismiss not only evangelists who base all their arguments on the Bible but apologists who take for granted that a divinely revealed book is possible. Increasingly over the last two centuries a relativistic worldview has entrenched itself in academia, in the media, and in the arts, a worldview most moderns absorb passively. And this relativism is felt not only in the field of ontology (the study of being, of the essential nature of things) but also in epistemology (the study of how we know and perceive things) and linguistics (how we communicate that knowledge) as well.

Though most relativists accept that absolute truth claims can be made in math and science, they disallow such claims in philosophy, theology, ethics, and the arts. Relativists, that is to say, are liable to doubt the very thing apologists take for granted—namely, that an infinite, personal God *can* exist (ontology) and *can* communicate to us through propositional truths—that is, theological/doctrinal formulas—that can be adequately known (epistemology) and reliably expressed in language (linguistics). Modernists, influenced by Nietzsche—even and especially if they have not read him—assume that all nonscience truths are man-made, culturally constructed opinions. That universal, absolute truths that transcend time and space might actually exist and serve as the foundation of all knowledge (sacred and secular) seems "medieval."

Granted, the relativist will admit that faith is real *for the believer* and has a personal, subjective force that can make him happy, but to move beyond this to claim a public, historical, objective status for the doctrines of Christianity is to be nonrational and unenlightened. In the previous chapter I argued that modern man is apt to dismiss the creeds of the church as mere opinions divorced from any absolute, eternal reality. Schaeffer argues that the situation is even worse than that. It is not just the tenets of the Nicene Creed that are relegated by modern relativism to the realm of opinions: *all* statements that cannot be expressed in terms of observed, repeatable facts are to be treated as mere opinions, as having no more claim to the realm of factual knowledge than the paintings of the Dadaists or the plays of the Theatre of the Absurd.

I find it telling that the late Stephen Jay Gould suggested that science and religion agree to abide by what he termed "non-overlapping magisteria" (or NOMA): that is, that the religious folks would leave the scientists alone to deal with the empirical world (the world that we can perceive and study with our five senses), while the scientific folks would leave the theologians alone to deal with issues of morality and ultimate meaning. Had Schaeffer lived to comment on Gould's "deal," he would likely have noted that the real upshot of NOMA is not to empower the theologians to make absolute, binding statements about the real nature of morality or the true purpose of humanity but to take away from them the prerogative to make *any* statements of an absolute or binding nature. Perhaps the best way to express this is to say that for those who have absorbed the worldview of NOMA, *systematic theology* is a contradiction in terms—for systems can only be built on facts, and the speculations of theology, like those of philosophy, ethics, and the arts, exist in a non-rational realm divorced from facts.

Modern man, explains Schaeffer, has fallen prey to a "divided field of knowledge." We have lost the ancient/medieval unity of truth and have split knowledge into mutually exclusive compartments (magisteria). Science, logic, and reason are confined to one realm (what Schaeffer terms the downstairs), while theology, philosophy, ethics, and the arts are confined to another (the upstairs). Only in the downstairs is it possible to make factual, verifiable statements that are either true or false, right or wrong, black or white. The upstairs, whatever it offers us in terms of personal satisfaction, is utterly divorced from reason and logic and cannot be defined or defended in terms of set categories. In the fully objective downstairs (what modernism terms the "real world"), man is rational but determined by forces he cannot control. In the fully subjective upstairs, he is free but finally irrational.

The existence of this divided field of knowledge forces us to make a terrible decision: either to live our lives in the public, external, mechanistic downstairs and thus surrender our yearnings for supernatural truth and transcendent beauty, or to leap into the private, internal, spiritual upper room and sacrifice all rational propositions and historical content. Unfortunately, when these two choices are extrapolated out to their logical ends, man is left stranded in one of two bleak worlds. To live in the former we must sacrifice free will; to live in the latter we must sacrifice meaning. A rigid downstairs reality yields in the end a *Nineteen Eighty-Four*-like dystopia: an antihumanistic, anthill totalitarianism that slowly devours the political, social, economic, and educational spheres. An equally rigid upstairs reality yields in the end a *Brave New World*-like dystopia of decadence, relativism, and doctrineless mysticism. In neither world can man, as a personal, meaningful creature made in the image of a personal, meaningful God, truly live and grow. In neither, in fact, can he be truly human at all.

## NATURE VS. GRACE

Schaeffer's great contribution to apologetics is how succinctly and cogently he traces the philosophical and theological steps that led us down the long descent to our present divided field. Schaeffer's tracing of this descent has been criticized (fairly) for being simplistic, for leaving out key thinkers, and for often ascribing the steps of the descent to the wrong thinker. Nevertheless, what Schaeffer's historical model lacks in nuance, it more than makes up for in its apologetic usefulness and its power to open our eyes to how strongly reason and faith have parted company in our modern (and now postmodern) world. In what follows, I will focus on trends rather than names, highlighting those parts of Schaeffer's model that I find most compelling and most true to Western intellectual history.

Whereas early patristic Christian apologetics was strongly Scripture-based and somewhat suspicious of fallen human reason unaided by direct revelation, the scholastics of the Middle Ages moved slowly toward a more reason-based natural theology that helped establish philosophy as a separate, autonomous sphere that could exist alongside theology. This led Christian theologians and philosophers—Schaeffer, unfairly, puts all the "blame" on Aquinas—to make too sharp a division between nature (the changing physical world known via reason) and grace (the unchanging, spiritual realm known via revelation). According to the Reformed Schaeffer, Aquinas made this "error" because he did not understand that the fall not only affected our will and our passions but our reason as well: whereas Catholics use the phrase "original sin" to refer to our fallen status, Calvinists prefer to use the stronger "total depravity."

Although I would disagree with Schaeffer's analysis of Aquinas (indeed, Reformed apologist R. C. Sproul has taken pains to exonerate Aquinas from this charge), and although I think Schaeffer pushes the nature/grace split too far back in history, his overall point is a compelling and vital one. Whenever nature is separated from grace and the intellect is rendered autonomous—that is, it is allowed to operate in total isolation from the greater theological truths revealed in the Bible—the way is paved for nature to eventually "eat up" grace. As already noted above, if Gould's NOMA were ever to be put fully into practice, and science and religion were to be segmented off in hermetically sealed containers, the result would be that scientific theories would eat up all religious claims to truth. If truth be told, NOMA *has* already been put into practice in secular universities across Europe and America, and the result *has* been to marginalize the truth claims of Christianity and render them irrelevant. In our secular universities, and even in many of our religious ones, on issues of morality (especially sexual behavior) and ultimate meaning (the purpose of life), statistics generated by the social sciences will always trump arguments based on Scripture or Christian doctrine.

But let us return to Schaeffer's historical account of how nature and grace parted ways. During the Renaissance, argues Schaeffer, early modern scientists like Copernicus, Bacon, and Newton stayed within a generally biblical framework, accepting the reality of the fall in both the moral and natural field, and allowing for religion to remedy the former even as science remedied the latter. In fact, early modern science would not have been developed at all had its founders not believed that the universe operated on the basis of laws put there by the Creator. This compromise position, sort of a kinder, gentler NOMA, allowed science to operate within the larger framework of creation and fall. The compromise, however, was soon abandoned as the line separating nature and grace became stronger and as the seventeenth- and eighteenth-century deans of science and reason, troubled by the growing split, sought to restore a unified field of knowledge. Unfortunately, they achieved this restoration not by renewing the upstairs and its revelation-based truths but by simply dismissing it altogether.

This dismissal led, in turn, to a crisis since, without the upstairs not only God but freedom, morality, love, significance, and beauty are cut off from their moorings in reality. Enter Kant, who sensed that if man were to be confined to a closed naturalistic downstairs, the result would be a rigid determinism that would rob man of his free will, his dignity, and ultimately his personhood. To preserve these things from the antihuman, mechanical nature of the downstairs, Kant sought to redefine the upstairs as the realm of the absolute, supersensible, autonomous individual. By so doing, he hoped to preserve the upstairs as a habitable refuge for humanity. His goal was a noble one, but in the end he only succeeded in furthering the divide and paving the way for a type of bohemian freedom that rejects all forms of restraint and puts the individual, rather than God or natural law or revealed truth, at the center of the universe. Upstairs man *would* gain freedom, but it would be merely a freedom *from* all "bourgeois" values rather than a freedom *to* live as creatures made in the image of a personal God who endowed us with purpose and revealed that purpose to us in the form of scriptural propositional truths.

Following in the footsteps of Kant, Kierkegaard, even more angst-ridden than Kant at the mechanistic nature of the downstairs, makes an existential leap of faith into a spiritual upstairs that he hopes will supply him with meaning but that he knows is nonrational and noncommunicable. Though Schaeffer also "blames" Kierkegaard too much, many moderns since 1850 (Schaeffer highlights Wittgenstein) *have* felt that the only way to escape from materialistic determinism is to "escape from reason." Rather than take a reasoned step of faith, as apologists like Chesterton, Lewis, Sayers, and Schaeffer would counsel us to do, Kierkegaard and his heirs would call on us to take an irrational leap into the void. Such a leap, argues Schaeffer, is too high a price to pay for spiritual meaning. For if our faith in Christ is based solely on emotion and experience rather than on the propositional truth claims revealed to us in the Scriptures, then by what standard can we distinguish faith in Christ from faith in Buddha or Zeus or Freud?

For Schaeffer, theology since Kierkegaard has been haunted by its inability to bridge the divide between nature and grace. Indeed, modern academic theologians, argues Schaeffer (controversially), have make little attempt to restore a unified field of knowledge grounded in an inerrant Word of God whose historical and propositional truth claims are foundational for both nature and grace, reason and morality, science and religion. While liberal theologians have sought to identify a historical Jesus stripped of all supernatural miracles (downstairs), neoorthodox theologians (Schaeffer highlights Karl Barth) have accepted a Christianity that surrenders history and propositional truth for the sake of a faith salvaged from naturalism (upstairs). The upshot of this divide within theology is that the doctrines of orthodox Christianity are cut off from their moorings in reason and logic and are left to compete on a level playing field with a host of other vehicles for leaping out of nature into a nonrational upstairs that promises freedom and meaning. In terms of the upstairs, Christian theology can exert no privilege of truth over surrealism, the occult, drugs, sex, or pornography. It is merely one of many escape routes from the mechanical determinism of the downstairs.

Because Christianity has been "demoted" to the nonrational sphere of self-expression, modern apologetics must often be preceded by a preapologetic stage in which the apologist argues for the possibility of rational discourse on faith, truth, freedom, and beauty. The apologist must argue that truth—whether scientific or spiritual—is a fixed, knowable entity that rests on solid logical principles rather than on personal preference and that the claims of Christ are not merely mythic but took place in real space-time history. Sharing Christianity in the modern world means not only presenting the Christian plan of salvation as the correct one but arguing that such a thing as a Christian plan of salvation can be expressed in rational, historical terms.

## PRESUPPOSITIONALISM

Francis Schaeffer was a pupil of Cornelius Van Til, the father of an apologetic school known as presuppositionalism. Practitioners of presuppositionalism insist that apologetics be grounded on Scripture as the ultimate source of truth and logic rather than on neutral grounds— Lewis's Tao, Chesterton's fairy tales, Sayers's human artist—that believers and nonbelievers share. They tend to be Reformed Calvinist in outlook, viewing man as totally depraved and viewing reason in its unregenerate state as too dark and feeble to build a foundation for faith.

Presuppositionalism may be contrasted with evidentialism, an apologetic school—or better, approach—that seeks to establish common ground by appealing to reason, natural law, and our shared spiritual longings. Though I find much merit in presuppositionalism, and though I believe apologists should seek to restore the broken unity of truth that continues to divide our post-Enlightenment world, I will in this book pursue an evidentialist approach. I have chosen to do so for three reasons: 1) Evidentialism is the mainstream modern approach that issues out of Lewis, and it is the one that speaks, I believe, to the widest possible audience of believers and nonbelievers. 2) Because presuppositionalism is so firmly grounded in Calvinism, it would take us away from Lewis's mere Christianity approach into long-standing Protestant/Catholic debates as well as struggles (often bitter) within Protestantism. 3) Presuppositionalism tends to get dry and academic, and I mean to maintain a firmly "middlebrow" approach. An additional reason for my choice, one that issues directly and unapologetically out of my own American-evangelical-pragmatic pedigree, is that evidentialism has shown itself to be far more effective and useful than presuppositionalism. Quite simply, it works.

Why then, the reader may ask, have I devoted a full chapter to Schaeffer? Because Schaeffer, despite his presuppositional background, was at least half an evidentialist at heart. As I noted at the head of this chapter, Schaeffer the apologist devoted much of his time and energy to engaging young bohemian skeptics at L'Abri. With great passion and vigor, he sought common ground with his dispossessed hippies by working to understand their countercultural art, literature, and film and trying to get to the root of their often rootless yearnings for truth. To reach out to them, he even adapted a unique strategy that blends presuppositional notions about truth with an evidentialist attempt to build bridges. Moderns, explains Schaeffer, will often fashion a protective "roof" over themselves so they don't have to face the full consequences (and horror!) of downstairs determinism and upstairs meaninglessness. Schaeffer the apologist uses Socratic dialogue to rip off that roof and to force them to acknowledge and face the personal consequences and metaphysical horror of the divide. Only through such a severe "reality check" can modern man's need for God and metaphysical truth be made clear.

# 12

# APOLOGETICS AMERICAN STYLE: THE LEGACY OF JOSH MCDOWELL

Something strange began to happen in the late 1960s and early 1970s. All over America, hippies who had forsaken what they saw as the narrow-minded, bourgeois values of their parents were embracing Christ as their Lord and Savior. The phenomenon came to be known as the Jesus Movement, and it exerted a strong and lasting influence on the American church. Though the hippies-turned-Christians traded in their free-love ethic for a more biblical sexual morality, they nevertheless retained their yearning for authenticity, their love of popular music (both rock and folk), and their preference for informal small-group intimacy. Most importantly, they put a strong emphasis on their personal relationship with Jesus Christ and on the born-again experience that made that relationship possible.

As they matured in their faith, their hunger to know Christ more closely and to study the Bible more carefully grew, and they began to search for books that would help instruct them in and assure them of the historical reliability of the Bible (especially the Gospels), the exact manner in which the prophecies of the Old Testament were fulfilled in the New, and the nature and import of Christ's claims and miracles. One of the apologists who helped answer their questions—and in the process helped give American apologetics a distinctive voice, style, and approach—was Josh McDowell.

Though never an official spokesman for the Jesus Movement, Josh brought apologetics to the common man, not only by writing a series of carefully argued but accessible books, but by debating the claims of Christ with students on campuses all over the United States. Josh has long been associated with Campus Crusade for Christ, a parachurch group that has spent the last half century directly engaging students with the gospel and the wider Christian worldview. I myself am a "product" of a group with a similar mission to that of Campus Crusade (InterVarsity Christian Fellowship), and I relied heavily on the work of Josh McDowell during my college years to help answer the challenges of secular graduates and undergraduates who viewed Christianity as little more than a fairy tale.

## EVIDENCE THAT DEMANDS A VERDICT

Unlike the more literary British apologists, not to mention the more cerebral, avant-garde Schaeffer, Josh spoke, and continues to speak today, in a down-home, conversational American idiom. His style is forthright and assured without being arrogant; though intellectually rigorous, he maintains a personal, informal tone (note that I follow the common practice of referring to Josh by his first name). In all his apologetic books, Josh puts a heavy emphasis on the presentation of evidence, relying often on the testimony of expert witnesses—including, and especially, witnesses who are not believers but feel compelled to concede the historical or logical probability of various Christian claims. The goal of Josh's genially confrontational approach is to shake his readers out of slothful complacency and force them to make a decision about the historical, theological, and philosophical claims of Christianity. Like a lawyer building a case, Josh lays out his evidence and testimonies in a logical, methodical fashion that impresses and convinces by its careful accumulation of detail. Indeed, one of his most enduring contributions to apologetics is titled, appropriately, *Evidence That Demands a Verdict*.

Like Schaeffer, Josh has never lost his love for young seekers hungry for meaning and truth. Whether in his books or in his almost-legendary open-air debates with college students, he has shown himself to be unafraid to question authority (there's that Jesus Movement hippie side) and eager to track down and test all claims, whether sacred or secular. Part of the reason Josh has been successful at this is that he, like Lewis, spent the first part of his life as a convinced atheist. In fact, his conversion followed an intense personal effort to *disprove* the claims of Christ and the historicity of the Resurrection. Josh's books, like those of Lewis's, never "preach to the choir" but engage directly and fearlessly with the kinds of doubts and concerns that plague the minds of skeptics who are intrigued by Christianity but fear that modern "science" has made faith in Christ intellectually untenable.

Though he did not "invent" American apologetics, Josh perfected an approach that complements rather than mimics Lewis's. Understanding well the paradoxes of the American psyche—we want just the facts, and yet we want to believe in people; we insist that seeing is believing, yet we truly want to believe in unseen realities; we question everything, yet we have a natural respect for the authority of the written word—Josh fashioned his pragmatic apologetics around three central elements. First, he quotes the Bible often to back up his claims but does not rely only on Scripture to prove his points; in fact, he spends much time defending the reliability of the Scriptures. Second, he keeps the focus firmly on Christ himself—particularly on his claims to divinity, his fulfillment of messianic prophecy, and the historicity of his death and resurrection. Third, he presents Christ as someone about whom we cannot be neutral by focusing on the reactions and testimonies of people, past and present, who have rejected or accepted him.

Josh's true successor has proven to be Lee Strobel, arguably the best current popular apologist writing in America. Like Josh, Strobel was also an atheist whose own intense study of the claims of Christianity brought him to Christ; like Josh and Lewis, he also does not preach to the choir. Strobel shares Josh's focus on expert witnesses and on the claims of Christ and the historicity of the Gospels; with the same lawyer-like skills, he builds logically solid cases. But Strobel adds something as well—firsthand experience as an investigative reporter. It should come as no surprise that the titles of Strobel's great apologetics trilogy are *The Case for Christ*, *The Case for Faith*, and *The Case for the Creator*. In constructing my arguments for part 2 of this book, I consulted often not only this trilogy but Josh's *Evidence That Demands a Verdict* and his ground-breaking book, *More Than a Carpenter*.

## APOLOGETICS 101

In *More than a Carpenter*, Josh lays out in miniature his apologetic approach. That approach begins immediately in his preface where he quotes two historians who were strong religious skeptics. The first is Victorian writer H. G. Wells. Though best known for such science fiction novels as *The War of the Worlds* and *The Time Machine*, Wells was also an influential secular humanist who felt science had superseded religion—a thesis that he sought to "prove" in his widely read *History of the World*. In *The Everlasting Man* and *The Problem of Pain*, Chesterton and Lewis respectively devote much energy to disputing Wells's secular theories of the origin of religion. The second historian Josh quotes is Ernest Renan, a theological liberal who embodied fully the Enlightenment rejection of supernatural claims. Renan was one of the first scholars to write a "psychological" biography of Jesus that stripped him of his miracles and divinity. Rather than dismiss or ignore the writings of these two skeptics, Josh carefully extracts from the work of each a statement about Christ. Though both men essentially denied Christ's divinity, both attested to his absolute uniqueness and to the indelible mark that he left on history.

Josh begins by quoting Wells and Renan to prove a simple but vital point: even skeptics are fascinated by Jesus Christ and cannot simply dismiss him. In fact, the first statement that greets readers when they open the front cover of *More Than a Carpenter* is this provocative question: "Why is it that you can talk about God and nobody gets upset, but as soon as you mention Jesus, people often want to stop the conversation? Why have men and women down through the ages been divided over the question, 'Who is Jesus?'" Why indeed? Why is it that I hear people all over the world take Jesus' name in vain, yet I have never heard a single person say, "Oh, Muhammad" or "Oh, Buddha" or "Oh, Socrates" or "Oh, Moses"?

The simple fact of the matter is that nearly every person in the world, whatever his religion or culture, respects Jesus as a great man and a good teacher. But is that really all that he was? Throughout the Gospels, Jesus himself purports to be much more than a prophet or teacher, to be, in fact, the Son of God—that is, equal with God. In chapter 17, I will conduct a careful survey of Jesus' claims. Suffice it to say for now that Christ's *enemies* knew he was claiming divinity—that is why they tried to stone him for blasphemy (John 8:59). In the Sanhedrin, heated debate raged as to what crime Jesus was guilty of, until he claimed before the high priest Caiaphas to be the Son of God. The moment he did so, Jesus was accused of blasphemy (Matthew 26:63–66), was condemned, and was turned over to Pilate.

Following in the footsteps of Lewis's liar-lunatic-Lord trilemma, Josh carefully sifts through all the options, demonstrating the illogicality of those who argue that Jesus was a good man but not God. That Jesus might have lied about his divinity is not only inconsistent with his universally acclaimed integrity but with the high premium his followers put on honesty. And besides, had Jesus set himself the goal of deceiving people into believing in his divinity, he would have surrounded himself with different followers. Rather than trying to convince the fiercely monotheistic Jews, he would have gone among the Egyptians or Greeks or Romans who were accustomed to ascribing divinity to such men as Rameses II, Alexander the Great, and Julius Caesar. As for being a lunatic, Christ's humility and incisive preaching are inconsistent with megalomania and other forms of self-delusion. The only logical, rational option that fits the evidence we know about Jesus is that he was, in fact, the Son of God.

Now Josh admits that there is one way a skeptic *could* refute the trilemma. He could simply refuse to believe that Jesus ever made any of his claims and argue instead that the Gospel writers put the claims of divinity into Jesus' mouth. But this option is finally untenable. A person who could have forged the sayings and claims of Jesus would have been more remarkable than Jesus himself! Indeed, we would have to posit half a dozen or so such theological geniuses, for *all* the New Testament writers give the same basic portrait of Jesus. Furthermore, even if we could convince ourselves that all the writers of the New Testament were remarkable men who could conjure up out of thin air the sayings and deeds of the most unique and important man who ever lived, we would still run into two further problems. First, no good Jew would have thought on his own to make Jesus divine. Second, nearly all the Jews, especially the disciples, were not looking for a divine scapegoat but a political messiah in the guise of David to overthrow Roman authority. The wholly unique portrait we find of Jesus in the Gospels and the Epistles *would not* and *could not* have been made up by the Jewish followers of Jesus. I will return to these issues in chapters 16 and 17 and present fuller evidence that the Gospel accounts are reliable.

Having repackaged Lewis's trilemma for modern American readers, Josh proceeds to investigate another way of testing the claims of Jesus—considering his impact on others. When Jesus was crucified, all his disciples but John ran away in fear. Their hopes of a political messiah had been dashed, and they were crushed with defeat and despair. But then something happened a few days later to turn the cowering disciples into such bold witnesses of Christ's power that all but one died painful deaths as martyrs. In chapter 18 I will defend the historicity of the resurrection; for now let us consider its reality and power on those who claimed to have witnessed it.

Though one man might have been deluded into seeing a ghostly apparition of Christ, all the apostles were as one in claiming to have seen the risen Christ. In fact, throughout the book of Acts their testimony to the risen Christ formed the cornerstone of their preaching. The early apostles presented themselves as witnesses of the resurrection, and it was on the basis of that rock-solid belief that they preached the good news to the Roman world. A few years later, a personal encounter with the risen Christ on the road to Damascus transformed a zealous, Christian- and Gentile-hating Pharisee named Saul into the apostle Paul. Paul and his fellow apostles did not risk life and limb to defend an idea or a myth or a legend; they were servants of a resurrected Savior whom they had met and spoken with and handled.

One final proof that Josh offers to substantiate the claims of Jesus are the more than three hundred Old Testament prophecies that were fulfilled by Christ—prophecies that Josh surveys briefly in *More Than a Carpenter* and catalogs in full in *Evidence That Demands a Verdict*. Nearly every detail of Christ's birth, life, death, and resurrection was prophesied hundreds of years earlier with uncanny accuracy. People who are aware of the number and accuracy of these prophecies will not be shocked to know that about half the libretto of Handel's *Messiah* is taken directly from the Old Testament. Long before his birth, the entire arc of Jesus' life and ministry was forecasted in the Jewish Scriptures.

Today, of course, many dispute whether Moses or David or Isaiah or Jeremiah actually wrote all the passages ascribed to them, but even if they did not, that does not take away from the remarkable accuracy of the prophecies. By about 200 b.c. the Old Testament existed in a Greek translation known as the Septuagint—which is to say that even the great-est biblical skeptic must admit that the prophecy-rich Old Testament existed in its present state two full centuries before Christ was born. Of course, there are also many today who claim that Jesus or his follow-ers might have so manipulated things as to fit in with the prophecies. Though this argument can account for some of the fulfilled prophecies, it cannot account for enough of them. There still exist scores and scores of prophecies—Jesus' birth in Bethlehem, his Davidic descent, the man-ner of his betrayal, his death by crucifixion, and so forth—that could not have been manipulated by Jesus or his followers. The odds of one man fulfilling all of these prophecies are astronomical. I for one do not have enough faith to believe that a combination of chance and messianic manipulation can account for them.

As an addendum to Josh's discussion of biblical prophecy, I would suggest another way of highlighting how truly unique are the messi-anic prophecies. Just as Christianity claims that the New Testament is a fulfillment of the Old, there are two other religions in the world today that follow a sacred book that they claim to be a sort of third testament fulfilling and superseding the first two. I speak of Islam and the Church of Jesus Christ of Latter-Day Saints, whose followers make this claim for the Qur'an and the Book of Mormon respectively. I do not mean to scorn or belittle either of these religions or their sacred books, but the simple fact remains that whereas Christ and the New Testament fulfilled hundreds of specific prophecies made in the Old, there is not a single shred of prophecy in the Bible to indicate the coming either of Muhammad or the Qur'an or of Joseph Smith or the Book of Mormon. Now many Muslim apologists will claim that Jesus' promise of a coming "Helper" (John 16:7; also translated as "Advocate," "Encourager," or "Counselor") refers to Muhammad; likewise, many Mormon apologists will claim that Jesus' reference to having other sheep (John 10:16) is a reference to the American Indian tribes to whom the risen Christ would appear, an event that would culminate with the writing and later discovery of the Book of Mormon. That is what they claim, but a simple reading of these two verses in their biblical context will show that the first is a clear reference to the coming of the Holy Spirit and the second a clear reference to the Gentiles. Please let me repeat: I do not point this out to criticize Muslims or Mormons but to highlight how utterly unique are the fulfilled prophecies that surround the life and ministry of Christ and the writings of the New Testament.

Josh ends his book by defending Christ as the only way to God and sharing his own personal testimony. I shall hold off discussion of the former until chapter 19. As for the latter, I would merely note that Josh's choice to conclude his apologetic arguments by moving from the rational to the personal, the theological to the experiential, is a common one among American apologists. Though Josh and his fellow apologists are committed to presenting evidence for Christianity that is logical and systematic, they also know that Christianity calls for a personal step of faith that transcends all human logic and earthly systems. And they know something more: Christ is not just a proposition or a proof but a living, active God who is still transforming lives today.

## THE MAN OF SORROWS

Before closing this chapter, I would like to highlight briefly two prophetic passages whose historical and theological accuracy are so remarkable that if these were the only messianic prophecies contained in the Old Testament, they would be enough, to my mind at least, to qualify Jesus as the Christ.

The first is taken from one of the Psalms of David:

> But I am a worm and not a man,
> > scorned by mankind and despised by the people.
> All who see me mock me;
> > they make mouths at me; they wag their heads;
> "He trusts in the Lord; let him deliver him;
> > let him rescue him, for he delights in him!" . . .
> I am poured out like water,
> > and all my bones are out of joint;
> my heart is like wax;
> > it is melted within my breast;
> my strength is dried up like a potsherd,
> > and my tongue sticks to my jaws;
> > you lay me in the dust of death.
> For dogs encompass me;
> > a company of evildoers encircles me;
> they have pierced my hands and feet—
> I can count all my bones—
> they stare and gloat over me;
> they divide my garments among them,
> > and for my clothing they cast lots. (Psalm 22:6–8, 14–18)

I do not exaggerate when I say that this passage reads like an eyewitness account of the events of Good Friday. All the details of the psalmist's torment—being poured out like water, the bones out of joint, the heart melted like wax, the piercing of hands and feet, the horror of looking down and counting one's bones—find a direct parallel in the excruciating process of death by crucifixion, a form of execution that did not exist when the psalm was written. In addition to describing the physical pain of crucifixion, the psalm also captures with uncanny accuracy the humiliation of such a death. When reading it, one feels as if David had been transported to the crucifixion and stood among the hostile crowd as they jeered and taunted Jesus and watched sadly as the callous Roman soldiers cast lots for his clothing.

Psalm 22 begins with the heart-rending cry, "My God, my God, why have you forsaken me?" If that verse sounds familiar, it is because Jesus himself quoted it as he hung on the cross. The suffering David expresses in Psalm 22 goes far beyond any sorrow he encountered in his own life to point prophetically forward to the Messiah, he who would, for a brief horrific moment, be forsaken even by the Father with whom he dwelled in eternal communion.

The second passage is taken from one of the messianic prophecies of Isaiah:

> He was despised and rejected by men;
>     a man of sorrows, and acquainted with grief;
> and as one from whom men hide their faces
>     he was despised, and we esteemed him not.
> Surely he has borne our griefs
>     and carried our sorrows;
> yet we esteemed him stricken,
>     smitten by God, and afflicted.
> But he was wounded for our transgressions;
>     he was crushed for our iniquities;
> upon him was the chastisement that brought us peace,
>     and with his stripes we are healed.
> All we like sheep have gone astray;
>     we have turned—every one—to his own way;
> and the LORD has laid on him
>     the iniquity of us all. (Isaiah 53:3–6)

If Psalm 22 reads like an eyewitness account of the crucifixion, then Isaiah 53 reads like a poem written by a church father in the third or fourth century to explain the Christian doctrine of the atonement. Indeed, if I wanted to explain to someone the true nature of the atonement—that by dying on the cross, Christ paid the penalty for our sins and bore the punishment of our guilt—I could do so without quoting a single verse from the New Testament. The full theological meaning of the atonement is expressed here in verses that were written hundreds of years before Jesus was born. Read in full, Isaiah 53 includes prophecies as well of the exact manner of Jesus' trial, execution, and burial, but what I have quoted should suffice to show that both the details of Jesus' life and death and the purpose of that life and death existed in the mind of God long before that first Christmas morning in Bethlehem.

# PART TWO

# MAKING THE CASE
# FOR FAITH IN A
# (POST)MODERN WORLD

# 13

# THE EXISTENCE OF GOD I:
# ARGUMENTS FROM LOGIC

In part 1 of this book, I focused on five specific apologists—Lewis, Chesterton, Sayers, Schaeffer, and McDowell—who have helped to initiate, to shape, and to popularize a certain type of modern Christian apologetic with the power to challenge the assumptions of North Americans and Europeans who have been raised (indoctrinated?) in a post-Enlightenment, secular humanist worldview that they rarely question. So successful have these five been in their endeavors that they have helped to inspire two generations of well-trained, highly educated, and extremely articulate successors to carry on their work. Among the scores of top-notch apologists working today, I would like to highlight a dozen and a half who have influenced me greatly and whose work will underlie many of the arguments presented in the next twelve chapters: William Lane Craig, Lee Strobel, Ravi Zacharias, Gary Habermas, Peter Kreeft, J. P. Moreland, Alister McGrath, Phillip E. Johnson, William Dembski, Hugh Ross, Don Richardson, Chuck Colson, Norman Geisler, John Stott, R. C. Sproul, Dinesh D'Souza, Timothy Keller, and N. T. Wright.

Needless to say, with so many fine apologists writing and speaking in England and America—I could easily have added an additional dozen and a half to my list—a considerable amount of overlap appears in their work. This is by no means a bad thing (most of the things we know well were impressed upon us through repetition and reinforcement), nor does it suggest any unoriginality on the part of the apologists. Nevertheless, the large and growing number of working apologists and the frequent overlapping of ideas suggest the need for a different approach in part 2 of this book. As such, my goal for part 2 will be to focus not on specific *apologists*, as I did in part 1, but on specific *apologetic arguments* that have played a key role in the work of numerous writers and that have shown themselves to be particularly effective in reaching the modern world. Indeed, only in cases where I use an argument that is unique to a single writer will I mention that writer by name. In most cases I will focus on arguments shared by nearly all apologists, giving them, when appropriate, my own personal perspective or "spin." Rather than quote directly from the works of the last two generations of apologists, I have provided in my appendices a Who's Who of major apologists and an extensive annotated bibliography of one hundred or so of the seminal apologetic works of the past century.

As for the chapters themselves, in the first six I will trace a traditional apologetic arc, moving from arguments for the existence of God to arguments for the authority of Scripture, the deity of Christ, and the historicity of the resurrection. In the second six I will take up more recent issues: intelligent design, the growth of neo-Gnosticism and neo-atheism, and the influence of postmodernism on apologetics. As already stated, in constructing these chapters, I will draw widely on the work of numerous apologists, seeking always to highlight the most successful and enduring arguments.

One last caveat before I begin. Modern apologists spend almost as much time defending the historic Christian faith from atheists and skeptics as from liberal Christians who deny key tenets of orthodoxy—the incarnation, the Trinity, the resurrection, the miracles of Jesus, the authority of Scripture, and so forth. It must be understood from the outset that when I use the word *liberal*, I will be using it in a theological, not a political, sense. The liberalism that I will be critiquing off and on over the next twelve chapters has nothing whatsoever to do with partisan politics. A liberal theologian is not someone who votes for the Democratic Party but someone who takes a nonsupernatural approach to Scripture, who privileges Jesus the reformer over Jesus the God-Man, and who questions, if not rejects, the exclusive doctrines of the church.

## THE ONTOLOGICAL ARGUMENT

Lewis begins *Mere Christianity* not with a defense of the Gospels or the claims of Christ or the resurrection but with an argument for the existence of God. Modern apologists, following Lewis's lead, have often felt a similar need to preface their defense of Christianity with a defense of theism. A modern skeptic who denies the existence of God will likely not be convinced by arguments that Jesus is the Son of God. Accordingly, before considering the specific claims of Christianity, I will devote three chapters to arguing for the existence of a personal God whose fingerprint can be discerned both in human reason and in the ordered cosmos and whose power and goodness can be reconciled with the existence in our world of pain and suffering. I will begin by considering three classic arguments for the existence of God: the ontological, the cosmological, and the teleological.

The first thing that must be admitted about these arguments is that they tend to carry less weight and force with modern readers. The major reason for this is that all three arguments make use of deductive rather than inductive logic, and although moderns still use deduction (often unconsciously), the last two centuries have seen a sharp rise in the reputation of induction. Put simply, induction is a form of logic that accumulates facts, figures, and observations and then works upward to construct the best hypothesis, or inference, possible. When a doctor takes your symptoms and then, on the basis of those symptoms, arrives at a hypothesis, he is making use of inductive reasoning. The same goes for a jury that is instructed to unburden itself of all previous assumptions and pay attention only to evidence and sworn testimonies. When the lawyers have finished making their cases, the jury is expected to deliberate and, on the basis of the evidence and testimonies they have seen and heard, come up with a verdict. Induction is concerned only with facts, with empirical evidence that we can perceive with our five senses and that we can verify through experimentation.

Deductive logic, on the other hand, often works with ideas, values, and beliefs that cannot be seen or smelled or heard or tasted or touched. It begins with assumptions and principles that are generally taken for granted and then works downward toward a specific conclusion. Aristotle, the father of logic, taught us to carry through deductive reasoning in the form of a three-part proof known as a syllogism. Syllogisms begin with a major premise, a general principle or assumption that is accepted as a given ("All men are mortal"), proceeds to a minor premise, usually a fact or observation ("Socrates is a man"), and ends with a conclusion that follows from the major and minor premises ("Socrates is mortal"). Of course, people rarely speak in syllogisms; they speak instead in what Aristotle called enthymemes—partial syllogisms in which the major premise is left unstated. Hence, the syllogism used above would more likely be expressed in the form of the following enthymeme: "Socrates is a man; therefore, he is mortal" (or, "Because Socrates is a man, he must be mortal"). Anyone who hears that statement will immediately fill in the missing major premise. Unfortunately, the fact that we speak in enthymemes rather than syllogisms causes many moderns to overlook the fact that many of the things they believe are based on deduction rather than induction. The Christian who says, "The Bible tells us that we must repent and accept Christ; therefore, we must repent and accept Christ," and the skeptic who says, "The Gospels claim that Jesus rose from the dead; therefore, this claim must be based on a cover-up story, on self-delusion, or on later legendary material," are often unaware of the unstated major premises that underlie their arguments—namely, that the Bible is the Word of God and that miracles do not happen.

Whereas classical, medieval, and Renaissance thinkers had little problem thinking in terms of syllogisms and resting their proofs on accepted, "unproven" assumptions, modern, post-Enlightenment skeptics tend to be both empirical and pragmatic in outlook. As a result of this modern preference—I almost said prejudice—for empiricism, I will, in the rest of this book, take a generally inductive approach, seeking to accumulate evidence in favor of the central truth claims of Christianity. Still, in an age when many dismiss Christianity as purely emotional, if not downright irrational, it is vital to assert that the mysteries of Christianity *do* rest on logical principles. The ontological, cosmological, and theological proofs for the existence of God are all built on the twin logical laws of noncontradiction (a thing cannot be itself and its opposite at the same time and in the same way) and of causality (if you have an effect, then you must have a cause to produce it). As such, though these proofs may not actually prove beyond the shadow of a doubt that God exists, they do demonstrate that belief in God is consistent with logic. For this reason, I and many other modern apologists find it helpful to restate these arguments in modern terms, without therefore resting our entire case for faith upon them.

The philosophical school of ontology (Greek for "the study of being") is concerned with the "thingness" of things, with defining and describing their essence. The ontological argument—most famously stated by Anselm in the eleventh century—seeks to substantiate God's existence by arguing *from* (not for) the divine, eternal essence of God. God, argues Anselm, is a being than which nothing greater can be conceived. This is the major premise with which Anselm begins, and, in its favor, we must admit that nearly all people have an innate, essential understanding of God as just such a being. Of course, apologists will readily admit that we can define something that nevertheless does not exist—a unicorn, for example—but the fact remains that unbelievers know immediately what is meant by the idea of God and accept the existence of that idea.

Anselm next presents his minor premise: something that exists in the mind *and* in reality is greater than something that only exists in the mind (or understanding). Things that truly exist, that is to say, are greater than those that live only in the imagination. But if that is so, Anselm concludes, then God *must* exist; otherwise, our idea about God (as the being than which nothing greater can be conceived) would be an impossible idea: for a God who exists in the mind but not in reality would not be the greatest thought we could conceive. God *must* exist, or there would be no origin for our idea of God as the being than which nothing greater can be conceived.

As admitted above, such feats of deductive logic do little to bring modern people to faith in Christ, or even in God, but Anselm's ontological argument may serve an indirect purpose. It reminds us of something our modern age rarely thinks about—ontological causality: that our ideas of God, love, truth, beauty, and so forth point back to an eternal, supernatural origin. One *could* reasonably claim that the Christian (and Platonic) belief that our earthly ideas have divine origins is not a proof but an assertion, but then the modern claim—found in Marx, Freud, and Nietzsche—that our divine ideas have human origins is also an assertion. The question then is not which view has been proved deductively but which view better accounts for our own (inductive) experience of our world and our ideas.

While Christianity teaches that human fatherhood is a (fallen) reflection of God's divine Fatherhood, the atheist Freud argued that our idea of God the Father is the result of our sublimation—our projection upward—of our experiences with our own earthly fathers. But how can someone know—as, alas, too many have known—that he has a "bad" father unless he (perhaps unconsciously) measures the actions of the "bad" father he knows against his innate, essential knowledge of the perfect heavenly Father he does not know? Or, as Lewis has argued, Freud's contention that divine love is a sublimation of earthly lust is better explained if we view lust as a degradation or falling away from love.

Our modern evolutionary mind-set has convinced us that progress is the controlling metaphor by which all things are to be understood. We think that the effect will always be greater than the cause, when the reverse is more often the case. As any artist will tell you, the fiery spark of inspiration that initiates the creation of a poem or symphony or painting is always purer and more perfect than the work it inspires. Just so, behind our most exalted ideas of the divine is an even greater God—one than whom nothing greater can be conceived!

## THE COSMOLOGICAL AND TELEOLOGICAL ARGUMENTS

Although I find it both helpful and worthwhile to recount and contemplate Anselm's ontological proof, I would nevertheless assert, along with most (though not all) other apologists, that the cosmological and teleological proofs for the existence of God are finally more convincing, especially to the modern mind. Like the former, the latter two proofs call for deductive logic and rest on assumptions that must be granted before the reasoning process can begin. Still, these two proofs seem to touch more closely on our lived experience of ourselves and our world and thus are more appealing to pragmatists living in an empirical age.

The cosmological argument—most famously associated with Aquinas, though it dates back to Aristotle—states that for the cosmos to function as it does, there must exist a First Cause to account for that functionality. That is the argument in a nutshell, but it must be understood that what philosophers and apologists refer to as the cosmological argument is really an umbrella term for several related proofs. Aquinas himself offers five different proofs that all rely on the same basic notion of causality. Perhaps the clearest of these five proofs can be stated thus: The fact that motion exists in the world proves there must be a prime or unmoved mover; if there were not, our cosmos would be subject (illogically) to infinite regress. Now, to be fair, it must be conceded that postmoderns like Derrida have maintained, in direct opposition to Aquinas, that the true nature of the cosmos is precisely infinite regress; but then the counterclaims of Aquinas and Derrida leave us in the same position as we were with the ontological argument—forced to determine which assertion best explains the world we know.

Of course, if we decide to accept the postmodern account of reality, then we will have to explain far more than the existence of motion. We will have to explain our own existence as contingent beings—as beings, that is, that might or might not exist. We as human beings are contingent because we do not possess life within ourselves; to the contrary, a time will come when we will cease to exist. But if a time will come when we will cease to exist, then there must have also been a time when we—and our equally contingent universe—did not exist. And if *that* is true, and if we accept the atheist position that there exists no eternal God who dwells outside of time and space, then the cosmos should, in fact, be empty—an obviously untrue conclusion.

According to a cosmological corollary of the law of causality known as the Kalam argument—which dates back to medieval Arabic philosophy, but which was made famous in America by William Lane Craig—anything that begins to exist must have a cause (or origin). Since we and our universe (as contingent beings) came into existence at some point, then there must be a cause for it, but that cause cannot be part of our contingent universe. Or to put it another way, it is logically impossible that the contingent universe could have brought itself into existence. To say that we (or our universe) created ourselves is ridiculous, for to do so we would have had to have existed before we existed. Interestingly, in *Paradise Lost* Milton has Satan claim (illogically) that he created himself; his "proof" is that he does not remember the moment that he came into being!

Since nothing can come out of nothing, there must have been an eternal something, a First Cause that brought everything into being; otherwise, nothing would exist. Many moderns misunderstand this argument and ask, "If God created us, then who created God?" But that is a fallacious question, for what makes God God is that he is an uncreated and uncaused being who possesses life within himself. If he were not that, he would not be God.

To the Kalam cosmological argument, we may add two further corollaries that flesh out more fully the need for an uncreated Creator who transcends our spatiotemporal reality. First, just as our contingent status demands an uncaused cause, so the fact that we and our cosmos exist in a perpetual state of death and decay demands the existence of an absolute, eternal Life in the universe that can prevent utter entropy and chaos. Second, the fact that there are degrees of perfection (better, nobler, more beautiful) on this earth necessitates an ultimate standard or touchstone against which all others can be measured; without this measure we end up, once again, with infinite regress.

The teleological argument—most famously associated with William Paley, an English theologian and philosopher who lived in the eighteenth-century Age of Enlightenment—holds that the purpose (*telos* in Greek) and design inherent in our universe points to a Designer. According to Paley's oft-borrowed analogy, if we find a watch on the ground, its complexity will convince us that the watch did not occur naturally but was designed. Since our universe—not to mention our fearfully and wonderfully made bodies—is infinitely more complex than the watch, logic demands an eternal Watchmaker who could have designed both us and our world.

Lewis once stated that the true atheist must be both blind and dumb, for every inch of the universe all but shouts out the presence of an omnipotent, creative God (see Psalm 19). In chapters 14 and 22 I will argue that advances in science have not weakened but strengthened the teleological argument. Here I will instead answer one of the common criticisms leveled against it. Many who accept the teleological argument claim that it points not to the personal God of the Bible but to the impersonal, uninvolved watchmaker God of Deism. If the only place we found design and purpose were in nature, that might be true, but we find that design and purpose most supremely expressed in man, the crown of creation. How could an impersonal, unconscious, purposeless, apathetic, amoral God design creatures who are so radically personal, conscious, purposeful, passionate, and ethical? Contra the contentions of Darwinian evolution—contentions that are *forced* upon them by their unproven but fiercely defended major premise ("all natural phenomena must have a material, physical origin")—an impersonal cause cannot produce a personal effect. Here, as in the other two proofs discussed above, logic falls on the side not of modern, post-Enlightenment naturalism but of classical-medieval-Renaissance theism.

# 14

# THE EXISTENCE OF GOD II: ARGUMENTS FROM SCIENCE

Many today see science as the foe of Christianity, but is our strongly held modernist belief that science and religion are enemies based on historical fact or on Enlightenment propaganda? Increasingly over the last two decades, a growing number of historians and apologists have labored nobly to explode the myth of the perpetual war between ethical, self-sacrificing scientists and an ignorant, superstitious, monolithic church. As many apologists have pointed out—I find the discussions in Alister McGrath's *The Twilight of Atheism* and Dinesh D'Souza's *What's So Great about Christianity* to be particularly helpful and accessible—this so-called war was really the invention of two influential but now discredited books by two crusading sons of Enlightenment secularism: John William Draper's *History of the Conflict between Religion and Science* (1874) and Andrew Dickson White's *History of the Warfare of Science with Theology in Christendom* (1876).

For nearly a century, public schoolchildren across Europe and America have been taught to interpret the relationship between science and religion on the basis of two (and *only* two) incidents: the trial of Galileo and the Scopes "monkey" trial. Even if we accept the historically flawed secularist readings of these two incidents—readings that have been powerfully enshrined in Bertolt Brecht's play *The Life of Galileo* and the film version of *Inherit the Wind*—the clear fact remains that what these incidents really represent in the history of science and religion is not business as usual but the rare *exception* that proves the rule. The trials of Galileo and Scopes are aberrations in an otherwise cordial and often invigorating interaction between Catholic scientists and their church (particularly in the Middle Ages) and Protestant scientists and their firm sense of being called by God to use their gifts to think God's thoughts after him and to uncover the wonders of his creation.

Indeed, the very reason that theoretical science developed in the West is that its greatest founders and architects (Roger and Francis Bacon, Boyle, Copernicus, Faraday, Galileo, Kelvin, Kepler, Mendel, Newton, Pascal) were all Christians, or at least strong theists, who believed they would find order and laws in nature because nature was created by a God of order and law. Though the Chinese were great inventors, mastering gunpowder and movable type long before these inventions reached Europe, they did not develop—did not even come close to developing—the theories and methods of Western science. And the same goes for India, Japan, and Egypt. The reason that the scientists of these countries did not develop modern science is not because they were intellectually inferior to their European counterparts, but because they did not believe in the fixed nature of matter or in a Creator separate from his creation. Of course, there were a number of pre-Christian Greek scientists (most notably Pythagoras, Aristotle, and Euclid) who helped lay the foundations of modern science, but then all of these thinkers distanced themselves from the pantheism of their fellow Greeks to catch a glimpse of a divine Mind or Logos, an unmoved Mover who had endowed the universe with rationality, balance, and harmony.

The central tradition of Christianity has long understood that God reveals himself to us through two books: the "book" of nature and the Book of the Law (the Bible, the Word of God). Through the first book, God speaks in general terms of his power and authority and of his care for the world and for humanity; theologians call this God's "general revelation." Through the second, God speaks directly of what he expects from and desires for man. This, God's "special revelation," is also demonstrated in his historical interactions with the Jews and, supremely, in the life, death, and resurrection of the incarnate Christ (one of whose divine titles is the Word of God). Though we cannot learn from studying nature and the universe that God is triune or that Jesus is the Son of God, nature does speak of God's glory and sovereignty.

This biblical truth is perhaps best expressed in Psalm 19, which begins with a resounding affirmation of God's clear presence in nature ("The heavens declare the glory of God, / and the sky above proclaims his handiwork.") and then proceeds, starting at verse 7, to celebrate his far clearer presence in the Torah. ("The law of the LORD is perfect, reviving the soul; / the testimony of the LORD is sure, making wise the simple.")

The great thinkers who laid the foundation for modern science most often saw themselves as performing a task similar to the great Christian ethicists. Just as the latter did not invent the moral code (Lewis's Tao) but sought to discover and clarify the divine precepts written in our consciences by God, so the former sought to discern in the movement of the planets and the cycles of the seasons and the circulation of our blood higher, transcendent laws of motion and purpose that could be expressed in that most divinely inspired of languages—mathematics.

True, for the last two centuries Western science has increasingly strayed from its theistic roots. Just as the drafters of the constitution of the European Union consciously excluded from the document all reference to Christianity, so many in the scientific establishment have fought hard to deny and discredit the essential role that theism played in the development of modern science. Nevertheless, despite the growing fierceness of these denials, most of the modern advances in science have strengthened rather than weakened the case for the existence of God.

## THE ANTHROPIC PRINCIPLE

Through much study and observation, modern physicists and astronomers have come to realize that our universe is incredibly, if not miraculously, fine-tuned. For our universe to continue functioning, and for earth to continue being habitable, a large number of cosmic forces need to operate within precise parameters. Among these cosmic forces, the five best known are gravity, electromagnetism, the weak nuclear force, the strong nuclear force, and the cosmological constant. Were any of these forces to shift up or down by the slightest degree, the universe would either fly apart or crush together; either way, life as we know it would be destroyed.

Modern science has taught us that our universe, and our life within that universe, is almost unfathomably unlikely; the odds against it are truly astronomical. If we run the odds against just one of the five constants being tuned the way it is, we get a number in the trillions; but when we calculate the likelihood of all five being in the necessary alignment, we get a number that exceeds the number of atoms in the known universe. Those who would have us believe that man could have evolved solely by time and chance expect us to believe that if a billion monkeys were set in front of a billion typewriters, one of them would, by chance, type out *King Lear*. For the universe to have achieved its fine-tuning by chance is equivalent to putting a single typewriter in front of a single monkey and having him type *King Lear* on the first try, or, be more accurate, having him type out the collected works of William Shakespeare.

Apologetics books abound with quotes from high-level agnostic or atheist scientists who have admitted that the evidence points toward some kind of supra-natural design. Here are three representative quotes that appear regularly in books of apologetics (all three can be found, for example, in Fred Heeren's *Show Me God*):

> The more I examine the universe and the details of its architecture, the more evidence I find that the universe in some sense must have known we were coming. (Freeman Dyson, physicist)

> A common sense interpretation of the facts suggests that a superintellect has monkeyed with physics, as well as with chemistry and biology, and that there are no blind forces worth speaking about in nature. The numbers one calculates from the facts seem to me so overwhelming as to put this conclusion almost beyond question. (Sir Fred Hoyle, astrophysicist)

> For the scientist who has lived by his faith in the power of reason, the story ends like a bad dream. He has scaled the mountains of ignorance; he is about to conquer the highest peak; as he pulls himself over the final rock, he is greeted by a band of theologians who have been sitting there for centuries. (Robert Jastrow, astronomer)

When studied inductively, free from any preexisting metaphysical assumptions, the cumulative evidence all but eliminates the possibility of chance. Everything we have learned over the last century about the fine-tuned nature of our universe has pointed away from chaos and coincidence toward order, purpose, and design. I noted above that the laws of nature and of the universe are written in the language of mathematics. Many nontheistic scientists—Richard Dawkins, Daniel Dennett, and the late Carl Sagan among them—view these cosmic mathematical laws with an almost religious awe; and yet it is the numbers themselves that testify most strongly against their atheistic faith. The odds against mere chance having formed the universe we inhabit are simply too enormous to be ignored—unless one has a previous, unshakable metaphysical commitment against the existence of God. In that case no amount of empirical, mathematical evidence will be sufficient to prove the existence of a supernatural Creator.

The shocking discovery that our universe has been fine-tuned in such a way as to make human life possible has been dubbed the anthropic principle (from the Greek word *anthropos*, "man"). One would think the anthropic principle would offer clear proof not only that there is a Designer but a personal Creator who *purposed* for man to exist, but many in the scientific community disagree. Indeed, the term anthropic principle (or AP) was partly coined as an alternative "scientific" shorthand for admitting the *appearance* of fine-tuning without conceding its clear theistic implications. It is as if a liberal theologian who knew that Christianity was born out of the apostles' eyewitness experience and proclamation of the resurrection but who refused—on metaphysical rather than empirical grounds—to accept the possibility of resurrection were to construct a naturalistic explanation for the birth of Christianity and then dub it the resurrection principle.

Those who have a previous metaphysical commitment to naturalism want to have it both ways. On the one hand, Carl Sagan founded the Search for Extraterrestrial Intelligence (SETI) in order to scour the night sky for any signs of alien intelligence. Had he found, say, a quasar beating out the prime numbers, he would have concluded triumphantly that aliens exist. On the other hand, when it comes to our world, scientists who share Sagan's militant agnosticism can study the astronomical precision that makes human life possible and fail to see the "alien" intelligence of a Creator. At times they will even resort to an argument that is metaphysically and scientifically fallacious. Man, they will say, cannot possibly have been a special creation of God's, for we and our planet are so insignificantly small compared to the vastness of the cosmos. I call this argument fallacious, for it not only illogically makes size a marker of value but it ignores the fact that the universe needs to be as vast and spread out as it is to make possible the production of the raw materials out of which our planet and our hominid bodies were formed. That is to say, the vastness of space is a central facet of AP; it is one of the cosmic preconditions for the existence of human life!

Most scientists today whose naturalist beliefs and presuppositions *compel* them to accept only physical, natural processes simply dismiss the supernatural implications of AP by saying, essentially, that we are here, so the odds obviously fell in our favor—end of debate! Such scientists might be compared to a naive and optimistic gambler who does not believe it possible for a person to cheat at cards. He then plays a game of poker in which one of his opponents draws five royal flushes in a row. Since he refuses to believe his opponent is capable of cheating, he simply concludes that his opponent *must* have been very, very lucky. Though the odds against drawing five royal flushes are astronomical, the gambler has no choice but to conclude that, impossible as it seems, "luck" must have been on the side of his opponent. If cheating is ruled out, then the "coincidence" can only be explained by reference to some shadowy "royal-flush principle."

Of course, not all metaphysical naturalists have been satisfied with this somewhat embarrassing cop-out. A number of bolder (cockier?) scientists, desperate to preserve a respectable "natural" explanation for AP, have concocted a theory straight out of science fiction. Granting the astronomical odds against the fine-tuning of our universe, they theorize that these odds would be lessened if there were, in fact, billions of universes out there. Borrowing a page from the equally sci-fi quantum physicists who theorize that an infinite number of quantum realities exist to account for all the possible actions we *might* have taken and all the potential consequences those potential actions might have caused, AP-phobic scientists have posited that our universe is but one of multiple universes (or multiverses). Given enough multiverses, they argue, it is not unreasonable to expect that one would end up like ours.

That respectable, even brilliant scientists would resort to the multiverse theory as an escape hatch from the theistic implications of AP exposes the weaknesses in a metaphysical naturalism that refuses to consider even the possibility of a supernatural God who is actively at work in the universe. Were I vacationing on a cruise ship, and I saw the captain abandon the ship to paddle off in a rotting canoe punctured with holes, I would know that the ship itself was doomed! I see the multiverse theory as just such a rotting canoe, a desperate, last-ditch effort to survive the impending collapse of metaphysical naturalism. And yet, ironically, even that rotting canoe cannot afford an escape; for even if the multiverse theory *could* be proven, the existence of a finely tuned cosmic soup that could *produce* all these universes would itself point to a Designer.

## THE BIG BANG

The theistic implications of AP are indeed strong and pose a major threat to scientists and others in the academy and media who are firmly committed to a worldview that excludes the supernatural. But the story does not end there. As strong as the theistic implications are for AP, they are even stronger for that other great discovery of the twentieth century— the big bang. In the century following the Enlightenment's dismissal of God as an unnecessary hypothesis, many scientists, aware of the strength of the Kalam cosmological argument (that a universe which came into being must have a cause) began to theorize an eternal universe. Even after Edwin Hubble demonstrated (in 1929) that our universe was expanding from a central point, many scientists continued to cling to a static (or "steady state") universe. Einstein himself, aware that to accept an expanding universe meant accepting a universe with a beginning, theorized a groundless "fudge factor" to explain away the apparent expansion. He later recanted his "fudge factor" as the greatest mistake in his scientific career and accepted, if grudgingly, that our universe was expanding.

By 1980 abundant evidence had been amassed to prove that the universe began in an explosive event dubbed the big bang, an event that created not only matter but the space-time continuum. Still, despite the evidence that our universe had a beginning, Carl Sagan began his successful and highly influential 1980 TV series *Cosmos* by *asserting* that the cosmos is all there is, all there has ever been, and all there will ever be. Sagan was certainly aware that a universe that begins with a big bang needs a "Big Banger" who exists outside of and separate from that universe to bring it into being, but this was something his philosophical (not scientific) presuppositions would not allow him to accept. Fifteen years earlier, Arno Penzias and Robert Wilson had discovered (by accident) the "smoking gun" of the big bang—background microwave radiation spread out smoothly across the vastness of space. Sagan knew of their discovery and knew what it meant—that our cosmos had not always existed; nevertheless, he, a supposedly "objective" scientist, used his media platform to try to convince an entire generation that our universe is eternal.

That the universe had a beginning, that there was a time when neither matter nor space nor time itself existed, came as an unpleasant shock to metaphysical naturalists like Sagan. It should, however, have come as no shock to Jews and Christians who believed in the revealed truth of Genesis 1:1 ("In the beginning, God created the heavens and the earth.") and Hebrews 11:3. ("By faith we understand that the universe was created by the word of God, so that what is seen was not made out of things that are visible.") Though few realize it, the Bible is the *only* ancient book to claim God created the world *ex nihilo* (out of nothing); all the other pagan nations, from the Greeks and Romans to the Egyptians and Babylonians to the Indians and Scandinavians, believed that matter, not spirit, came first. Unlike the eternal God of the Jews, the one whose name is I AM, the gods of the Gentiles were born *out of* the initial chaos and then used their powers to shape that chaos. Outside the Bible, the belief was not "in the beginning, God," but "in the beginning, stuff."

Today nearly all scientists accept the big bang, placing it about fourteen billion years ago—a time frame, incidentally, that is far too short to account for the kind of slow evolution theorized by Darwin and his heirs. That, of course, does not mean all scientists accept the theistic implications of the big bang. The science-fiction scenarios of the multiverse theorists have also been applied to the big bang, but they bear as much resemblance to real science as mermaid legends do to ichthyology. Indeed, further research into what happened in the first few seconds of the big bang has revealed an even greater fine-tuned precision that boggles the mind. The message that the big bang is telling us, if only we will have ears to hear it, is that there exists an eternal "something" outside of our space-time continuum. In the absence of that "something," neither our planet nor our universe would exist. There would be nothing.

Empirical, inductive science has demonstrated both that our universe had a beginning and that it is incredibly fine-tuned. Why then don't the vast majority of scientists follow the evidence of AP and the big bang to its logical and unavoidable conclusion—that God exists? I have suggested thus far that the refusal on the part of the scientific community to acknowledge the overwhelming theistic implications of AP and the big bang can be accounted for by the entrenched, monolithic position that metaphysical naturalism holds in the academy. But there is, I believe, a second moral-spiritual reason for this refusal that must be raised. According to Christianity, though we were made in, and continue to bear, God's image, we are all of us born with a sinful, depraved nature.

I am aware that by invoking the doctrine of original sin I risk sounding more like a preacher than an apologist, but this doctrine is central to apologetics in at least three ways. First, the problem of pain cannot be "solved" apart from our admission that we exist in a state of rebellion against our Creator and that we are guilty of pride and disobedience. Second, apart from this admission, the gospel message that Christ died for our sins on the cross becomes irrelevant, and Christ becomes not a savior but a moral cheerleader. Third, only the doctrine of original sin enables us to understand Paul's contention (in Romans 1:18–23) that God has revealed his eternal power and divine nature to mankind through the glory of his creation, but men *choose* not to heed him.

It is with this third implication of original sin that I am concerned. Agnostics and atheists like Bertrand Russell and Richard Dawkins often claim that if God would show himself clearly to them, they would believe in him; yet, when his presence *is* demonstrated clearly through something like AP or the big bang, they immediately defuse the evidence via a "scientific" explanation—even one as ludicrous as the multiverse theory. Such skeptics, of course, will claim that their conclusions are born out of logic, observation, and the scientific method. But is that really the case? Might it not be pride and sin rather than intellect and reason that impels skeptics to reject scientific evidence for God's presence?

# 15

# THE EXISTENCE OF GOD III: WHY BAD THINGS HAPPEN TO GOOD PEOPLE

The ubiquitous presence of pain and evil in our world is, to my mind, the only argument against the existence of God that carries any real weight. It is also the number-one reason people give for denying—or, better, giving up on—God. Confronted with terrible illnesses and tragic accidents, the death of the young and innocent, the horrors of war and oppression, and the ravages of natural disasters, many moderns find it intellectually and emotionally impossible to believe in the existence of God—at least not the all-powerful, all-loving God who is revealed in the Bible. Although I have already offered some tentative answers to this dilemma (see chapter 4), I believe that the issues raised by pain and suffering are too real and pressing to be dealt with in a single chapter. For that reason, I will devote this chapter as well to exploring and wrestling with this key apologetic concern.

Let us begin with a question that is seldom raised: why is it that the last two generations of Americans and Europeans, generations that have seen a vast *decrease* in human suffering, have struggled *more* with the problem of pain than all previous generations? Despite the phenomenal growth in health, education, freedom, and labor-saving technology, our modern age has shown itself less able to deal with pain and more quick either to blame God for suffering or to deny his existence—or, paradoxically, to do both at the same time! And that inability has only increased further since the end of the Cold War. The greater our quality of life, it seems, the more apt we are to reject God on account of the suffering in our world. How can this be?

The reason for this paradox, I believe, can be traced back to one of the most influential writers of the eighteenth century, Jean-Jacques Rousseau. Before Rousseau, the Enlightenment, and the French Revolution (out of which the romantic age was born), Christian Europe accepted that the problem with man, the reason he could never build a perfect world or free himself from evil and suffering, was his inborn propensity for sin, pride, and disobedience. That is to say, the doctrine of original sin was understood to have repercussions not only in the sphere of ethics and morality but in the natural, social, and political spheres as well. After Rousseau, however, more and more people in the West distanced themselves from original sin and came to believe that man, at least in his natural state, was inherently good. Rousseau argued that the problem with man was not sin, pride, and disobedience but ignorance and poverty. Eliminate those, promised Rousseau, and we can return to an innocent, Edenic state of peace and plenty.

Rousseau's optimistic, secular faith in man's innate goodness galvanized eighteenth- and nineteenth-century Europe and America, filling them—and us, their heirs—with the hope that if we could eliminate sickness, ignorance, and poverty and purify man and society from systemic greed and injustice, we could build utopia. It was a lovely dream, but it led, as Chesterton correctly prophesied, to great horrors. Throughout the twentieth century, totalitarian regimes, denying original sin, sought to eliminate evil by purging "bad" groups that were too corrupt to be reformed: Jews, kulaks, landlords, Kurds, and so forth. And they were absolutely ruthless in their purges, for the "nobility" of what they were trying to achieve—the purification of man and society—justified their by-any-means-necessary approach.

The liberal democracies fared better, but they, by puffing us up with promises of our "inalienable" right to health, happiness, and prosperity, left us spoiled, disappointed, and thankless. Because we misunderstand—or refuse to accept—that we are fallen, we imagine that we ourselves (apart from God) can eradicate all evil and suffering through state-run public education, universal health care, and free-market capitalism. Alas, because we feel entitled to all of these things, and more, we are left angry and bitter when we do not get what we think we deserve. In response to our disappointment, we do not question our Rousseauian assumptions but blame God for not bailing us out.

Worse yet, as the denial of original sin combined with the belief that man was evolved from lower forms rather than created in the image of

God, the totalitarian *and* liberal West adopted a deterministic view of man that robbed us of our status as full moral agents. The ascendancy of biological and environmental determinism freed us from responsibility for our actions and left us feeling victimized when things went wrong. When suffering occurs, our first response is to blame society (the "system"), our DNA (the "selfish gene"), or God (for "making me this way"), rather than considering that it might be the result of our misuse of free will or a spur to test and purify our moral character and faith.

## HUME'S CHALLENGE AND PLANTINGA'S REPLY

To exacerbate the influence of Rousseau's "optimistic" view of man, the Enlightenment exchanged the active God of the Bible with the passive God of the philosophers. Yes, God existed and had philosophically defined attributes (omnipotence, omniscience, omnipresence, omnibenevolence), but he was not a personal God one could know, love, or trust. Indeed, one of the reasons that I devoted only one chapter of this book to logical proofs for the existence of God (chapter 13) is that I wanted to avoid a danger that Lewis exposes in *The Great Divorce*. In chapter 9 of that brilliant study of the narcissism and idolatry that leads to hell, Lewis warns against a kind of passionless apologetics that becomes so obsessed with proving the existence of God that it comes to care nothing for God himself! In our day the deistic God of the philosophers—whose only job seems to be to exist—has morphed into a "user-friendly" God whom we can ignore when things go well and against whom we can rage when thing go wrong.

Indeed, it is precisely this depersonalized Enlightenment God who has proven to be an easy target for agnostic debunkers who project onto this inactive, impassive deity all their rage against the evils and indignities of our world. The most successful of these skeptics was David Hume, who claimed to have logically disproved God's existence by arguing that God's attributes of A) omnipotence and B) omnibenevolence were inconsistent with C) the existence of pain. Since, Hume concluded triumphantly, our observations of C cannot be reconciled with A and B, God must either not exist or does not possess the qualities of power and goodness that the Bible ascribes to him. Modern skeptics continue to parrot Hume's "proof," while ignoring the fact that the "God" Hume debunks is the God of the philosophers, not the God and Father of our Lord Jesus Christ. I will devote the rest of this chapter to defending the latter God; before doing so, however, I must mention that Hume's logical disproof of God was soundly rebutted in the 1970s by a man widely considered to be one of the foremost living philosophers, Alvin Plantinga.

Plantinga argues that the statements *God is all-powerful, God is all-loving,* and *there is evil in the world* do not, as Hume and his heirs claim, constitute a formal contradiction. They do not because the two major premises that lurk beneath the first two statements (*an all-powerful God could eliminate suffering*; *an all-loving God would desire to do so*) are premises that need to be modified and added to before the skeptic can claim a contradiction. The first needs to be modified to say: *an all-powerful God can do anything he wants*; the second to say: *an all-loving God would desire in all cases to eliminate suffering.* If these modified premises were true, then indeed, the presence of pain and suffering in our world would be inconsistent with God's nature. But *are* they true?

To rebut the first modified premise (*an all-powerful God can do anything he wants*), Plantinga argues that God cannot do something irrational—make a square circle, for example, or simultaneously give and not give us free will. To rebut the second (*an all-loving God would desire in all cases to eliminate suffering*), he argues that many scenarios exist by which God can use evil for good. Interestingly, Plantinga insists that the theist does not have to explain *how* God uses evil or pain for good; to refute Hume he need only show that God can logically have loving reasons for allowing pain. Lewis, as we saw in chapter 4, offers a number of reasons in *The Problem of Pain* as to why God might allow suffering for our good: to ensure the reality of our free will, to shape us into the masterpieces he wishes us to be, to draw our attention away from ourselves and our illusory self-sufficiency, and so forth. Plantinga accepts the power of such arguments but insists again that they are not necessary to refute the oft-repeated argument of Hume. Essentially Plantinga uses logic to show that it is not illogical to believe in an all-loving and all-powerful God—even in the midst of pain and suffering.

## A SAVIOR WHO KNOWS SORROW

Despite the power of Plantinga's logic and Lewis's free will theodicy, a full answer to the problem of pain demands a direct wrestling with the incarnation, the crucifixion, and the resurrection. The God of the Bible, unlike the God of the philosophers, is a living, active, dynamic God who (quite literally) invaded our world and who desires to know each of us personally. When we, in our grief, anger, and despair, come face-to-face with the God-Man who died and rose again, we move into a region that does not obliterate but transcends logic. Plantinga himself admits that logical answers can only take us halfway to resolving the problem of pain; pastoral care is needed if we are to reconcile our individual suffering with the person and promises of Christ

In "On Obstinacy in Belief" (anthologized in *The World's Last Night and Other Essays*), Lewis makes a similar admission: the question the believer should ask is not "how can I rationalize my pain? but, will I or will I not trust God? When the risen Christ tells doubting Thomas that the blessed ones are those who do not see and yet believe (John 20:29), he rebukes not a philosophical antagonist but a friend. His words are "not addressed to a philosopher enquiring whether God exists . . . [but] to a man who already believed that, who already had long acquaintance with a particular Person. . . . It is a rebuke not to skepticism in the philosophic sense but to the psychological quality of being 'suspicious.' It says in effect, 'You should have known me better.'"

While modern skeptics claim that Christianity is a religion that is accepted for emotional reasons and then rejected for intellectual ones, Lewis argues that the reverse is true. We accept the claims of Christ because they make sense and then abandon them when a painful or confusing situation causes us to be overcome by feelings of fear or guilt. What would you think of a man who vowed to love and honor his wife and then, every time she looked at another man, immediately accused her of adultery? You would think him a boor and a fool, and yet that is how our modern, skeptical world expects the believer to behave toward God. When bad things happen in my life, I continue to trust in God, not because I allow my "blind" faith to obliterate my higher rational faculties, but because I trust that the same God who wore my skin and bore my sin will guide me through my present suffering. Once you vow to follow Christ, Lewis explains, "You are no longer faced with an argument which demands your assent, but with a Person who demands your confidence." The Christian who does not abandon God in the face of evil and suffering does not act illogically or irrationally; he merely maintains his trust in a God who suffers and saves.

In *Where Is God When It Hurts?* Philip Yancey presents evidence, both scholarly and personal, that experiences of pain, suffering, and loss do not, in and of themselves, either strengthen or tear apart families. More often than not, the experience—whether it be the loss of a child, the sudden onset of a debilitating disease in one's spouse, or the care of a severely injured family member—exacerbates what was already there.

If the love between husband and wife is strong to begin with, the loss of their son will drive them closer together; if their relationship is not grounded in deep and unconditional love, the same tragedy will more often than not drive them away from each other. The same is true for our relationship with God. If my faith in God is secure, pain and loss will drive me closer to, not farther away from, his divine presence and care.

And I, together with hundreds of millions of believers, know that I can trust in that presence and care, for I know that the final answer to the problem of pain is to be found on the cross. God *has* shown us the full power and extent of his love, but he did not do so by removing all evil and pain from our world. If he had, he would have robbed us of free will and prevented us from growing into the creatures he created us to be. No, Christ demonstrated his love—indeed, *proved* his love—by entering our world, living as a poor man, and suffering the full consequences of evil and pain.

The God revealed in Christ is not the God of the Deists—removed and aloof from the cares and struggles of men. Nor is he like the Stoic and Epicurean gods of Greece and Rome—feasting on nectar and ambrosia while arbitrarily raining down benevolence or destruction on us puny, insignificant mortals below. In the incarnation and crucifixion of Christ, we encounter instead a God who not only suffers *for* us but *alongside* us as well. Only Christianity has made and can make this profession of its God: "For we do not have a high priest who is unable to sympathize with our weaknesses, but one who in every respect has been tempted as we are, yet without sin" (Hebrews 4:15). God can identify with the fullness of our suffering, for he experienced himself that fullness and did not turn away from it. All the pains and the indignities, the loneliness and the frustration, the fevers and fatigues, the stubbed toes and upset stomachs and pounding headaches, even the futile rage against the system, he experienced them all—and not on his own terms but on the cruel, inflexible terms of our fallen world.

When Christ suffered and died on the cross, he took upon himself not only the full weight of human sin but the full weight of human evil and pain—and something more, something, I believe, that was worse than the horrific pain of crucifixion. He bore that which is more painful than pain: public rejection, betrayal, humiliation, and scorn. And, miraculously, for he was himself God, he bore the emotional and spiritual devastation, the utter and absolute isolation that comes when one is cut off from God. We heirs of Sartre and Camus speak so glibly of existential despair; in that terrible moment when Christ cried out, "My God, my God, why have you forsaken me?" (Matthew 27:46), he not only experienced existential despair—he became it. Christ learned in that moment what it means to feel lost and abandoned in a world without meaning or purpose or hope.

But the story, thank God, did not end there. On the third day he rose again, proving once and for all that good can come out of evil and that God can transform the deepest defeat into the greatest victory. Christians who cling to God's promise that all things work together for good (Romans 8:28) are not trusting in pie in the sky but in the One who said, "I am the resurrection and the life. Whoever believes in me, though he die, yet shall he live" (John 11:25). Christ defeated evil and suffering, not by ignoring or avoiding it, but by going *through* it to find the hope and victory that lie on the other side. To paraphrase the Easter hymn sung across the world by Orthodox Christians, it was *by* death that Christ trampled *upon* death and so brought freedom and light to those in bondage.

Such is the paradoxical claim of Christian theology, but it is a claim whose truth is daily substantiated by a curious fact: it is those who have suffered the most—not those who have suffered little—who have the strongest faith in God. In the modern Western world, it is invariably healthy, prosperous academics who work in clean, well-lit offices who complain the most about the problem of pain. When a businessman once asked Mother Theresa where God is when a child is dying on the streets, she purportedly replied, "God is with that child," and then added, "The real question is not where God is, but where you are." I do not say this to scoff or accuse; I say it because it is true. The great saints and martyrs of the Bible and the church age from Moses and Joseph to Daniel and Jeremiah to Peter and John to St. Francis and Luther to Bonhoeffer and Mother Theresa all suffered in body and spirit—and then went forth to relieve as best they could the pain and suffering of others.

When Paul himself begged God to remove from him "a thorn . . . in the flesh," he was told, "My grace is sufficient for you, for my power is made perfect in weakness" (2 Corinthians 12:7, 9). Academics (like me!) who have been blessed with relatively easy lives face the ongoing temptation to take their own "reasonable" natures and project them onto God. "I would never allow suffering in the world or send people to hell," we muse and then conclude that if God were truly God, he wouldn't either.

So Job thought until God spoke to him from the whirlwind, reminding him that we are the creature and not the Creator, that God made us in his image and not vice versa:

> Who is this that darkens counsel by words without knowledge?
> Dress for action like a man;
> I will question you, and you make it known to me. (Job 38:2–3)

# 16

# THE BIBLE TELLS ME SO: DEFENDING THE AUTHORITY OF SCRIPTURE

One of the essential components of "mere" Christianity is a belief that the Bible is divinely inspired and wholly trustworthy and holds authority in the church and in the life of the believer. Granted, between (and within) denominations debate continues as to what parts of the Bible should be taken literally and what figuratively, what the exact relationship should be between Scripture and sacred tradition, and how such phrases as *inerrancy* and *plenary inspiration* should be defined and applied. But all orthodox Christians will accede to the inspiration, trustworthiness, and authority of the Old and New Testaments. Over the last century, numerous apologists have arisen to defend the inspiration and/or inerrancy of Scripture in response to those in Enlightenment-inspired universities and seminaries who have sought to question, problematize, and deconstruct the claims of the Bible.

Although I applaud the work of these defenders of the Word, and although I believe that the Bible, like Jesus himself, is fully human and fully divine, in the chapters that follow I will not be arguing for or even assuming that the Bible was directly inspired by God. This statement may strike many of my readers as odd and even disturbing, especially those who share my evangelical Protestant perspective. But I think it is a necessary, if preliminary, concession that needs to be made if the twenty-first century apologist is to find common ground with a modern and postmodern world whose first instinct is to question authority, especially religious authority.

In order to substantiate the basic claims of Christ and the essential doctrines of Christianity, the apologist need not prove the inspiration or inerrancy of the Bible; he need only show the Bible to be *reliable* in its account of Jewish and Christian history. The role of the post-Enlightenment, popular apologist who would convince modern skeptics of the accuracy of the biblical record consists simply in this: to demonstrate that the Bible, though written by several dozen authors over the space of a millennium, offers a unified and reliable chronicle of God's actions and interactions in human history.

## A FAITH GROUNDED IN HISTORY

The Bible, it must be acknowledged, contains a great deal of poetry: psalms that praise, wisdom literature that instructs, prophetic literature that warns and guides, and so forth. Nevertheless, despite the Bible's heavy reliance upon poetic, nonliteral forms, its focus remains firmly on history. Most of David's psalms are closely linked to troubled or exultant moments in his long bid for power and his even longer reign. Prophecies demand that the reader have a thorough knowledge of the history of Israel and the power politics that defined, and continue to define, the life and destiny of the Middle East. Even divine promises and theological doctrines emerge in the context of God's interventions in historical time. Above all, the bloodline of the Messiah, which wends its way not only through charismatic leaders (Abraham, David, Solomon, Hezekiah) and powerless exiles but also through women of suspect sexuality (Tamar, Rahab, Bathsheba), is inextricably linked to the historical triumphs and defeats of God's chosen people.

In contrast to other holy books of the ancient world, the Bible focuses not on legendary or mythic heroes (Achilles, Gilgamesh, Krishna) but on real human characters who live in real space-time, fight historical battles, and interact with actual kingdoms. One of the most poetic, outlandish, seemingly ahistorical images in the Old Testament—Nebuchadnezzar's dream of a giant image made out of four metals (Daniel 2)—points not to abstract religious ideas but to the four great kingdoms that shaped the destiny of Asia Minor for over five centuries: Babylon, Persia, Greece, and Rome. And the climax of that dream, the destruction and replacement of the giant by a stone uncut by human hands, points to one of the most shocking transitions in human history: the waning of the Roman Empire and the waxing of the Roman Catholic Church.

We may call the Bible a book of faith, but it is a faith fully grounded in historical events—past, present, and yet to come. Indeed, take away the historical truth of Abraham and Moses, Joshua and Samuel, David and Solomon, Ezra and Nehemiah, John the Baptist and Jesus, and you no longer have Christianity. This important element of Christianity, one that is too often overlooked by moderns, distinguishes it from all other religions (except, of course, Judaism). Hinduism and Buddhism rely on legends and/or precepts that need no grounding in historical reality; in many ways such religions rest on a denial of history, at least in any straight, linear sense. The same is essentially true of the various forms of pantheism, monism, Gnosticism, occultism, and neo-paganism that have sprung up again and again in the Western world. As for Islam, though it may seem on the surface to be historical (mostly because the Qur'an piggybacks on the Bible), the faith of the Muslim, like that of the Western Deist, is finally divorced from a dynamic, involved God who acts and interacts in human history and who, in the person of Jesus Christ, entered into it.

I think it significant that critics of religion rarely concentrate their energy on "disproving" such holy books as the Qur'an or the Gita or the Analects—unless, of course, the religion happens to be Christianity and the holy book happens to be the Bible. Since the Enlightenment, secular humanists and liberal Bible scholars have been unrelenting in their attempts to undermine, if not explode, the historical accuracy of the Scriptures. Throughout the nineteenth and early twentieth centuries, such critics seemed to be winning the battle for the Bible; however, the last several decades have effected a stunning, if not always acknowledged, reversal. Again and again modern archaeology has shown the Bible to be consistently reliable in its historical, cultural, and political details.

True, archaeology cannot "prove" the Bible to be inspired, but then no respectable apologist ever claimed that it could. No archaeological find can prove that God spoke directly to Moses or David or John. What archaeology *can* do, and what it has done time and again over the last century, is verify the historical details that form the backdrop to the biblical narrative. The Old Testament abounds with the names of people and places, and it is no exaggeration to say that every major dig in the Holy Land has unearthed place and people names that match those recorded in the Bible. The same holds true for the wording of ancient oaths and treaties that give structure to such books as Genesis, Deuteronomy, and Esther and for the names, locations, and histories of Israel's enemies—Canaanites, Philistines, Moabites, etc. Archaeology has also substantiated the general shape of Israelite history as it is presented in the Hebrew Scriptures, including and especially the chronologies of Israel's kings. No, not every detail in the Bible has been verified by an archaeological finding, but no major finding has ever contradicted its basic historical accuracy.

In many cases, archaeology has actually *vindicated* the Bible from its critics. In the early decades of the twentieth century, liberal scholars had, they thought, "proven" Genesis to be unreliable because it had invented a "nonexistent" people group, the Hittites. To add to their triumphalism, they also claimed to have "proven" the Gospel of John to be a late-second-century text because its theology, so it was argued, was too highly "evolved" for the first century. These findings were widely touted until, later in the century, archaeologists uncovered detailed evidence of the existence of the Hittites and found in the sands of Egypt a scrap of papyri that decisively dated the Gospel of John to the late first century, the traditional date of its composition.

Despite continued media and academic claims that the Bible is historically suspect, the fact remains that every phase of Jewish history—from the patriarchs to the exodus to the conquest of Canaan to the united and divided Kingdoms of David and his heirs to the exile and return—has yielded artifacts and extrabiblical texts that square with the biblical accounts. Further, archaeology has often shown that linguistic or cultural details recorded in the Bible are true of the historical age in which they are set but not true of later ages. That is to say, archaeologists have discovered that many of the names and physical details mentioned in Genesis existed in the age of the patriarchs (first half of the second millennium B.C.) but disappeared in the first millennium (when liberal scholars claim Genesis was actually written). In contrast, *the Iliad*, though often correct about place names, records numerous details—like the practice of cremation—that did not exist in the Mycenaean age of Agamemnon (1250 B.C.) but that were widespread in Homer's age (750 B.C.).

Perhaps the best case study to prove the unwillingness of many in the academy, the media, and the liberal seminaries to acknowledge the historical accuracy of the Bible is that of the Dead Sea Scrolls. Though there remains a strong popular suspicion, often fueled by scholars who should know better, that the Dead Sea Scrolls "contradict" the Bible, the truth is exactly the opposite. First, the Dead Sea Scrolls provide us with the oldest surviving texts of most of the books of the Old Testament—texts that substantiate the accuracy of the Bible in use today. Second, the portrait of first-century Palestine that the Scrolls provide us with is consistent with that presented in the New Testament. The Gospels and Scrolls offer similar details of Jewish rites and rituals (like the stone jars mentioned in John 2) and of religious and political sects (for example, the Pharisees, Sadducees, and Herodians).

Though liberal scholars and secular skeptics continue to attack the Bible as nonhistorical, their criticism is flawed, for it rests on, and is driven by, an unproven *a priori* assumption: miracles don't happen. Most liberal scholars begin not with an inductive search for truth but with an unsubstantiated prejudice against the supernatural. Such scholars *take for granted* that if a Bible story contains a miracle, it *cannot* be historical. By doing so, however, they beg the question of the Bible's authority, which is grounded not only on the specific miracles that surround the ministries of Moses, Joshua, Elijah, and Jesus but on the more general miracle of God's continued interventions in human affairs. A proper, unbiased procedure would say that since the Bible has been shown to be accurate in its small details, there is good reason to believe that it is also reliable in its larger claims. Unfortunately, the miracle-denying scholar takes a backward approach, *beginning* with the rejection of the larger claim and then dismissing or distorting the accuracy of the smaller details.

Biblical authority, not to mention biblical inerrancy, also rests, as we saw in chapter 12, on the two hundred plus prophecies fulfilled by Jesus' birth, ministry, death, and resurrection. The odds against his having fulfilled all the prophecies "by chance" are as astronomical as those related to the fine-tuning of the universe. Unfortunately, since liberal scholarship not only proscribes miracles but prophecy as well, much of the most compelling, if not *decisive*, evidence for biblical authority is simply thrown out. Most liberal scholarship insulates itself from ever weighing fairly or facing directly the claim that God is a miracle-working, history-invading, prophecy-making God!

Imagine if you suspected that someone in your family was possessed by a demon, and you invited a highly credentialed priest to come to your house to test whether your suspicion was true. Imagine further that when you greeted the priest at the door, he informed you that he himself categorically denied the existence of angels and demons. Would you, *could* you, put any credence in the man's assessment of whether your family member was possessed? Of course not! And yet for nearly two centuries our modern culture has entrusted a matter of highest importance—whether the Bible is accurate and reliable—to a group of scholars who deny *a priori* the miraculous and prophetic claims around which the Bible is structured.

Meanwhile, outside the walls of academia, in the land of John Q. Public and the man on the street, the most common critique of the Bible is, simply, that it is "full of contradictions." This critique, I have found, is usually made by people who can't think of one offhand but who "know" the critique is true. As it turns out, when these contradictions are actually listed, they turn out to be few in number, and most can be resolved either by some help from history or archaeology or by a more careful reading of the text. For example, those who maintain that the Old and New Testaments contradict each other by giving us a God of wrath followed by a God of love are generally guilty of the same vice practiced by millions of college students: laziness. A closer, more-focused reading of the Bible will reveal several places in the Old Testament (like the stories of Rahab, Ruth, and Jonah) that show God's mercy toward Gentiles, and several places in the New (like Jesus' cleansing of the Temple and his condemnation of the Pharisees and most of Revelation) that reveal the wrath and anger of Christ. As for the few legitimate "contradictions" that remain after careful study has eliminated the lion's share of supposed ones, nearly all can be shown to be a result either of minor textual errors in transmission or of the fact that much of the Bible, especially the Gospels, is based on eyewitness accounts that complement rather than contradict each other. In any case, none of these minor contradictions alters any central teaching of the Bible or the creeds.

Indeed, they are precisely the kinds of "contradictions" we should expect once we accept the Bible on its own terms. It is too often forgotten by extremists on both sides of the debate that were the Bible meant to be the kind of scientific textbook that fundamentalists claim it to be and liberals attack it for not being, it would have far less poetry and would be far less redundant and repetitive. There would, for example, be only one Gospel and two or three Pauline epistles, not four Gospels and over a dozen epistles that have sent many a New Testament harmonizer to bed with headache and eye strain. The Bible, we must remember, is not a "modern" book. Though it holds up remarkably well against all modern "tests," it is not concerned with fulfilling modern notions of "scientific" verification. It is both unscholarly and unfair to force the Bible to adhere to a system of verification that did not exist when the documents were written, that did not, in fact, exist until the eighteenth century!

Far more could be said in defense of the historical accuracy of the Bible, but I will conclude with two observations that are often overlooked. First, the continued existence of the historic Jewish people, despite numerous attempts to destroy them, reinforces the Bible's claim that the Jews are God's chosen people. Second, whereas many people think that Christians believe first in the authority of Scripture and then in the deity of Christ, the reverse is more often the case. For those who have placed their faith in Christ, the strongest evidence of the reliability of the Old Testament is that Christ himself testified to its absolute authority.

As for the New Testament, its reliability rests not only on the testimony and central presence of Christ but on a number of concrete, objective, textual factors that simply cannot be ignored by anyone familiar with the study of ancient texts.

## THE ACCURACY OF THE NEW TESTAMENT DOCUMENTS

If the New Testament were not the New Testament, it would be hailed by *all* critics, liberal and orthodox alike, as the most reliable text of the ancient world, if not, indeed, of the premodern world. The relentless barrage of liberal, media-hyped attacks on the Bible obscures the fact that by the scholarly, objective standards of textual criticism, the New Testament gets very high marks.

Textual criticism determines the reliability of an ancient (pre-printing press) text by considering three factors: 1) the length of time between the original writings and the earliest extant manuscripts; 2) the number of early copies of the manuscripts; and 3) the variations between the copies. As anyone who has studied textual criticism knows, the vast majority of ancient texts from the classical period—whether they be historical, literary, or philosophical—are based on very few manuscripts that appear many centuries after the original. And yet, despite the shaky history of textual transmission that hangs over most of the works of antiquity, no scholar doubts the authenticity of works by Homer, Hesiod, Aeschylus, Sophocles, Euripides, Plato, Aristotle, Virgil, Horace, Cicero, Ovid, and dozens of others.

One of the first modern apologists to inform a public audience of this situation was F. F. Bruce, and all apologists who have followed in his footsteps owe him a debt of gratitude. In his many books (most notably *The New Testament Documents: Are They Reliable?*), Bruce explains that the historical writings of Julius Caesar and Tacitus are preserved in manuscripts that are some eight hundred years later than the original, while those of Greek historians Herodotus and Thucydides come a full thirteen hundred years later—and in each case we have only about ten copies. One of the very few ancient manuscripts to boast copies in the hundreds are Homer's *The Iliad* and *The Odyssey*, but the earliest of those manuscripts date to a full millennium after Homer!

In contrast, there are more than five thousand extant Greek copies of the New Testament. Though the oldest full copy dates to A.D. 340, significant portions of the Gospels and Epistles date as early as 200, with the scrap of the Gospel of John mentioned above dating to about 100. Just as important, if we put together the epistles and sermons of such early church fathers as Clement, Ignatius, and Justin Martyr, all of whom quote extensively from the Bible, we can reconstruct almost the entire New Testament. To add to the abundance of Greek manuscripts and to the corroborating evidence of the fathers, we also possess numerous early copies of the New Testament in Coptic, Syriac, Armenian, and Slavic. And yet when we compare these thousands of extant manuscripts, we find *very* little variance in the texts. As noted above, nearly all variances that do exist can be accounted for by minor scribal errors, and none of the variations alters any central doctrine or teaching of the church.

Judged by modern, *secular* textual standards, the New Testament is extremely reliable. Indeed, I do not exaggerate when I assert, together with Bruce and a growing cadre of scholars, that if the New Testament documents are not reliable, then neither are any manuscripts from the ancient world. Throw out the historical witness of the Gospels and of Acts, and we must throw out as well the historical writings of Herodotus, Thucydides, Xenophon, Polybius, Cicero, Livy, Tacitus, and Plutarch! To trust in the historical record presented by the New Testament is to rely, not on blind faith, but on man's innate desire and ability to preserve such a record. To reject the New Testament record is tantamount to rejecting the very possibility of history.

Though all the Gospels hold up well to historical "checking," the one that shows the highest degree of reliability—higher, perhaps, than any other historical work of antiquity—is the Gospel of Luke. Judged by academic, nonreligious criteria, Luke, who wrote both the Gospel that bears his name and the book of Acts, emerges as one of the finest historians of the ancient world. He carefully dates all events by reference to Roman emperors, governors, and other public officials and is highly accurate in his geographic, political, and cultural details. Though Luke was not one of the twelve apostles, he traveled with Paul, who, shortly after his conversion, met with the apostles and Jesus' brother (James) in Jerusalem. Luke also carefully interviewed eyewitnesses, including, according to many scholars, Jesus' mother.

As for the other three Gospels, all were written by men who were either eyewitnesses of the events or worked closely with eyewitnesses. Matthew and John were both disciples who knew Jesus firsthand. Mark was too young to be a disciple, but he knew and worked with Paul and served as the apostle Peter's right-hand man for many years. The rest of the New Testament consists of letters written by Paul to various churches, general letters by James, John, and Jude (probably another brother of Jesus), and the book of Revelation, which is traditionally ascribed to John the apostle but may have been written by a different John.

Extrabiblical witnesses to the New Testament increase its historical reliability. Though secular historians say little about the initially minor and generally despised Christian "sect," we can cull enough information from such sources as Tacitus, Suetonius, Josephus, and Pliny to substantiate the basic historical contours of Christ's life. Even outside the New Testament, the life, ministry, and death of Christ are attested to by what the modern court system would call hostile witnesses!

Of course, as expected, the antisupernatural scholars mentioned above have questioned the miracles that punctuate the Gospels, using them as handy devices for casting doubt upon the historical reliability of the New Testament. Those who do so, however, have repeatedly failed to distinguish the miracles of Jesus from those recorded in such contemporary pagan works as Ovid's *Metamorphoses*. Unlike the arbitrary, often terrifying "miracles" that appear in pagan texts, those recorded in the Gospels are always consistent with the character of God and of Christ and serve not to deconstruct but to legitimize Jesus' claims. In fact, unlike Matthew, Mark, and Luke, who use the Greek word for "power" (*dunamis*) to denote Jesus' miracles, John uses the Greek word for "sign" (*semion*). The miracles of Jesus are neither fairy tales nor aberrations, but signs and markers that authorize the deeds and words of Jesus—deeds and words that are themselves reliably recorded in the New Testament.

# 17

# IN SEARCH OF THE HISTORICAL JESUS

To my mind, Lewis's trilemma—that Jesus was either a liar, lunatic, or Lord—remains the greatest logical proof for Jesus' deity. Nevertheless, for all its power, Lewis's proof only "works" if we can say with certainty that Jesus said the things recorded in the Gospels. If we can trust that the words in red (in New Testaments that identify the words of Jesus in that way) were actually spoken by Jesus of Nazareth, then, as I shall argue in the second half of this chapter, there can be little doubt that Christ himself claimed to be divine. And if he did make that claim, then Lewis's trilemma must be taken seriously by any fair reader of the Gospels. For, to paraphrase Lewis, no mere mortal who made the claims that Jesus did can be considered a good man. Either he was, in fact, the Son of God, or he was a deceiver and blasphemer of a very high and wicked order, or he was a crazy, deluded prophet whom all rational people should shun as they would a madman who claimed to be the archangel Gabriel.

But did Jesus actually speak the words in red? For the last few centuries, several generations of liberal scholars have contended that there is a distinction between the "Jesus of history" and the "Jesus of faith." The incarnate Son of God constructed by the later church should not be confused, they argue, with the humble itinerant preacher or the polished cynical sage or the gruff revolutionary who wandered through Galilee and Judea with his band of followers and fell afoul of the Romans. Indeed, in an act of hubris so shameless that it comes perilously close to self-parody, the self-proclaimed Jesus Seminar published a version of the Gospels in which the words of Christ were printed in four different colors to indicate sayings that he definitely said, probably said, likely didn't say, and almost surely did not say. Their method for determining which color to assign? They voted!

It is very appealing to the modern mind, this notion of a "real," "historical" Jesus who was kidnapped by evil, deceptive ecclesiastics, but the theory (I almost said conspiracy theory) is divorced both from demonstrable facts and from common sense. The Gospels know nothing of a "Jesus of history" separate from a "Jesus of faith"; rather, they present us with a single historical Jesus in whom to put our faith. Those who read the Gospels without a preexisting, and unproven, bias against the supernatural will encounter a real flesh-and-blood Jesus; there is *nothing* "mythic" or "legendary" about him. Indeed, Lewis has argued that, aside from Socrates, there is no other person from the past whom we know so well; we feel we *know* the kinds of things Jesus would or would not say. Alas, the liberals of the Jesus Seminar, who represent a fraction of scholars and who work mostly on the fringe of biblical studies, seem unable to hear the authentic voice of Jesus ringing through *all* of the words in red; further, they seem oblivious to the fact that the Gospel portrait of Jesus is both historical and consistent.

## EYEWITNESS ACCOUNTS

In the last chapter I argued that the New Testament documents, when measured against the criteria of modern textual criticism, emerge as the most reliable and well-attested texts of the ancient world. There should be little doubt in the mind of anyone who has surveyed the facts that the New Testament we have today is essentially identical with the one written down in the first century. But when exactly, we must ask, *were* the books of the New Testament originally written down? The scrap of the Gospel of John discovered in Egypt verified that the Gospel of John could not have been written later than the 90s A.D., but that discovery alone is not enough to offer assurance to modern readers that the words in red are authentic. If all four Gospels were written in the 90s, that puts a gap of sixty years between the crucifixion and the writing of the Gospels—a gap large enough to leave room for some "tampering" with the words of Christ.

Enter a learned and aggressive group of modern apologists—most notably Gary Habermas, J. P. Moreland, and Craig Blomberg—who have offered compelling evidence for dating the Gospels (at least the Synoptic Gospels—Matthew, Mark, and Luke) to no later than A.D. 60. Such apologists generally begin by noting that the book of Acts makes no mention of the destruction of Jerusalem (A.D. 70), Nero's persecution of Christians following the great fire in Rome (64), or the martyrdoms of Peter and Paul (65 or earlier). This triple omission of significant historical events that exerted a profound influence on the members of the early church strongly suggests that Luke wrote Acts before 64, if not before 62. Since Acts is a sequel to Luke's Gospel, the latter must have been written closer to 60, and nearly all scholars (liberal or orthodox) believe Mark was written earlier than Luke.

The Gospel of Mark most likely was composed in the early to middle 50s; in any case, it certainly was written no later than 60—twenty-five to thirty years after the crucifixion (A.D. 30–33). Mark, that is to say, was written, at the most, one generation after the events it records. And that means that when Mark's Gospel was circulating, there were hundreds, if not thousands, of people alive who were eyewitnesses to Jesus' ministry. Further, since the pre-A.D. 70 church was based in Jerusalem, the Gospel of Mark was circulating in the very city where Jesus did much of his public teaching. The fact that numerous eyewitnesses were still alive in the city where Mark's Gospel, not to mention those of Matthew and Luke, was circulating means that if the Gospel writers had not been faithful to Jesus' words, the eyewitnesses would have risen to challenge those Gospels. But no such challenge occurred, even from the enemies of the church. Indeed, not only did Jesus' enemies not dispute that Jesus had said the things he did, they did not dispute that he had worked miracles and performed exorcisms. Rather than deny his words or his deeds, they accused him of speaking blasphemy and of performing miracles in violation of God's law (on the Sabbath) and by the power of Satan. Jesus' enemies understood full well the nature of Lewis's trilemma—they simply opted for the liar or lunatic option over that of Lord!

And something else about the early church and its status vis-à-vis its many and powerful enemies must be kept in mind. Modern and postmodern skeptics love to invent scenarios whereby corrupt, power-hungry churchmen imposed their "oppressive" doctrines upon ignorant, intimidated adherents. What these conspiracy theorists forget is that for the first three centuries of its existence, the church was weak, scattered, and under constant threat of persecution. The church of the second century, not to mention that of the first, was in no position to exert "censorship" powers; it was too busy trying to survive!

Putting aside issues of faith and inspiration, the historical evidence alone provides us with firm reasons to believe that the Gospels contain a trustworthy and accurate record of Jesus' words and deeds. Josh McDowell, Lee Strobel, and other apologists go even further than this to argue (convincingly) that the evidence presented in the Gospels would hold up in any court in the land. What we encounter in the Gospels are eyewitness testimonies that corroborate with one another but are not so exactly identical as to suggest collusion. And, as already stated, no eyewitnesses rose up to counter these testimonies; to the contrary, the hostile witnesses, by interpreting Jesus' words and deeds as evidence of blasphemy, insanity, or possession, further corroborate the Gospel records.

The mounting evidence that the Gospels were written within a generation of Jesus' death has helped establish their reliability, but it has also done something else. For the last hundred years, liberal scholars working in the shadow of Rudolf Bultmann have claimed that the Gospels are composed mostly of legendary or mythic material. That the Gospels were in circulation by A.D. 60 gives the lie to this oft-touted theory. One generation is simply not enough time for myths and legends to spring up; it takes a good three generations (or more) for legendary material to attach itself to heroic figures.

Besides, the Gospel writers do not present Jesus in mythic terms; nor does Paul, whose epistles were written earlier than the Gospels, perhaps a decade earlier. As long as we don't allow an antisupernatural bias to *force* us to read the miracle accounts as mythic interpolations, we will be able to recognize the Gospels for what they are: sober, antisensational eyewitness accounts of Christ's ministry in word and deed. In fact, there's even a moment in John's Gospel (21:23) when the Gospel writer himself makes a point of exposing a false (legendary) rumor that Jesus had told John he would not die until Christ's return.

Everything about the Gospels rings with truth. First, the Gospel writers remain true to details that put them in an unflattering light or that highlight both priestly and popular resistance to Jesus. Second, they depict Jesus as fully committed to the truth—so much so that if they were untruthful in their accounts, they would have violated the very teachings of Jesus that they record. Third, the Gospel writers had no motivation to lie, since the claims they put in Jesus' mouth were those that led to his crucifixion. By faithfully recording them, they did not conspire to gain fame and fortune but risked persecution by the same forces that put Jesus to death.

More proof of the reliability of the Gospels is to be found in yet another aspect of Matthew, Mark, Luke, and John that is immediately evident to anyone who reads them in an unbiased way. The Gospels, both separately and when taken together, provide us with a type of character that even the greatest novelist has never been able to conceive: a truly sinless man. Not just morally but psychologically, Jesus is the perfect man. He possesses a full emotional range (sorrow, joy, and anger), yet his feelings never drive him into sin; he makes incredible claims, yet remains humble; he is pure, yet never appears prudish or self-righteous. And Jesus' character is drawn against a first-century Palestinian background that is as detailed as any novel by Dickens or Dostoyevsky or Zola. Nothing about the Gospels is abstract, mythic, or ahistorical; all of it takes place in real space and time.

Before concluding this section and moving on to survey the actual claims made by Christ, let me briefly address three aspects of the chronology and authorship of the New Testament that are often misunderstood. First, though the Gospels appear first in the New Testament, they were actually written after the epistles of Paul and served a different purpose. Paul's preaching and epistles sought partly to convince unbelievers of the truth of Christianity; the Synoptic Gospels, in contrast, were written to provide *believers* with a record of Christ's ministry. That is to say, their *primary* purpose was more pastoral and didactic than evangelical or apologetic. Second, the traditions that ascribe certain Gospels and epistles to certain writers are all quite old and, except for a few minor books (2 Peter, 2 and 3 John, Jude) and Revelation (which some attributed to John the apostle and others to John the elder), were not contested. Finally, though John's Gospel is usually dated later than the Synoptics (Matthew, Mark, and Luke), it was *clearly* written by an eyewitness. Its portrait of Jesus is consistent with the Synoptics, and despite its long discourses, it is grounded in historical detail. In fact, it is John's Gospel, not the Synoptics, that allows us to date the three years of Jesus' ministry. I might also add that though most date John's Gospel to A.D. 90, some have suggested more recently that John's failure to mention the fall of Jerusalem suggests a date in the 60s.

## THE CLAIMS OF CHRIST

I trust that what I have written thus far will convince the believer and the skeptic alike that the Gospels are not later works of Christian myth making but reliable eyewitness accounts of the words and deeds of Jesus of Nazareth. Having established this, but one task remains for the apologist who would prove, or at least validate, the truth and force of Lewis's trilemma—to demonstrate that Jesus did, in fact, claim to be divine. Although Jesus makes this claim in all of the Gospels, his strongest claims are recorded in the discourses of John's Gospel.

Unlike the three Synoptic writers, John organizes his Gospel around seven, and only seven, miracles performed by Jesus. These miracles (or signs) not only verify the power and authority of Jesus but point to some aspect of his nature—his glory, his power over nature, his status as light-bearer and life-giver, and so forth. To drive home the connection, John records lengthy sermons (or discourses) delivered by Jesus to the crowds who witnessed his miraculous signs. Many of these discourses include shocking self-statements that, if Jesus were not the Son of God, would be those of a megalomaniac or blasphemer: "I am the bread of life" (6:35), "I am the light of the world" (8:12), "I am the door [to salvation]" (10:9), "I am the good shepherd" (10:11), and "I am the resurrection and the life" (11:25). On the night before his crucifixion, Jesus added to these five self-statements two more: "I am the way, and the truth, and the life" (14:6) and "I am the true vine" (15:1).

These statements, shocking in themselves, are rendered even more shocking by Jesus' appropriation of the divine name of God. When Moses asked God his name (Exodus 3:13), God answered, "I AM WHO I AM" (v. 14). This name, known as the tetragrammaton (Greek for "four letters"), is composed of four Hebrew consonants (YHWH) that are closely related to the Hebrew verb meaning "to be." Depending on what vowels are filled in between the consonants, God's name can be written as Yahweh or Jehovah, though nearly all English Bibles follow the tradition of writing the divine name as "LORD." This name was so holy that it would not be spoken by pious Jews, and each time scribes copied the name, they would pause to cleanse themselves ritually.

Despite the sacredness of the Name, Jesus identified himself with it on numerous occasions, even daring to link it to attributes possessed by the Lord of Israel alone—he who fed the Israelites with manna (bread of life), created light and life out of darkness and lifelessness (Genesis 1), and was the true shepherd and vine that guided and sustained the children of Israel. However, Jesus' most brazen appropriation of the Name is found in John 8:58 when he boldly proclaimed to a group of skeptical religious leaders who questioned his authority, "Before Abraham was, I am." He did not say, as we would expect, "Before Abraham was, I *was*," but "Before Abraham was, I *am*"—a clear claim to be equal with the eternal God who did not come into being, as did Abraham, but who simply *is*. That the religious leaders recognized the blasphemy in Jesus' words is made clear by their response: "they picked up stones to throw at him" (v. 59). As stoning was the prescribed punishment for blasphemy in biblical times, we can assume that the religious leaders recognized Jesus' statement as a claim to be equal with God. As noted above, the reaction of the hostile witnesses offers perhaps the clearest testimony to the audacity of Jesus' claims.

An earlier example of Jesus' multiple claims to divinity can be found in the very first chapter of John, when Jesus began to gather his disciples. To one of these disciples, Nathanael, he made an astonishing promise: "Truly, truly, I say to you, you will see heaven opened, and the angels of God ascending and descending on the Son of Man" (1:51). By making this promise, Jesus called up the image of Jacob's ladder (Genesis 28:12), upon which the angels of God were seen ascending and descending. That Jesus would equate himself, the Son of Man, with Jacob's ladder is tantamount to proclaiming himself the divine bridge between God and man.

Two chapters later, while speaking to a Pharisee named Nicodemus, Jesus again made a startling promise/prophecy: "As Moses lifted up the serpent in the wilderness, so must the Son of Man be lifted up, that whoever believes in him may have eternal life" (3:14–15). Looked at in isolation, this verse is scandalous: Jesus is telling a Pharisee, a man set apart to God and the Law, that the path to salvation is not to believe in God but to believe in him! Looked at in the context of the Hebrew Scriptures, it is even more scandalous. During the forty-year sojourn of the Israelites in the wilderness, God punished their eternal grumbling by sending fiery serpents among them. As, one by one, they began to die from the poisonous bites of the serpents, they repented of their sins before Moses and asked him to intercede for them with God. Moses prayed to the Lord, and the Lord commanded Moses: "Make a fiery serpent and set it on a pole, and everyone who is bitten, when he sees it, shall live" (Numbers 21:8). In calling up the serpent in the wilderness, Jesus prophesied not only the crucifixion (Jesus would be lifted on the cross as the serpent was on the pole) but the atonement as well (the Israelites were saved by looking up to an image of a serpent, the very thing that was killing them; that which kills us, sin, is the very thing that Jesus became for us on the cross).

In his last public discourse, Jesus said, "Whoever believes in me, believes not in me but in him who sent me. And whoever sees me sees him who sent me" (John 12:44–45). Later he told his disciples, "Whoever has seen me has seen the Father" (14:9). The Jesus we encounter in John's Gospel is the revelation of God: to see and know him is equivalent to seeing and knowing the Father. This great truth, central to John's Gospel, was also expressed in negative terms when Jesus admonished the Pharisees, "You know neither me nor my Father. If you knew me, you would know my Father also" (8:19). As John explains in the prologue to his Gospel, "No one has ever seen God; the only God, who is at the Father's side, he has made him known" (1:18).

One would think the numerous claims Jesus makes in the Gospel of John would be sufficient to demonstrate that he viewed himself as the incarnate Son of God. Unfortunately, the same liberal scholars who have driven a wedge between the "Jesus of faith" and the "Jesus of history" have also driven a wedge between John and the Synoptics, claiming (or at least implying) that the more theological, and later, Gospel of John somehow thrust upon Jesus a divine dimension that is absent from Matthew, Mark, and Luke. In matter of fact, Jesus' claims to divinity are just as pronounced in the Synoptics—and this is true even if one focuses only on the "bare bones" Gospel of Mark, which nearly all scholars believe was written first.

Let us survey quickly some of the more shocking claims that Mark records:

- Jesus claims the right to forgive sins (2:5), a right that belongs only to God, who is the wronged party when we sin. The teachers of the Law clearly recognized his claim as blasphemous and were appropriately scandalized (2:6–7).
- Jesus claims not only to be the Lord of the Sabbath (2:28) but to have the right to reinterpret the Law; and when he does reinterpret it, he does so on his *own* authority (10:2–12).
- Jesus' teachings put the focus on *him*, not on God: "For whoever is ashamed of me and of my words in this adulterous and sinful generation, of him will the Son of Man also be ashamed when he comes in the glory of his Father with the holy angels" (8:38). Note that Jesus prophesied that he would come again in glory with the Father!
- To accept Jesus is to accept God: "Whoever receives one such child in my name receives me, and whoever receives me, receives not me but him who sent me" (9:37). Note that here, as throughout Mark and the other Gospels, Jesus generally spoke of God, not in isolation, but in relationship to himself.
- Jesus promises that those who give up home and family *for his sake* will receive their reward (10:29–30); or, more strongly, "For whoever would save his life will lose it, but whoever loses his life for my sake and the gospel's will save it" (8:35).
- When Caiaphas asked Jesus directly if he was "the Christ, the Son of the Blessed," Jesus replied, "I am, and you will see the Son of Man seated at the right hand of Power, and coming with the clouds of heaven." In response, Caiaphas ripped his cloak and declared Jesus guilty of blasphemy, a sentence to which all agreed (14:61–64). Unless Jesus was, in

fact, the Incarnate Son of God, his words to Caiaphas were indeed blasphemous and worthy of death by Jewish law. If we view them, however, within their Old Testament context, we will discover that they are even more blasphemous than they may at first seem. For Jesus' words allude directly to a passage in Daniel that is not only messianic but that presents the Messiah in deified terms:

I saw in the night visions,
and behold, with the clouds of heaven
    there came one like a son of man,
and he came to the Ancient of Days
    and was presented before him.
And to him was given dominion
    and glory and a kingdom,
that all peoples, nations, and languages
    should serve him;
his dominion is an everlasting dominion,
    which shall not pass away,
and his kingdom one
    that shall not be destroyed. (7:13–14)

None of the Gospels allows us to say what so many would like to say—that Jesus was just a good man or a rabbi or a prophet and nothing more. In the person of Jesus we are brought face-to-face with a man whom we must either condemn, institutionalize, or worship. Neither Jesus nor the Gospel writers presents us with a fourth option!

# 18

# THE CASE FOR THE RESURRECTION OF CHRIST

In 2007 a maverick archaeologist named Simcha Jacobovici caused something of a media sensation by claiming that he had discovered the family tomb of Jesus of Nazareth. In the TV special that quickly followed, Jacobovici invited his viewers to consider a group of stone ossuaries (containers into which the Jews of Jesus' day placed the bones of their dead) bearing names familiar to readers of the Gospels, among them Mary, Matthew, and Jesus son of Joseph. Might not the bones in the ossuary labeled "Jesus," he asked, belong to the man whom Christians have long believed rose bodily from the dead on the first Easter morning?

As is typical with such sensational finds, the vast majority of archaeologists, whether Christian, Jewish, or secular, rejected Jacobovici's conclusions as unsound, and the matter quickly migrated from newspaper headlines to Internet purgatory. Something from that media event, however, caught my attention, something that should make any self-respecting apologist wince. In the wake of Jacobovici's "discovery," several liberal Christian scholars asserted that if the bones in the ossuary could be proven to be those of Jesus, that revelation would not affect their faith in the least. I've tried to avoid being too blunt in this book, but a Christian scholar who could make such a ludicrous remark really does not deserve to bear the title "Christian scholar." Only a Christian who rejected miracles and the deity of Christ out of hand and who blithely set himself in direct opposition to the universal witness of the early church could indulge in such a scandalous claim.

All opinion and rhetoric aside, the simple fact remains that the truth of Christ's claims and of Christianity itself rests firmly and non-negotiably on a literal, historical resurrection. Even a cursory reading of the Book of Acts will reveal that *the* central message of the apostles was the resurrection of Jesus Christ, an event of which they were eye-witnesses. Consider this sampling from the many apostolic sermons recorded in Acts:

- This Jesus God raised up, and of that we all are witnesses. (2:32)
- And you killed the Author of life, whom God raised from the dead. To this we are witnesses. (3:15)
- The God of our fathers raised Jesus, whom you killed by hanging him on a tree. God exalted him at his right hand as Leader and Savior, to give repentance to Israel and forgiveness of sins. And we are witnesses to these things, and so is the Holy Spirit, whom God has given to those who obey him. (5:30–32)
- And we are witnesses of all that he did both in the country of the Jews and in Jerusalem. They put him to death by hanging him on a tree, but God raised him on the third day and made him to appear, not to all the people but to us who had been chosen by God as witnesses, who ate and drank with him after he rose from the dead. (10:39–41)
- And when they had carried out all that was written of him, they took him down from the tree and laid him in a tomb. But God raised him from the dead, and for many days he appeared to those who had come up with him from Galilee to Jerusalem, who are now his witnesses to the people. (13:29–31)

At the core of apostolic preaching was not Christ's earthly ministry but his bodily resurrection from the dead. Everything hinged on that single, history-changing event. Paul himself proclaimed clearly, boldly, and unswervingly, "If Christ has not been raised, then our preaching is in vain and your faith is in vain," and again, "If Christ has not been raised, your faith is futile and you are still in your sins" (1 Corinthians 15:14, 17). The resurrection is not a doctrine to be taken up or left at will, but a reality on which all other doctrines rest.

Philosopher Karl Popper has argued that one of the characteristics of a true, scientifically valid system is falsifiability, that it can be refuted by empirical evidence. Freudianism is a nonfalsifiable system, for any proof leveled against it can be explained away as a conscious (or, if that doesn't work, an unconscious) resistance to psychoanalysis and psychoanalytical theory. Multiverses, too, are nonfalsifiable, for they cannot be observed or measured and therefore cannot be disproved by any form of experimentation; they cannot even be logically refuted, for they work outside the boundaries of human logic.

Christianity, in contrast, is subject to falsifiability, for it could have been killed at its very inception if someone could have produced the body of Jesus. Even today, if the bones in the "Jesus tomb" could be authenticated beyond a shadow of a doubt, Christianity would be exposed as false, and anyone who continued to believe in it would be a fool. How much of a fool? If I may be blunt again, a Christian who said his faith would not be affected in the least by categorical proof that Jesus did not rise from the dead would be the equivalent of an orthodox Muslim or Mormon claiming that his faith would be undisturbed if he were presented with an authentic, incontestable affidavit by Muhammad or Joseph Smith including his sworn confession that he had "made up" the Koran or the Book of Mormon out of his own head. Such a discovery, of course, would render both Islam and Mormonism defunct. If it could be shown that Jesus did not rise bodily from the dead, Christianity would be rendered equally defunct. More than that, it would be exposed as the greatest hoax, the greatest confidence trick in human history!

The ultimate proof of Christianity rests not on emotion or wishful thinking or even on faith but on a physical, historical event that either did or did not happen—an event that modern research has shown to be historically verifiable.

## THE EMPTY TOMB

As with Christ's claims to deity, liberal scholars for the last two centuries have attempted to dismiss the resurrection as a later, mythic accretion tacked on to the life of the "historical Jesus." To refute this critique, recent apologists have pointed to this vital passage from the letters of Paul:

> For I delivered to you as of first importance what I also received: that Christ died for our sins in accordance with the Scriptures, that he was buried, that he was raised on the third day in accordance with the Scriptures, and that he appeared to Cephas [Peter], then to the twelve. Then he appeared to more than five hundred brothers at one time, most of whom are still alive, though some have fallen asleep. Then he appeared to James, then to all the apostles. Last of all, as to one untimely born, he appeared also to me. (1 Corinthians 15:3–8)

Nearly all scholars, whether liberal or orthodox, accept the Pauline authorship of 1 Corinthians, which certainly dates to no later than the 50s. But the passage quoted dates to even earlier. Paul does not speak for himself but passes down what is clearly a very early creed of the church that he seems to have learned from the apostles themselves. Since Paul met with Peter and James (the brother of Jesus and leader of the Jerusalem church) in the 30s, the creed dates to only a few years after the events it describes.

A whole generation is not enough time for a "resurrection myth" to form, much less a few years. Besides, Paul delivers not a myth but a list of eyewitnesses to a historical event. And most of those eyewitnesses were still living when Paul wrote his epistle. As with the Gospels, if Paul had been making things up, hundreds, if not thousands, of hostile witnesses would have risen up to refute his claim. But they could not do so, for most of the eyewitnesses that Paul lists were still alive and living in Jerusalem. Paul provides his readers not with a vision or a myth or a legend but a list that could have been checked by any of the numerous enemies of the church.

Before moving on to the details of the resurrection, it should be noted that this early creed also refutes liberal claims that the "original" church was concerned only with following the precepts of Jesus, not with "mythic" doctrinal claims about the atonement and the resurrection. The creed Paul records gives the lie to that argument. Here, at the very birth of Christianity, the focus *already* rests not on Jesus as a moral teacher but on the good news of a risen Messiah who died for our sins. Further, when Paul says that Christ died for our sins and rose again "in accordance with the Scriptures," he points to the central Christian claim that Jesus fulfilled in his birth, ministry, death, and resurrection the Old Testament prophecies of the Messiah.

To corroborate this early creed recorded by Paul, history provides us with an indisputable fact that no sources, Christian or otherwise, ever disputed: the tomb into which Jesus' body was laid on Good Friday was empty on Easter morning. One would have to search hard to find a respectable scholar of the New Testament who would not concede the historical truth of the empty tomb. The real question is not whether the tomb was empty but what happened to the body of Jesus. I, along with dozens of top-notch apologists and historians, believe that the historical truth of the resurrection can be verified by a simple process of elimination.

According to that most logical of detectives, Sherlock Holmes, "When you have eliminated the impossible, whatever remains, however improbable, must be the truth." If it can be shown that no possible natural, "scientific" explanation can account for the empty tomb, then, however improbable it may seem to the modern materialistic mind, the resurrection presents itself as the best answer to the riddle. Let us then eliminate the chief naturalistic explanations:

- Some say the Pharisees or the Romans might have stolen the body, but if they had, they would have produced it and thus ended Christianity at its very birth. Both groups would have been happy to strangle Christianity in its crib. The fact that they did not do so by turning over the body is clear proof that they did not have it.
- Others say thieves might have stolen the body, but if they had, they would have taken not the body but the expensive burial cloths. And even if they had taken the body, they would have sold it to the Pharisees for a small fortune.
- The majority of critics claim the disciples stole the body; indeed, Matthew 28:11–15 reveals this claim to be the first "natural" explanation offered by critics of Christianity. Such a claim, however, is logically unsound. History presents us with people who have been willing to die for something they believed (often falsely) to be true, but if the disciples stole the body, then they died painful deaths as martyrs for something they *knew was a hoax*. Such a notion is psychologically untenable.
- Of course, it has been claimed that the disciples just imagined they saw the risen body of Christ, that what they called a miracle was just a hallucination. But the eyewitness evidence does not bear this theory out. Jesus was seen not only by individuals but by groups of varying sizes and at different locales and times of day. Furthermore, the eyewitnesses claimed not only to have seen Jesus but to have touched him and even to have watched him eat (Luke 24:37–43; John 20:27; 21:15). Indeed, when they first saw Jesus, they thought he was a ghost; Jesus had to *invite* them to touch him (Luke 24:37–39).
- Proponents of the "swoon theory" claim that Jesus was still alive when he was put in the tomb, but based on what we now know about Roman crucifixion techniques, that is untenable. Besides, even if Jesus could have survived and pushed aside the stone blocking his tomb, his near-dead state would have convinced no one that he had triumphed over death.
- Proponents of the "wrong tomb theory" claim that the women, being in an agitated state, entered the wrong tomb on Easter Sunday and jumped to the false conclusion that Jesus had risen. But if that were the case, then there would still have been a body for the Pharisees to find and produce.

As difficult as it may be for the modern mind to accept, the apostles' historical claim that Jesus rose bodily from the dead offers the only logical answer to the question, what happened to Jesus' body? The historical resurrection of Jesus of Nazareth is forced upon us not by faith or wishful thinking but by the preponderance of evidence.

Please note that I have arrived at this conclusion by using inductive, not deductive logic. I have not even assumed that the Gospel accounts were inspired by God. My arguments in this chapter and the previous one have all been based on textual and eyewitness evidence. What I have presented, that is to say, is not a deductive argument that begins by assuming the inerrancy of Scripture or the deity of Christ but exactly the kind of inductive argument that a lawyer might present before a judge. In response, I ask you, the reader, to respond as a jury might: sifting and weighing the evidence and the eyewitness testimonies in order to arrive at the inference (or verdict) that best explains the known facts. If you will do so fairly, I believe that you will find the force of history, inductive logic, and empirical evidence pushing you inexorably toward accepting, together with Peter, James, and the other eyewitnesses, that Jesus rose on the third day in accordance with the Scriptures.

## THE FILLED APOSTLES

So we have history, logic, evidence . . . and something more: a remarkable, inexplicable change in the disciples that cannot be accounted for by any other event short of the Resurrection. When Jesus was crucified, all the disciples (except John) fled in terror. As far as they were concerned, the one they thought was the Messiah had failed; the dream was over. When Jesus appeared to them, they were not boldly proclaiming the teachings of their Master but were huddled together in the upper room where they had celebrated the Last Supper. Far from being witnesses of the words and deeds of Jesus, they were a defeated and despairing group.

And yet, a few days later this same defeated group rose up to defend with superhuman courage their belief that, to paraphrase Paul, Christ had died for their sins and risen from the grave. What could possibly have changed them in such a brief time? What could have galvanized them to sacrifice everything for a religious leader who was executed as a criminal?

Paul's creed highlights three people whose transformations were most amazing. Peter, the leader of the disciples who had been the first to confess Jesus as the Christ, had publicly denied three times that he knew Christ; yet he would go on to became the boldest martyr of all. The James mentioned by Paul is not the apostle James (John's brother) but the brother of Jesus who, along with his siblings, did not originally accept Jesus' claims (John 7:5). Yet something happened that radically changed James. He would become the first official leader of the church (the Bishop of Jerusalem) and would die as a martyr. Paul himself, to whom the risen Christ appeared on the road to Damascus (Acts 9:3–6), began his life as Saul of Tarsus, a Pharisee who zealously persecuted the church. But something changed the pharisaical, ethnocentric Paul, transforming him into a fearless missionary and a lover of Gentiles, and radically altering his reading of the Old Testament. What event could have so utterly changed the lives of these three very different apostles? The resurrection is too wide-ranging and too personal in its effects to be explained naturally as some form of mass hypnosis.

The resurrection is further attested to by two supposed weaknesses in the accounts of Mathew, Mark, Luke, and John. It is very strange that all four Gospels insist that the first eyewitnesses of the resurrection were a group of women, since in that day and culture female testimony was not accepted in court. If the disciples had conspired to make up the resurrection accounts, they would not have cast women in this role. They would have claimed that one of the male disciples (say, Peter or John) or one of the two Pharisees who believed Jesus' testimony (Nicodemus and Joseph of Arimathea) were the first witnesses to the resurrection. Indeed, there is only one logical explanation for their insistence that it was Mary Magdalene and the other women who first encountered the risen Christ: that is how it actually happened!

A second seeming weakness in the four resurrection accounts—the fact that they contain minor discrepancies that make them difficult to harmonize—has been used frequently by skeptics to cast doubt on the historicity of the resurrection. Ironically, these discrepancies, much touted as proof against the resurrection, actually strengthen the reliability of the Gospels. The Gospels claim to present us with separate, eyewitness-based accounts of the resurrection of Christ. Were all four accounts to read as exact replicas of one another, it would suggest collusion between the writers. Instead we get four accounts that complement (not contradict) one another, and from which we can extract a clear, consistent, and reliable narrative of the resurrection of Christ. As I noted earlier, the Gospel accounts of the life, deeds, and claims of Christ would all fare well in any court of law; the same holds true for the Gospel accounts of what is, if true, the most important event in human history.

In *The Case for Christ*, Lee Strobel interviews apologist J. P. Moreland on the subject of the resurrection. In his responses to Strobel, Moreland suggests further intriguing evidence for the resurrection that builds on our growing knowledge of the interplay between Judaism and the early church. After reminding us of a fact that is too often forgotten by Christians and skeptics alike—namely, that the original Christians were all Jews—Moreland argues that only an event like the resurrection could have so radically changed five key pillars of Jewish religious and cultural identity that would have been sacrosanct to the twelve disciples and their initial converts.

First, the early Christians immediately eliminated animal sacrifices, a practice that was essential to Judaism. The destruction of the Temple in A.D. 70 would eventually put an end to such sacrifices among Jews as well, but the early Christians ceased the practice long before that time. The only thing that could have convinced them to do so was their firm belief that the crucifixion and resurrection of Christ had rendered animal sacrifice obsolete. Second, although Judaism was grounded in the Law of Moses, which itself demanded blood sacrifice for the atonement of sin, the early Christians shifted the focus of religion from law to grace—a grace that had been released into the world by the power of the resurrection. Their belief that Jesus rose again also caused the first Christians to do two things that would otherwise have been unthinkable to pious, fiercely monotheistic Jews: shift the Sabbath from Saturday to Sunday and proclaim Jesus as a God worthy not only of imitation but of worship (Matthew 28:17). Finally, though the Jews of the first century continued to await a political Messiah who would rescue them from Roman control—expectations that led to two disastrous Jewish revolts in the first and second centuries—the early Christians adapted themselves to Roman rule and worshiped Christ as a spiritual Messiah whose kingdom was not of this world.

A second recent apologist, who is also a first-rate theologian, has contributed yet further proof of the historical reliability of the Resurrection—proof that also relies on our growing understanding of first-century Judaism. In his magisterial *The Resurrection of the Son of God*, N. T. Wright explains how shocking and unprecedented was the early church's belief in the resurrection of Christ. Despite the fact that the Pharisees saw the resurrection of the body as occurring at the end of time (see Martha's comment to Jesus at John 11:24) and that the pagans, especially those influenced by Plato, rejected the notion as nonsense (see the Stoic and Epicurean response to Paul in Acts 17:32), the early church—composed of former Jews and pagans—believed unanimously that the resurrection had happened *now* to Christ. Resurrection, Wright explains, had never been central to Judaism; it was seen, rather, as a far-off event unrelated to the world in its present state. And yet, despite this fact, the early church made it the central teaching. *Only* an actual resurrection could have sparked such an innovation in the beliefs and culture of Judaism.

Wright also takes his own close look at the Gospel accounts of the resurrection and discerns in them a primitive oral tradition stripped of the deeper theological reflection that appears in Paul's letters. He further notes the fact that Paul in the 50s does not mention the women at the tomb, but the Gospels do, suggesting that whereas the Gospels stayed true to the bare-bones story, Paul "cleaned up" the slightly embarrassing bit about female eyewitnesses. Far from casting suspicion on the Gospels, both of Wright's observations strengthen the essential reliability of the resurrection accounts. The tomb was empty, and the risen Christ appeared to many—that is the essence of the story and of the central Christian claim. It is the message that the angels spoke to the frightened women, a message that more than two thousand years have not dulled, altered, or destroyed:

> Why do you seek the living among the dead? He is not here, but has risen. Remember how he told you, while he was still in Galilee, that the Son of Man must be delivered into the hands of sinful men and be crucified and on the third day rise. (Luke 24:5–7)

# 19

# WHY CHRIST IS THE ONLY WAY: CHRISTIANITY AND OTHER RELIGIONS

In one sense Christianity should carry a strong appeal to those living in an increasingly global and pluralistic society. The good news of Jesus Christ cuts across all racial, ethnic, and cultural boundaries and promises love, forgiveness, tolerance, and understanding. Jesus did not confine his message to the powerful religious leaders of his day but reached out to the sinners, the prostitutes, and the tax collectors. Indeed, it was more often the social outcasts than the Pharisees and Sadducees who followed Jesus and clung to his words.

Jesus treated men and women, rich and poor, educated and illiterate with equal respect and dignity and affirmed the intrinsic value of all human beings. He called on his followers to love their neighbors as themselves—even if those neighbors were enemies!—and instructed those who would be leaders in his stead to act not as overlords but as stewards. In his first public sermon (Luke 4:17–27), he proclaimed, in fulfillment of messianic prophecy, release to the captives, freedom to the oppressed, and sight to the blind. Then he went on to remind his fiercely ethnocentric Jewish audience that even in the Old Testament, God showed favor to the Gentiles; worse yet, those Gentiles often showed more faith than the people of Israel! And Jesus lived out this multi-ethnic vision by speaking publicly to a half-breed Samaritan woman of questionable character (John 4), healing the servant of a Roman centurion (Matthew 8:5–13), and casting out a demon from the daughter of a Gentile (Matthew 15:21–28).

I repeat, Christianity *should* appeal to modern pluralists who yearn to see a world united by love, tolerance, and philanthropy. And yet those very people in the universities, the media, and the government who long to build a utopia of universal peace, plenty, and brotherhood are often the most hostile to Christianity. The reason for this seemingly contradictory state of affairs is not difficult to discern. Christianity, though it preaches the eternal, God-given worth of the human person, is *not* an inclusivist religion, at least not in the way that modern people would like it to be. Yes, like the Statue of Liberty it opens its arms and its doors to the tired and the poor, the huddled masses, the wretched refuse of our fallen and despairing world, but it opens neither its arms nor its doors to those who would deny or pervert its key doctrines (the Trinity, the incarnation, the atonement, the resurrection) or who would demote the Lord and Savior Jesus Christ to the status of one option among many.

As unpopular as it may be to make such a pronouncement in our modern (or, better, postmodern) world, the fact remains that the personal claims of Christ and the doctrinal claims of the church are necessarily exclusivist in nature. In response to this nonnegotiable aspect of Christianity, the modern apologist must seek to answer a number of questions: Can Jesus' exclusivist claims be taken seriously in a pluralistic society? In a world of so many religions is Christianity not a hindrance to global peace and understanding? Isn't the claim that Jesus is the only way a form of religious imperialism?

## EXCLUSIVISM VS. PLURALISM

In one of the best recent apologetics books to tackle the exclusivity of Christ, *Is Jesus the Only Savior?*, James Edwards reminds us that Christianity was born and came of age not in the midst of a monolithic culture but in a radically pluralistic one. Just as in our own day, first-century believers had a host of religions, truths, and moralities from which they could choose. Rome may have been imperialistic in politics, but she was not so in religion! As long as other philosophical systems and religious cults did not break the law, threaten the peace, or challenge the authority of Rome and her emperor, she was happy to allow them the freedom to worship as they saw fit. Yes, they were expected to participate in the imperial cult, but for the vast majority of Romans, paying religious homage to the emperor caused no more cognitive dissonance or spiritual distress to followers of the Persian Mithras or the Egyptian Isis or the Greek Bacchus than listening to Christmas carols does to (nonpoliticized) Jews, Muslims, Hindus, and atheists in our own country.

The early Christians were well aware that their religion was not only distinctive from the Mosaic Law but was incompatible both with the public, universalizing cult of the Caesars and the more personal, intimate mystery religions practiced in secret by numerous cultic groups across the Roman Empire. Nevertheless, though there were strong contemporary forces to dissuade them from doing so, the early church continued to preach—in the face of persecution—the reality of sin, the need for grace, and the universal, cross-cultural truth of the Christian story of creation, fall, and redemption. That is not to say that the early Christians were rebels against the political control of the emperors. On the contrary, the early church retained a pacifist stance, even when the law courts of Rome condemned them to death for refusing to pay religious homage to the genius, or divine spirit, of the Caesars.

By studying carefully the historical, political, and cultural context in which Christianity was born and flourished, Edwards substantiates his argument that Christianity is *both* exclusivist in its theology and cross-cultural in its reach. And his argument has been further substantiated in recent years by the tremendous growth of Christianity in Africa and Latin America—what many refer to today as the Global South. Whereas Africa was only 5 percent Christian in 1900, recent statistics show that half the population confesses Christ as Lord. Meanwhile, throughout Asia, Christianity is spreading like wildfire. By percentage of population, South Korea is the most Christian country in the world; the number of orthodox Christians in China far exceeds those in Europe. And the Christians in China and South Korea have shown a fearless missionary zeal, enduring persecution for their faith that is equivalent to that faced by first-century martyrs. Indeed, as if they have not already suffered enough in their own countries, large numbers of Asian missionaries have committed themselves to a movement called Back to Jerusalem. Their plan is to take the gospel from their homelands and return it to its birthplace in Jerusalem, a journey that is guaranteed to land many of them in Muslim jails.

The changing face of Christianity, as historian Philip Jenkins has documented, is increasingly poor, nonwhite, and non-Western. And yet, though African, Asian, and Hispanic believers have shown themselves open to the basic values of democracy and the free market, they have not therefore sought to make themselves over as modern Westerners. The strongest churches in these countries hold firmly to orthodox teaching and traditional morality, though their worship styles tend to be more emotional. In fact, within the global Anglican Communion, it has been the African bishops who have called their Western brothers and sisters to reject modern liberal notions of biblical accommodationism and sexual experimentation and to reaffirm classic Christian orthodoxy. Many African Christian groups have also gotten bolder in rejecting liberal Western solutions for fighting HIV/AIDS (based on condom use and an ethic of sexual liberation) in favor of a more orthodox approach that affirms celibacy and biblical sexual morality. Indeed, in Africa today Western secular humanism, not orthodox Christianity, has been the cultural solvent that has quickened the erosion of traditional African virtues and values.

Christianity is veritably exploding in Asia and the Global South, and yet, ironically, at the same moment that black, yellow, and brown believers are committing themselves to the One whom they believe is the only Savior of the world, religious pluralists in America and Europe continue to claim, loudly but falsely, that all religions ultimately teach the same thing. I already argued in chapter 8, along with Chesterton, that the modern belief that religions are the same at the core, differing only in their externals, is demonstrably false. To the contrary, it is in their external practices—prayer, fasting, almsgiving, and so forth—that religions are the same; it is in their core theological doctrines that they differ widely. Though moderns are loath to admit it, the Christian claim that Jesus Christ was God incarnate and the Muslim claim that he was a prophet but not the Son of God are *mutually exclusive* claims. According to the law of noncontradiction—a law without which logic falls apart—both claims cannot be true at the same time and in the same way. Likewise, the Christian claim that God created the world as a thing separate from himself and the Hindu claim that God is part of the world cannot both be true. If one is correct, then the other must be incorrect. It is not faith but reason that insists on this!

Some pluralists and relativists, it must be conceded, make a less sweeping claim. Rather than say that all religions teach the same doctrines, they argue that each religion only has a piece of the truth. Such thinkers often tell the parable of four blind men who encounter an elephant: each gives a different account depending on whether he touches the elephant's trunk, tail, ear, or leg. And yet, as a number of modern apologists have pointed out, the pluralist subtly alters the meaning of the parable. First, he forgets that an absolute truth really does exist: the elephant. Second, he misses the fact that Christianity *agrees* we are all blind to the true and full nature of God, but then goes on to claim that

God remedied our spiritual, intellectual, and moral blindness by taking the initiative in revealing himself to us through Christ and the Bible.

The late missionary Lesslie Newbigin, who has had a profound influence on a generation of apologists who have sought to be both orthodox (exclusivist) and global (inclusivist) in focus, has pointed out a third way in which modern and postmodern thinkers have twisted the parable. The pluralist, argues Newbigin, claims that while the orthodox devotees of various religions are blind, he sees the elephant clearly and thus knows the truth that the blind men can't see: namely, that no religion can know or teach absolute truth. But the moment the pluralist makes this (absolute) claim, he ceases to be a true pluralist, for his absolute claim that no religion can know the truth is itself a religious claim. Whether he realizes it or not, the pluralist claims that direct revelation from God is impossible, something that cannot be proved by reason, logic, or experimentation. Rather than actually disprove the claims of Christ and the Bible, the pluralist, guilty of Lewis's chronological snobbery, simply dismisses the possibility of such claims. Just as the naturalist refuses even to consider that Christ might have risen bodily from the dead, so the pluralist refuses to consider that Christ might have been who he claimed to be: God incarnate.

In the face of such a categorical refusal, our world, hungry for truth and revelation, can only seek answers to questions that are irrelevant to the truth claims of Christianity: Which culture is better? How do sociological forces shape religious belief? How do political and economic structures affect our conception of God? I don't mean to say that these are necessarily bad or false questions. I merely contend that they are irrelevant to the real issue at hand. Christianity does not claim Christ is the only way because his teachings are "superior" or because he was nurtured by a more "enlightened" culture. Christ is the only way because Christ is God, and therefore to be with God one must be *in* Christ. If Christ is, as he claimed, the truth and the life (John 14:6), then apart from him there can be neither truth nor life. Christians are not remade by following the *example* of Jesus, though Christians, of course, strive to do so. Christians are remade by dying to their old self and being reborn *through and in* Christ.

If the Bible (the revealed Word of God) is correct in assessing man's problem as original sin, then Christ (the incarnate Word of God) is the only adequate solution. God did not send his Son to earth to die a painful death to provide us with an "option"; he did it because the incarnation

(Christmas), the atonement (Good Friday), and the Resurrection (Easter) offered the only possible remedy to the problem of original sin. The Christian gospel represents extreme measures on the part of God, and moderns scarcely honor God's costly solution by treating it as one of many competing paths to God. Salvation means spending eternity worshiping God, and if Christ is indeed one with God, then salvation means spending eternity worshiping Christ.

## CONTRASTING TRUTH CLAIMS

The necessarily exclusivist claims of Christianity can be better assessed by contrasting them with the truth claims made by other major world religions—Judaism, Islam, Hinduism, and Buddhism. Only by facing squarely the radical differences that separate Christianity from all other religions will the modern/postmodern seeker be empowered to see how absolutely unique are the personal claims of Christ and the doctrinal claims of the church.

Although Christianity was born out of Judaism and cannot be understood apart from it, the two religions preach different paths to salvation and different conceptions of God's nature. Although I find personally appealing the popular belief that God has two different methods of salvation, one for the Jew and one for the Gentile, such a belief is finally incompatible with the claims of Christ and the Bible. Central to Christian doctrine is the teaching that man cannot be justified through practicing the Law. Yes, the Law is good and God given, but we cannot follow it perfectly and thus cannot be made righteous through it. If the Jews could have followed it, the sacrifice of Christ would not have been necessary; but again, no one can follow it.

Man's inability to follow the Law is made clear as far back as Genesis and Exodus, and that is why the Psalms and prophetic books of the Old Testament are filled with foreshadowings of a fuller revelation to come that would restore Israel and, through her, the world. Through the mouths of the prophets, God promises to establish a new covenant with the Jews (Jeremiah 31:31–34), to give them a new heart (Ezekiel 36:26–27), and to gather a faithful remnant under the Messiah, the "anointed" son of David whose rule will bless the Jews as well the Gentiles (Isaiah 9:1–7; 11). If Jesus was not the Christ (that is, the Messiah), then the promises have failed, and Israel and the Gentiles are both lost.

In Nebuchadnezzar's dream recorded in Daniel 2 (see chapter 16), God presents a succession of four pagan kingdoms (Babylon, Persia,

Greece, Rome) who would rule over the Jews with increasing tyranny. During the reign of the fourth kingdom, however, God promises to establish his own kingdom that will spread across the world and never end. That fifth kingdom comes in the form of a stone uncut by human hands that crushes the other four. In Luke 20:17–18, Christ, referencing also Psalm 118:22, Isaiah 8:14, and Isaiah 28:16, compares himself to a stone that crushes some but is the cornerstone for others (see 1 Peter 2:4–8). Indeed, Christ teaches a sad paradox: the very stone that was rejected by the builders (the Jewish leaders) and over which they stumbled became the foundation for all the nations. Christ was rejected by the leaders of Israel, not because there are many different paths to God and the Pharisees simply chose another path, but because Christ *scandalized* them by his radical claims (the Greek word translated "stone of stumbling" in 1 Peter 2:8 is *petra scandalou*). Today people of all ethnic and religious backgrounds continue to be scandalized both by Jesus' claims to be the Son of God and by the Crucifixion, an event that reveals the full extent of our sinfulness by revealing the extreme measures to which God had to resort to atone for our sin and bring us back into a right relationship with himself.

In Romans 11, Paul elaborates on the post-resurrection relationship between Christians and Jews by comparing Israel to an olive tree, some of whose branches have been broken off so wild olive shoots (Gentiles) could be grafted in. Today a growing number of messianic Jews (ethnic Jews who still practice Jewish cultural and religious rites but who confess Jesus as Messiah and Lord) cling to Paul's promise that God can graft back in the broken branches. Though many in the church rejoice at the growing number of Jewish converts to Christ, others, both inside and outside the church, see evangelism to Jews as anti-Semitic. I find this claim to be an odd and even illogical view, for much Jewish evangelism today is inspired by a rejection of replacement theology (the belief that God's promises to Israel have been superseded by the church) and by a desire to see Jews accept Messiah without rejecting their Jewishness.

After Judaism the religion that appears closest to Christianity is Islam. Certainly, the modern pluralist says, Muslims worship the same monotheistic God as the Christians. It is a nice thought and a compelling one, but it is simply untrue. Though Islam and Christianity share many of the same moral beliefs and ethical practices, they are, on the theological level, incompatible. The central, distinctive theological teachings of Christianity, that God is three in one (the Trinity) and that Christ is fully

God and fully man (the incarnation), are *categorically denied by the Qur'an.* Islam marks not a growth out of Christianity but a rejection of it and a return to the radical monotheism of Judaism. The essential Christian confession that Jesus is Lord is not only rejected by Islam, it is considered the highest blasphemy.

Though Islam claims to respect the Gospels, it directly contradicts both the historical and theological claims that are made in them. According to the Qur'an, Jesus neither died on the cross nor rose bodily from the dead; yes, he was a prophet who spoke good words and performed good deeds, but his death did not atone for our sins, and he does not share in the godhead of Allah. Some pluralists will claim that Islam merely substitutes Muhammad for Jesus, but this is not the case. The Islamic faith does not rest on Muhammad but on the Qur'an, which Muslims consider to be the divinely dictated (rather than inspired) Word of God. Whereas Christians hold an incarnational view of both Christ and the Bible, Muslims view Muhammad as only human and the Qur'an as only divine. Islam, like all religions, has a mystical branch called Sufism, but her rejection of any mystical, incarnational trafficking between God and man has made her radically antisacramental and iconoclastic.

The God of Islam dwells apart and alone in absolute unity and oneness, and the religion he oversees is essentially fatalistic. Christian salvation, in contrast, means participating in the dynamic activity and mutual love of the Trinity, and that dynamism extends into the perennial Christian paradox of predestination and free will—both of which are affirmed by Christ and the Scriptures. The words *Muslim* and *Islam* both come from an Arabic word that means "submission," and submission to God, not love for God or union with God, lies at the core of the teachings of Muhammad. But Christianity calls for much more than submission; it calls on its followers to be born again into the eternal, indestructible life of Christ.

Though Christianity, Judaism, and Islam share a basic faith in the existence of a single transcendent God who created the universe, their understandings of the nature of that one God and of his Son Jesus Christ are incompatible. Still, the Christian worldview differs far more radically from that of Hinduism. While Judaism and Islam reject Christ's divine nature, Hinduism rejects his human nature. In Hinduism the physical world is ultimately an illusion (or maya) and the flesh something from which to escape. Salvation comes not through Christ's bodily triumph over sin, Satan, and death and the grace that act imparted to the world, but either through a change in our perception (according to the more "refined" branch) or through the accumulation of karmic "brownie points." Hinduism does not redeem the world but rejects it! Indeed, at the core of Hinduism is not the drawing together of God and man in an incarnational union but a monistic denial of the very body/spirit distinction that Christianity holds in paradoxical tension.

On the one hand, Hinduism and Christianity may seem compatible, for Hinduism shares the Christian belief that God has visited the earth in physical form. Just as God became man in Christ, so the God Vishnu has entered into our physical realm through a series of animal and human incarnations known as avatars. There are, however, at least three major differences between the incarnation of Christ and the avatars of Vishnu. First, the avatars of Vishnu do not mark an incarnational fusion of human and divine. Vishnu did not actually *become* a man; he merely appeared as one for a time and then returned to the spiritual realm. Christ, in contrast, by rising *bodily* from the grave, continues, even in heaven, to be fully man and fully God. Second, Vishnu has appeared in a number of different forms (Rama, Krishna, etc.), while Christ is the *only-begotten* Son of God. Third, whereas Jesus was born under Caesar Augustus and died under Tiberius, the avatars of Vishnu take place not in historical but in mythic/legendary time.

Finally, the Hindu (and Buddhist) teaching of reincarnation violates the essence of human personality that Christianity safeguards by its teaching that we are incarnational fusions of one body and one soul. And this violation continues beyond samsara (the cycle of reincarnation). Unlike the Christian view of heaven as a marriage between Christ and the church that results in pure joy, the Hindu (and Buddhist) view of nirvana, achieved when we break free from samsara, is of a place where joy, emotion, and personality are utterly extinguished.

Ironically, while Christianity differs radically from such "sophisticated" religions as Judaism, Islam, and Hinduism, it has shown itself able to fulfill the deepest yearnings of isolated tribes who practice "primitive" folk religions. As missionary and apologist Don Richardson has documented in *Eternity in Their Hearts*, dozens of animistic tribal groups spread across Africa and Asia harbor, behind their strange rituals and occult practices, an ancient secret: there is a single holy God who created the world and who does not dwell in temples built by human hands. Most of these tribal groups retain a generations-old memory that their forefathers lost contact with the One God and became enslaved to spirits whom they serve out of fear, not love. In contrast to Enlightenment theories of religion that claim that monotheism evolved out of animism, the presence of these groups suggests that the opposite is more likely the case—that monotheism was the *original* state of mankind but we *fell* into animism and other forms of superstition.

Like Melchizedek meeting Abraham (Genesis 14:18–20), when tribes like the Karen of Burma, the Santal of India, and the Gedeo of Ethiopia first came in contact with Christian missionaries, they immediately recognized them as bearers of good news from the One God that would free them from their bondage to spirits. Many even reported that God had promised their ancestors that he would one day send them a "white brother" bearing a "lost book" that would teach them how to be reconciled with God.

In *Peace Child*, Don Richardson, working with a New Guinea tribe known as the Sawi, learned of a ritual in which the chief gave his son to be raised by the chief of a warring tribe—an exchange that brought peace and mutual trust. Richardson converted most of the Sawi by presenting Jesus as God's peace child. And he did so not by obliterating their native culture, as "imperialistic" secular humanist "missionaries" have done time and again, but by helping to bring to fulfillment the deepest, most ancient longings of their religion and culture.

20

# BEYOND *THE DA VINCI CODE*: ANSWERING THE NEO-GNOSTICS

In chapter 18, I made reference to the media sensation that was sparked by Simcha Jacobovici's claim that he had uncovered the family tomb of Jesus of Nazareth. As media sensations go, however, this one turned out to be surprisingly brief and garnered few critiques from apologists. Indeed, I cannot help but think that the intense, if brief attention that Jacobovici's claim received was due mostly to its riding on the crest of a far greater wave—that generated by the almost unprecedented popularity of Dan Brown's novel, *The Da Vinci Code*. Selling well in excess of forty million copies, *The Da Vinci Code* kept secular humanists, liberal theologians, and orthodox apologists busy sifting through its outrageous claims and weighing in on its historical and theological accuracy. And it kept them busy for several years!

In what follows I shall attempt not only to answer the criticisms leveled against Christianity by *The Da Vinci Code* but to demonstrate that much of what appeals to readers in Dan Brown's novel is better answered by orthodox Christianity than by the repackaged Gnosticism that Brown offers us in his novel.

## CHRIST AND CONSTANTINE

It is no exaggeration to say that nearly all the historical and theological claims made by *The Da Vinci Code* are either false or grossly distorted. And yet, oddly, the one that got the most press, that Jesus was married, is actually the least problematic of Brown's conspiratorial allegations. Though the claim that Jesus was married to Mary Magdalene has no biblical or historical support, it is at least theoretically possible that Jesus might have married at, say, age fifteen, only to have his wife die when he was thirty, the age at which he began his public ministry. Though this scenario is highly unlikely, if it could be proved, it would necessitate *no major change in Christian theology*. True, such a revelation would likely cause the Catholic Church to change its policy on clerical celibacy, but that policy represents not a doctrine but a discipline and could be changed by Rome without violating any essential teachings of the church.

Though the thought that Jesus might have been married may make many of my readers uneasy, I nevertheless insist that Jesus' sinlessness would not be compromised in the least if he'd engaged in marital sex. Indeed, since Jesus was fully man, it is even theologically possible, though *extremely* unlikely, that he might have had children with his wife. Still, it must be emphasized that there is not a shred of historical evidence that Jesus had children with Mary Magdalene and that their "royal bloodline" passed down through the Merovingian line. It makes for a good story, but as history, it is just plain silly. I only wish that I could say the same about Brown's other claims.

The real controversy over *The Da Vinci Code* comes not from Brown's slightly titillating suggestion that Jesus might have had sex with his lawful wife, but from his bold and heretical dismissal of the divinity of Jesus as a fourth-century invention of the Emperor Constantine and his clerical cronies. I already argued in chapter 17 that Jesus, in the historically reliable Gospels, clearly identifies himself as the divine Son of God. I further argued in chapter 18 that the apostles, after witnessing firsthand Jesus' resurrection, immediately began to refer to Jesus as Lord—that is, as Yahweh (or "Lord"), the covenant God of the Old Testament.

Contra Brown's historically inaccurate claims, belief in Jesus' divinity is not a later development. It is attested to not only in the Gospels but throughout the earlier-written epistles of Paul. Consider the following two passages:

> Have this mind among yourselves, which is yours in Christ Jesus, who, though he was in the form of God, did not count equality with God a thing to be grasped, but made himself nothing, taking the form of a servant, being born in the likeness of men. And being found in human form, he humbled himself by becoming obedient to the point of death, even death on a cross. Therefore God has highly exalted him and bestowed on him the name that is above every name, so that at the name of Jesus every knee should bow, in heaven and on earth and under the earth, and every tongue confess that Jesus Christ is Lord, to the glory of God the Father. (Philippians 2:5–11)

> He is the image of the invisible God, the firstborn of all creation. For by him all things were created, in heaven and on earth, visible and invisible, whether thrones or dominions or rulers or authorities—all things were created through him and for him. And he is before all things, and in him all things hold together. And he is the head of the body, the church. He is the beginning, the firstborn from the dead, that in everything he might be preeminent. For in him all the fullness of God was pleased to dwell, and through him to reconcile to himself all things, whether on earth or in heaven, making peace by the blood of his cross. (Colossians 1:15–20)

Although these passages were, of course, written before Paul's death in about A.D. 65, many New Testament scholars would date them much earlier. Paul seems here to be quoting two early hymns of the church that he likely learned when he visited Jerusalem in the late 30s, less than a decade after Jesus' death and resurrection. These passages leave little doubt that the early church viewed Jesus as equal with God and worthy of worship. No Jew would have used such language of a mere man, even if he were greater than Abraham, Moses, and David combined.

The poetic prologue to John's Gospel also reads like an early church hymn on Christ's deity:

> In the beginning was the Word, and the Word was with God, and the Word was God. He was in the beginning with God. All things were made through him, and without him was not any thing made that was made. In him was life, and the life was the light of men. The light shines in the darkness, and the darkness has not overcome it. (John 1:1–5)

Again, no one in the Old Testament, not the greatest king or prophet, is spoken of in such terms. A Jewish writer would save such language for God alone. Of course, those liberal scholars who attempted to "prove" that the Gospel of John was written a full century after John's death (see chapter 16) knew this quite well; hence their (failed) attempt to ascribe to it a late second-century date. What John offers us here is nothing less than a sophisticated meditation on the deity of Christ in the first century, a meditation that continues on to give one of the simplest but most elegant descriptions of the incarnation in the New Testament: "And the Word became flesh and dwelt among us, and we have seen his glory, glory as of the only Son from the Father, full of grace and truth" (1:14).

The Gospels and Epistles offer a unified testimony to the incarnation, a testimony that can be found as well in the earliest extrabiblical writings of the church—most notably in the early letters of Clement, third bishop of Rome (A.D. 96), and Ignatius (A.D. 110) and in the writings of second-century theologians Justin and Irenaeus. All four predate Constantine by two centuries, and all four attest clearly and unapologetically to the deity of Christ.

Now, to give Brown some credit, it is true that the emperor Constantine convened the Council of Nicea in 325 to issue a formal creedal statement on church doctrine, particularly the doctrine of the incarnation. What Brown misconstrues, or perhaps simply misunderstands, is that the Council and its resulting statement (the Nicene Creed) did not create but *confirmed* long-standing orthodox teaching. As I explained in chapter 10, it was only when the church was threatened from without and within by heretical groups indulging in fanciful speculations that contradicted several centuries of church teaching that she put into philosophical language the doctrines she had always believed.

Beginning slowly in the first century and increasing in the second and third, the church had to fight fringe heretical groups that denied either the deity or the humanity of Christ.

While the Ebionites and Arians taught that Jesus was man but not God, the Docetists taught that Jesus only appeared (*dokew* in Greek) to inhabit a human body. The Docetists were one of several neo-Platonic, Gnostic groups that viewed matter as inherently evil (the aborted creation of a lesser God) and the flesh as a prison house of the soul. As such, they denied the possibility—or even desirability—of a divine/human incarnation. Interestingly, because of its low view of the body, Gnosticism often manifested itself in terms of two opposing extremes—a rigid asceticism that tortured the flesh or an orgiastic overindulgence meant to exhaust the flesh.

The highly elitist Gnostics believed salvation came not from the bodily crucifixion and resurrection of Christ but through the acquisition of secret knowledge (*gnosis* in Greek). Gnostics like Valentinus (A.D. 140) even invented elaborate, convoluted mythologies of divine emanations. There were also a number of minor heresies that either collapsed or divided the two natures of Christ or the three persons of the Trinity. In each case, the church rejected these heresies as incompatible with the unified witness of Christ, the New Testament, and the early church fathers.

Starting in the mid-second century, some of the bolder Gnostic groups put together their own secret "gospels" of Christ. Brown, along with many liberal theologians, believes these Gnostic gospels give us a "truer," more accurate account of the life and teachings of Christ. This claim, however, betrays not only a misunderstanding of the early church and the early heretics but an inability to distinguish between one literary genre and another. An unbiased reading of, say, the Gospel of Thomas—which the Jesus Seminar published together with the canonical Gospels in their four-color edition—reveals it to be profoundly *nonhistorical*. Not only does the Gospel of Thomas lack the eyewitness details that give the canonical Gospels their veracity, it exists parasitically on them, merely using Jesus as a mouthpiece for Gnostic sayings. The best test to show that Thomas and the other Gnostic gospels are nonhistorical is to remove Jesus from the gospel and replace him with Buddha; the substitution changes nothing!

In addition to the nonhistorical, if not *anti*historical, nature of these "gospels," the fact remains that none of them was ever seriously considered by the clergy or laity of the church, and all were rejected long before Constantine—and at a time when the church had no political power! Granted, a few New Testament books were debated (2 and 3 John, 2 Peter, Jude, and, far less so, James and Revelation), but the canonicity of the four Gospels, Acts, and the Pauline epistles were always considered beyond dispute. Just as the Nicene Creed did not appear until the third century, in direct response to Arian and Gnostic heresies, so authorized lists of the already-accepted canon did not begin to appear until the second century, in direct response to the heretical teachings of a man named Marcion. Marcion, in contrast to the unified witness of the church, rejected the Old Testament "God of wrath" (and, with him, the Old Testament itself) as a lesser deity and proclaimed Christ as the true "God of love." Needless to say, this heresy is still with us today!

## THE TRUE CODE BOOK

No matter his religion, his age, or his cultural background, no reader of *The Da Vinci Code* can help but be delighted and intrigued by the circuitous trail of clues, codes, and puzzles that face the heroes of Brown's exciting, fast-paced novel. Indeed, I believe that much of the appeal of the novel is due to the innate desire we all possess to solve a riddle and gain hidden wisdom. Brown would have us fulfill these desires by turning to Gnostic gospels and societies, but I would suggest a better method for doing so. I know of a book—an even bigger and more international best seller than *The Da Vinci Code*—that is packed with more riddles, revelations, and reconciliations than all the "code books" ever written. I speak, of course, of the Bible.

Though the Old Testament is a book complete in itself, when it is read in conjunction with the New Testament, its second, hidden meaning slowly rises to the surface. More than a history of the Jewish people and a collection of their proverbial and prophetic wisdom, the Old Testament is a vast riddle book encoded with hundreds of clues that point forward to the coming of the promised Messiah. Until the birth, death, and resurrection of Christ, most of those clues seemed impossible to decipher, understand, or reconcile. When viewed, however, from the hindsight of the New Testament, the clues assemble themselves into a rich, meaningful tapestry.

In the Old Testament, God sets his chosen people a seemingly unsolvable riddle by speaking through his prophets two seemingly incompatible sets of prophecies about the Messiah: that he would be a suffering servant (Psalm 22; Isaiah 53) and that he would be a political leader like King David (Psalm 2; Isaiah 11). Only in the light of the New Testament would it become clear that the two sets of prophecies referred, in fact, to two separate comings of the Messiah—his first coming as a poor carpenter who would give his life for the world; his second (and still awaited) coming as a heavenly ruler who will destroy all earthly wickedness and set up his eternal throne.

The Da Vinci Code intrigues us with the fanciful, unbelievably remote possibility that there are people alive today who are direct descendants, via the Merovingian Dynasty, of a two thousand-year-old bloodline that began with Jesus and Mary Magdalene. The Bible presents us with a historical, two thousand-year-long bloodline that stretches from Abraham to David to Christ. Every kind of threat—from war to slavery to barrenness—threatens to destroy the sacred bloodline, yet it endures and persists. The bloodline is mostly royal, yet it embraces some (like Ruth) who are not Jewish, ends with two poor rustics (Mary and Joseph), and includes at least three women of suspect sexuality (Tamar, Rahab, and Bathsheba).

Yes, Brown's novel offers some nifty riddles, but consider this sampling of three brief biblical conundrums:

- Isaiah 53 includes the following prophecy of the Messiah: "And they made his grave with the wicked / and with a rich man in his death, / although he had done no violence, / and there was no deceit in his mouth" (v. 9). How can an innocent man of peace and truth be assigned a grave with the wicked? And how can one so assigned yet be with the rich in his death? The verse is like a double riddle that folds back on itself. And yet that is exactly what occurred on Good Friday. A sinless man, falsely accused of evil, was crucified between two thieves; but when his body was removed from the cross, a rich man (Joseph of Arimathea) gave up his own tomb to receive the body.

- King David begins Psalm 110 with these words, "The LORD says to my Lord: / 'Sit at my right hand, / until I make your enemies your footstool.'" Jesus himself (Luke 20:41–44) pushes the crowd to think carefully through this seemingly contradictory verse. If the Messiah is only the "son" of David, then why does King David address him as "Lord"? Who are these two Lords that both surpass Israel's king? Hidden within this single verse is not only the revelation that the Messiah will be something more than the son of David, but a brief, Old Testament glimpse of the later Christian understanding of the Trinity.
- In the same psalm, David goes on to say something even more puzzling about the Messiah: "The LORD has sworn / and will not change his mind, / 'You are a priest forever / after the order of Melchizedek'" (v. 4). Hebrews devotes an entire chapter (chapter 7) to mining the full meaning of this brief verse—a verse that points both backward toward one of the most enigmatic figures of Genesis (14:18–20) and forward toward some as yet unclear qualification of the Messiah. As it turns out, the qualification that both Christ and Melchizedek share is that they, unique in Jewish history, are both kings and priests. But Hebrews 7 is not content to stop merely with this connection. Melchizedek also foreshadows the Incarnate Son of God in that his shadowy presence in Genesis allows him to function as a type of One who is without beginning or ending and who mediates a covenant that surpasses, because it precedes, that of Moses.

The Old Testament is rife with such riddling verses, but these prophetic verses do not exhaust the encoded nature of the Hebrew Bible. In addition to the actual prophecies, the Old Testament offers a series of figures, events, and tales that foreshadow—in a more narrative sense—the gospel story of Christ. These include the heel bitten by the seed of the serpent (Genesis 3:15), Abraham's near-sacrifice of Isaac (Genesis 22), the Exodus story, the episode of the brazen serpent (Numbers 21:4–9; John 3:14–15), Zechariah's stricken shepherd (Zechariah 13:7–9), the ministry of Elisha, and the suffering and triumph of Joseph.

But my favorite of all the Old Testament prefigurements of Christ is to be found in the well-known story of the first Passover. According to Exodus 11–12, God prophesied through Moses that he would send throughout Egypt the Angel of Death, who would kill the firstborn of all things, whether man or beast, Egyptian or Jew. For his chosen people, however, God provided a way of escape. If they would take a spotless lamb, sacrifice it, and then smear its blood over their doorposts, when the Angel of Death saw the blood, he would pass over the house, and those inside would not die.

Here in this old, old tale is the very blueprint of Christian salvation. For we, like the firstborn of Egypt, are, on account of our sins, under sentence of death. But for us as well, the God of the Passover has provided a way of escape. Christ the spotless Lamb—spotless because he was without sin—was sacrificed upon the altar of the cross. If we take his shed blood and, figuratively, smear it over our sinful selves, when we come before the judgment seat of God, he will see not us or our sin but the blood of his Son—and we shall therefore pass out of judgment. Neither we nor the Jews of the Exodus deserve to be saved from the Angel of Death (who is God himself); it is only on account of the blood of the Lamb that we can survive the deadly ordeal.

Paul says it all in one brief sentence: "For Christ, our Passover lamb, has been sacrificed" (1 Corinthians 5:7).

Riddles upon riddles. Clues upon clues. If what we desire is a code that needs to be broken, a hidden key that needs to be turned, then we need look no further than the family Bible on the shelf. There shall we find both prophecies and fulfillments, questions and answers aplenty—enough for a lifetime of searching!

Appearing in the midst of a modern, scientific age that privileges simple, concrete solutions over mystery and ambiguity, the riddle-filled *Da Vinci Code* offers a much needed antidote to the dangers of excessive rationalism. Though Brown's characters use the masculine virtues of reason and logic to help solve the riddles, they rely just as strongly on the more feminine virtues of emotion, intuition, and faith. Indeed, part of Brown's project—and a good and worthwhile project it is—is to reclaim what he calls "the sacred feminine" as a positive and healing force. The trouble is that Brown misidentifies the true enemies of the sacred feminine.

The real suppression of the feminine virtues did not occur during the early church or the catholic Middle Ages—both of which held masculinity and femininity in a tense but creative balance—but during the secular Enlightenment. It was the architects of the eighteenth-century Age of Reason who privileged reason and logic over emotion, intuition, and revelation—that is to say, masculinity over femininity. Yes, much of the Protestant church absorbed—mostly unconsciously—this

Enlightenment dismissal of the feminine perspective, but the origin of the dismissal was secular rather than ecclesiastical. In fact, during this time period it was the Catholic Church—whom Brown unfairly pillories throughout his novel—that mounted perhaps the strongest resistance to the tyranny of rationalism.

Dan Brown seeks the sacred feminine in the writings and rituals of the Gnostics, when in fact the real impetus behind Gnosticism is not the preservation and exaltation of the feminine but the collapsing of masculinity and femininity into a bland, sexless androgyny. As with the Enlightenment, many in the church have jumped on the androgyny bandwagon, but they do so despite, not in keeping with, the traditional teachings of Christianity. In the Gnostic Gospel of Thomas, Jesus promises to do the following for Mary Magdalene: "I myself shall lead her in order to make her male, so that she too may become a living spirit resembling you males. For every woman who will make herself male will enter the kingdom of heaven." Hardly a text to promote the integrity and value of the sacred feminine! It is the true church, and not the promoters of the Gnostic gospels, who are best poised to protect and foster femininity in an age that would collapse the sexes and render the sacred feminine obsolete.

Please remember: it was the Gnostics, not the Catholic Church, who dismissed the physical body as evil and inherently fallen. Yes, there were many in the Catholic Church who, at times, embraced the Gnostics' low view of the body (Augustine, a convert from the Gnostic Manicheans, often fell prey to this temptation); but when they did so, they were moving away from—not toward—Christian orthodoxy. The Bible and the church have always denied that our bodies are inherently evil. If they were, God could not have become incarnate in Jesus, and the belief that we will be clothed in resurrection bodies in heaven would be considered heretical rather than centrally orthodox.

Again and again *The Da Vinci Code* calls for a sacramental mingling of earth and heaven, physical and spiritual, human and divine, but only the incarnation, which Brown rejects, can shatter the Gnostic denial of the flesh and exalt the physical as a potential container for divine presence.

# 21

# THE RETURN TO MYTH: APOLOGETICS FOR POSTMODERNS

Although most of this book has focused on logical, evidence-based proofs for Christianity, many recent apologists, sensing a widespread cultural change, have sought a less rationalistic approach. That cultural change goes by the name of postmodernism, a worldview that has consciously broken from modernism's focus on system, structure, science, and empiricism. Whereas modernism is very compartmental in its attempt to categorize all knowledge and phenomena in discrete boxes, postmodernism takes a more holistic approach. Postmoderns yearn to break out of the box in search of mystery, wonder, and awe. As a result, they tend to privilege intuition, imagination, and synthesis over logic, reason, and analysis. They think less like Western surgeons, who divide up the body, and more like Eastern chiropractors or acupuncturists, who see the parts of the body as being intimately connected.

And they think this way, too, about the arts, religion, and language. Modernism wants all forms of expression—whether scientific or aesthetic, secular or sacred—to "behave," to line up in a clear, logical series of one-to-one correspondences and mechanical causes and effects. Postmodernism, in contrast, yearns for an aesthetic and sacred language that is less fixed and systematic, that is more strange and startling and slippery. People who identify with the postmodern worldview find *both* science and the Church to be too constrictive, too black and white. They can find no place in either of these "institutions" to breathe or grow or create. They long to resolve rather than to solve, to experience rather than to figure out, to embrace the mystery rather than to capture and tame it. And the same goes for our interaction with the natural world. Modernism has reduced nature to an object to be studied; postmodernism seeks to restore meaning to the cosmos, to return to a sympathetic universe in which the turnings of the seasons and the orbits of the planets have something to do with us. For a postmodern, the universe is our *home*; for a modern, it is only our house.

## MIXED BLESSING

On the one hand, postmodernism poses a major threat to orthodox Christianity and to apologists who would defend Christianity as a worldview that is rational, consistent, and universal. Many today who yearn for a sympathetic universe reject the (Western) church and its "overly constrictive" creedal statements in favor of a smorgasbord of (Eastern) spiritualities: horoscopes, Transcendental Meditation, the occult, yoga, Indian spirit guides, tarot cards, cabalism, mediums, martial arts, and so forth. Such postmoderns are still referred to as New Agers, but they might better be called neo-pagans, for they tend to share a pantheistic worldview in which God is not viewed as the Creator of nature but as a part of nature. Pantheists direct their worship not to the personal God of the Bible but to an impersonal force or spirit that pervades all things.

Though the majority of these neo-pagans seek not power (black magic) but spiritual connection (white magic), they nevertheless find Christian doctrine to be cold, confining, and exclusivist. For the neo-pagan the staleness and rigidity of Christian doctrine can't compete with the awe and beauty of myth. Where, they ask, is the story, the adventure, the romance? What do those old, dusty biblical stories have to do with me? What role do I play in the sacred narrative? How can I feel-experience-know a spiritual reality that is locked up in old books and creeds?

Meanwhile, within academic circles postmodernism has led to a resurgence not of ancient Greek paganism but of Athenian sophistry. Like Socrates' and Plato's enemies, the Sophists, many postmoderns consider truth and morality to be relative, changing from culture to culture and polis to polis—even individual to individual! Rather than treat words as potential containers of absolute truth, postmoderns sever the words we use (signifiers) from the meaning they purportedly point back to (signifieds). The postmodern school of deconstruction posits a breakdown between signifiers and signifieds that prevents us from getting back to any fixed, originary meaning. Every time we try to trace a signifier back to a signified, it turns out to be yet another signifier; in the end we get caught in a swirl of signifiers that lead nowhere.

Deconstruction, I would argue, has brought back the three propositions put forward by one of Plato's nemeses, Gorgias the Sophist. Gorgias rejected the existence of any kind of original, fixed, transcendent Meaning (like Plato's Forms) and posited instead that 1) nothing exists, 2) if it exists, it cannot be known, and 3) if it can be known, it cannot be communicated. Modern deconstructionists like Derrida have affirmed Gorgias' cosmic and linguistic skepticism by essentially reasserting his three propositions: 1) there are no signifieds to fix meaning, and no single Transcendental Signified that can fix the meaning of the signifieds; 2) fixed, originary Meaning, even if does exist, cannot enter into our playhouse world of signifiers; 3) even if Meaning were to exist, and even if it could somehow enter our world, human language would not be able to contain or express it. For a religion like Christianity, whose faith rests not only on a book (the Bible) that is considered to be the revealed Word of God but on a Savior who is himself the Word of God in human flesh, deconstruction poses a clear and present danger. If the commands and promises of God can be neither known nor communicated, either in the form of an inspired book or of an incarnate Savior, then Christianity loses its claim to be God's ordained path to salvation, truth, and eternal life. The third book in Schaeffer's apologetics trilogy is titled *He Is There and He Is Not Silent*. By declaring war on all signifieds, deconstruction has turned God's presence into absence; by cutting signifiers adrift from any final meaning, it has turned God's voice into gibberish.

Postmodernism, it would seem, can only pose a threat to the integrity of Christ, the Bible, and Christianity. Surely, therefore, modern apologists should avoid it at all costs.

Though there is, alas, much truth in those last two statements, I nevertheless believe that, if handled properly, postmodernism can provide Christian apologists with a challenge and an opportunity to reach out to a generation of people hungry for spirituality and purpose. But it can only do so if apologists are willing to think outside the box—that is to say, to extend their vision to pre-Enlightenment and, yes, pre-Reformation ideals that can coexist and even be strengthened by a little postmodern slipperiness!

Though the modern world has taught us to dismiss (unfairly) the Catholic Middle Ages as dark, ignorant, and superstitious, the medieval vision was wider than our own and better enabled its adherents to embrace mystery and to perceive wonder and magic in the world around them. There was no need for neo-paganism in the Middle Ages, for the medievals already *lived* in a sympathetic universe. Though the Latin word *universe,* which suggests "unity in diversity," points to the dynamic vision of nature held by the medievals, their other word, *cosmos,* better embodies the fullness of their vision. *Cosmos* comes from a Greek word whose root meaning is "ornament," an etymological detail that captures perfectly the medieval faith that the universe is the ornament of God, a thing of beauty to be loved and known rather than merely studied.

In keeping with this medieval view of the connectedness of all aspects of God's creation, Francis of Assisi wrote hymns to Brother Sun and Sister Moon and called the animals his brothers. Rather than dismiss nature as "pagan" or study it as a dead object, Saint Francis reclaimed nature from the pantheists and, through it, celebrated God's presence in the world. Two centuries later, Dante invited readers of his *Divine Comedy* to join him on an exciting, whirlwind tour of our God-fashioned sympathetic universe. On his way through the heaven of the fixed stars, Dante passes by the constellation of Gemini (his "horoscope") and thanks it for shining down on him the gift of creativity. No, neither Dante nor his fellow-medieval Christians believed that the stars controlled us, but they did believe that the stars *influenced* us with their particular virtues. Today most nonbelievers *and* believers are likely to reject as foolish (or heretical) the idea that the motion of the stars or planets or seasons can influence us; yet scientists believe that microscopic strands of DNA determine everything about us, while Christians believe that it was a "star" (most likely a conjunction of stars) that led the Magi to Christ and an eclipse of the sun that marked his death.

The medievals knew that the world was good and meaningful, for not only had God fashioned it and called it good—he had even deigned to enter into his creation in the form of his Son. Granted, nature and man are fallen and in decay, but God's entry into man and nature redeemed both. There is no greater miracle, no greater *magic* than the incarnation. Christianity alone of all religions fully affirms the value and significance of flesh while fully affirming the reality of the spiritual realm. Can there be a more exciting story than that of a supreme, limitless God who stoops down and confines himself to the limits of flesh that he might win his bride, the church, and rescue her from the grip of the devil? Christianity has the best story to tell, and it needs to be told to postmoderns who yearn to participate in such a story.

As for Christianity being too exclusivist to appeal to postmoderns, we saw in chapter 7 that paganism at its highest points forward to Christ. That is why Michelangelo included pagan sibyls on the Sistine Chapel. We saw as well in chapter 20 that Christianity has the greatest Code Book, the one that affirms most fully the sacred feminine and that sacramentally joins heaven and earth. Though Dan Brown's claim that Constantine invented the incarnation is false, Constantine did help influence the way we celebrate Christmas. Faced with the monumental task of converting a pagan empire into a Christian one, the fourth-century church, probably guided by Constantine, wisely chose to celebrate Christmas on December 25, at the time of the winter solstice.

In addition to marking the first day of winter, December 25 stood at the convergence of two popular pagan celebrations—the birthday of the Unconquerable Sun and the Saturnalia (an anarchic, Mardi Gras-like festival that hearkened back to a lost golden age). The early church fathers who agreed to celebrate Christ's birth on a day when pagans were already open to the kind of sacramental magic that was ushered into our world by the incarnation were not guilty of "watering down" Christian doctrine but of attempting to build a bridge to people hungry for the True Myth, for what John calls "the true light, which enlightens everyone" (John 1:9). They understood, as post-Enlightenment Christians often do not, that Christ does not kill but consummates the yearning for myth and the desire to return to Eden. And they knew something else that modern apologists would do well to learn: rather than browbeat pagans (or neo-pagans) into blowing out their mythic candles, we can encourage them instead to trade them for the Sun (the full Truth revealed through Christ and the Bible).

The apologist who would reach postmoderns with the gospel must not be ashamed of the mythic qualities that hang around the gospel story. Rather, he must embrace the suprarational mysteries of the Trinity, the incarnation, the atonement, and the resurrection and then present those mysteries as the answer to mankind's yearning for a magic that connects, synthesizes, and transforms. He must gain eyes to see the paradoxes that underlie the Christian faith, and he must be courageous enough to face those paradoxes in the Bible as well. Only by doing so will he be properly equipped to confront the challenges of neo-paganism and deconstruction by offering in their stead a higher, redemptive postmodernism.

Far from demanding a one-to-one correspondence, the Bible is rich with poems, symbols, parables, and prophecies that are decidedly slippery. When the early and medieval church fathers read the Bible, they discerned in its stories and images not one but four overlapping levels of meaning. Dante, who factored these four levels of meaning into his

*Divine Comedy*, offers, in a letter to one of his patrons, just such a fourfold reading of a single verse from the Bible: "When Israel went out from Egypt . . ." (Psalm 114:1). Taken *literally*, this verse refers to the exodus; *allegorically*, it signifies how Christ freed us from sin; *morally*, it describes the conversion of the soul from bondage to sin to freedom in Christ; *anagogically*, it prophesies that final, glorious moment when the soul will leave behind the body's slavery to death and corruption and enter the Promised Land of heaven. For Dante and the medievals, these four meanings, though they can be described in terms of an ascending ladder of spiritual revelation, exist simultaneously. Rather than deconstruct or cancel each other out, they are held in tension within the overall biblical narrative. They are slippery, but it is a kind slipperiness that leads toward rather than away from meaning and truth.

And this redemptive slipperiness extends from the Bible to Christ himself. In the incarnation, God (the Transcendental Signified) emptied himself and took on the form of a lowly signifier (Jesus of Nazareth) while continuing to be a signified (fully God as well as fully man). As with the four levels of meaning, the incarnation reveals that our world is more open than modernists like to admit, but that openness does not lead, as a postmodernist might claim, toward relativism and meaninglessness but toward the mystical yoking of heaven and earth, the spiritual and physical, the eternal and temporal, God and man.

That is why the best answer to Gorgias's three propositions is not to be found in a formal proof or syllogism but in the highly literary, decidedly slippery prologue of John's Gospel (1:1–18). For each proposition of Gorgias's, John offers a verse that asserts the true existence, knowability, and communicability of the Triune God: 1) "In the beginning was the Word, and the Word was with God, and the Word was God" (v. 1); 2) "And the Word became flesh and dwelt among us, and we have seen his glory, glory as of the only Son from the Father, full of grace and truth" (v. 14); 3) "No one has ever seen God; the only God, who is at the Father's side, he has made him known" (v. 18).

## NONAPOLOGETIC APOLOGISTS

Though I have been calling in this chapter for a new kind of postmodern apologetics, I am aware that the very phrase *postmodern apologetics* is something of an oxymoron. How, after all, can one present a rational defense of the Christian faith if one privileges emotion, mystery, and slipperiness over logic, system, and evidence? If an apologist accepts the ground rules of postmodernism, will he not, by so doing, sacrifice the absolute truth claims on which Christianity rests? In some cases, I am grieved to say, the desire on the part of well-meaning Christians to accommodate the relativistic perspective and worldview of postmodernism has led to a fatal downplaying of key Christian doctrines (indeed, of the very idea *of* doctrine), a suicidal dilution, if not a dismissal, of biblical authority, and/ or a self-destructive compromising of basic biblical morality.

Still, Christians who are eager to reach out to neo-pagans and to present the gospel in a language that postmoderns can understand and receive should not be discouraged. Though the danger always exists that the would-be apologist or evangelist will succumb to the relativism, syncretism, and radical individualism of the postmodern ethos, if he will keep himself grounded in the central creedal statements of Christianity and place himself under the authority of the incarnate Christ, the revealed Word of God, and (please do not misunderstand me, my fellow evangelical brothers and sisters) the sacred tradition of the one holy, catholic (universal), and apostolic church, then he need not be afraid. I have already suggested above ways in which a vigorous and centered postmodern apologetics can be constructed by rehabilitating medieval notions of the sympathetic universe and the four levels of meaning. I would now like to suggest a second method for reaching postmoderns that involves emphasizing the narrative and restorative aspects of the Christian faith while not compromising the basic tenets of orthodox Christianity. To illustrate this second method, I will consider briefly three recent works that, though they may not technically be works of apologetics, point the way toward a type of engagement with the postmodern world that I find both effective and fruitful.

In *Epic*, John Eldredge helps bring to life the sacred narrative of the Bible by linking it to some of the greatest and best-known fantasy stories. With great passion and bravado, Eldredge draws fascinating parallels between the Bible's story of creation, the fall, and redemption and such books and films as The Lord of the Rings; *The Lion, the Witch and the Wardrobe*; *Gladiator*; *Paradise Lost*; *The Lion King*; and the Harry Potter series. By drawing these connections, Eldredge not only keeps his postmodern audience alert and entertained but invites them to participate in a great struggle that began long before they were born.

The great stories move us, argues Eldredge, because we are *in* one. In the beginning, the Bible assures us, there was a time of perfect fellowship, a golden age of innocence that is not only recorded in the account of Eden in Genesis 2–3 but that breaks through in those thousand beguiling glimpses that greet us in the pages of our favorite fairy tales. Unfortunately, that fellowship and that innocence are shattered by the appearance of a villain (Satan, Sauron, the White Witch, Voldemort) who breaks into Eden and ignites a struggle between good and evil. In the end, however, a hero, a long-awaited messiah (Christ, Aragorn, Aslan, Harry Potter) appears and brings victory (the resurrection) out of what seemed to be utter defeat (the crucifixion). But the story does not stop there, for the restored and renewed Messiah leaves us with the promise that a time will come, and already is, when he will make all things new. Until we understand this story and our place in it, argues Eldredge, we will feel displaced, unsure of our true identity and purpose. Until our eyes are opened to the true nature of our world, we will understand neither the danger that surrounds us nor the glory that awaits us.

In *Blue Like Jazz*, Donald Miller also seeks to open our eyes to the true nature of our world and of ourselves, but he does so by reflecting not on the great stories and fairy tales but on the everyday trials of his own Christian walk. Through confessing his own struggles and temptations and sharing his own little triumphs, Miller also makes Christianity come to life as something that is both real and relevant to our postmodern world. In a nonlinear, fragmented, improvisatory style, he presents the Christian life not as rigid or restrictive but as something that fosters humility, growth, and community. It is only by accepting God's free grace and unconditional love, he argues (or better, demonstrates), that we can be freed to forgive ourselves and others, to move out of our existential isolation, to take emotional risks, and to accept others as they are. And since we cannot be fully alive, or even fully human, until we can do those four things, the Christian message becomes not only a means for salvation in the next world but for self-actualization in this one.

Like one of his key mentors, postmodern guru Brian McLaren, Miller connects with his postmodern audience by privileging authenticity over social conformity, by rejecting all forms of self-righteousness, and by embracing the myriad mysteries that meet us at every turning of the road. For Miller, as for most "postmodern apologists," two counterintuitive principles stand at the center of his dynamic vision: 1) the journey is as important as the destination, and we are therefore more in need of guides than preachers; 2) Christian community is not something we join after we are saved, but something whose reality and genuineness lead us to salvation.

In *True Story*, James Choung, another disciple of McLaren, also attempts to expand our vision of Christian salvation by presenting the gospel not just as a get-out-of-hell-free card but as the only force that can renew and transform our world. Choung, who is more an evangelist than an apologist, presents his fuller gospel through a series of four circles that unintentionally parallel the four acts of Eldredge's epic story, though from a more sociopolitical perspective. And, in true postmodern fashion, he does so not in the form of a systematic slide presentation but through the mediation of a fictional narrative—a "true story" that he hopes will encourage his readers to participate in the greater "true story" of the gospel.

Choung's first circle presents us with a picture of our world as it was meant to be, a world of perfect harmony between God, man, and nature. Unfortunately, that original plan has been shattered, and so the second circle represents our world as it actually is—broken, unjust, rife with pain and oppression. We all know our world is like this, argues Choung; yet we all know in our hearts that it should not be in this state. The third circle embodies the inner restoration that Christ effected through his death and resurrection. In the fourth, Christians extend that inner restoration to the world, that they might bring about the vision of the Lord's Prayer: "Your kingdom come, your will be done, on earth as it is in heaven" (Matthew 6:10). Just as moderns must realize that the gospel is not complete until it is extended outward to encompass this circle-four vision, so postmoderns hungry to bring social justice, political reconciliation, and environmental harmony to our torn world must realize that we are powerless to carry out this vision until we have been restored from within by the power of the atonement (circle three).

# 22

# INTELLIGENT DESIGN:
# BEYOND THE BIG BANG

Though a growing number of scientists will admit that the big bang and anthropic principle (see chapter 14) carry theistic implications, most draw the line when it comes to the evolution of life. Indeed, if you were to take a national poll of university professors on the subject of the three founding fathers of the modern world (Marx, Freud, and Darwin), you would find that though most of them would be quite willing to criticize, often harshly, the theories of the first two, they would be extremely reticent to say anything negative about the third. That is because whereas the monolithic theories of Marx and Freud have been discredited by the very academics who used to be their most avid defenders, Darwinian evolution (slightly modified) continues to reign triumphant not only in the academy and in the scientific establishment but in elite media and political circles as well.

In nearly every school, college, and university today, whether it be secular or religious in orientation, all branches of the natural and social sciences and most of the humanistic disciplines are undergirded by an evolutionary paradigm that itself rests on naturalism—a philosophical (rather than scientific) system that forbids recourse to supernatural or nonmaterial causes or explanations. Naturalism does not necessitate atheism; it simply forbids any reference to a designer outside the closed system of nature. Material processes can and *must* explain all things. Naturalism, I would argue, marks the categorical opposite not of Christianity but of superstition. In the case of the latter, all phenomena must be explained by spiritual causes whose source and origin are supranatural; in the case of the former, all phenomena must be explained by physical causes whose source and origin are material. In either case, it's all or nothing!

Naturalism, *both* methodological and philosophical, has become so deeply ingrained in the European and American psyche that Christian academics and scientists are as likely as secular ones to defend Darwinism at all costs. As a result, they not only strongly oppose those who would advocate a six-day creation based on a literal reading of Genesis 1 but those who would argue—on the basis of empirical observation rather than biblical interpretation—that an Intelligent Designer must have played a direct role (past the initial big bang) in the formation of the various species and life forms that inhabit our planet. Though many persist in claiming that there is no middle option between Darwinian evolution and six-day creationism, a growing and multifaceted movement known as intelligent design (ID) has placed itself in the precarious no-man's-land between those who would force science to bend to naturalism and those who would force it to bend to biblical literalism. ID theorists, many (but not all!) of whom are Christians, do not argue that a literal reading of Genesis should be the touchstone for science. To the contrary, they argue that a close study of nature and of man reveals abundant evidence for a kind of specified complexity that could not have evolved solely by natural, unguided forces.

Alas, in daring to argue that a close, unbiased study of nature points to the work of an intelligent, supranatural designer, ID theorists like Phillip E. Johnson—whose 1991 book *Darwin on Trial* formally announced the presence of ID to the world—have provoked unbelievable wrath. As Tom Woodward has documented in his book *Darwin Strikes Back*, and as Ben Stein has visualized in his documentary *Expelled*, secular *and* Christian critics have used censorship, intimidation, and character assassination to stifle the voice of ID in the academy and the media. Again and again these increasingly hostile critics have falsely labeled ID as six-day creationism in disguise, libeled it as pseudoscience, and refused to publish its results in peer-reviewed journals. Rather than engage in or trace the history of this often bitter and vindictive controversy, I will devote this chapter to laying out the basic ID argument and leave readers to draw their own conclusions.

I only ask that my readers keep in mind two things as they sift through the evidence and decide for themselves. First, when Galileo defended Copernicus's heliocentric model of the universe, he was opposed by *both* the church and the scientific establishment. Second, it is the pioneers of ID, not the tenured Darwinists, who share the most in common with Galileo, for it is they who have risked scorn from their colleagues, the loss of their jobs, and the questioning of their credentials in order to poke a few holes in the pretensions of a monolithic scientific establishment that takes the theory of evolution as a universal, incontestable fact.

## DARWIN ON TRIAL

Though the truth of Christianity does not rest on ID, and though ID is not technically a branch of apologetics (it claims only that the evidence points to a designer), ID's success at carrying the theistic implications of the big bang from physics and astronomy into biology makes it a fit subject for discussion in a book devoted to modern defenses of the existence of God and of his actions and interactions in the world. Put simply, if ID could prove that nature is not a closed system, or at least problematize the nonnegotiable Darwinian claim that it is, then it would have the effect of opening nature to divine influence and empowering us to discern in the intricacies of life the fingerprint of a personal, involved, even invasive God.

In *Darwin on Trial*, Johnson, a lawyer, begins his case against Darwinism by rejecting the distinction between the *fact* and *theory* of evolution. Whereas Darwinists claim that though the theory is always being modified, the fact that evolution occurred is beyond question, ID theorists maintain that there is no such thing as the fact of evolution, for that so-called fact rests not on empirical science but on a naturalistic philosophy that *demands* a material explanation for life. To maintain this artificial and inaccurate distinction, Darwinists have co-opted the word *evolution*—using it to mean *both* microevolution (observed adaptation within species) *and* macroevolution (the unproven assumption that one species can evolve into another by physical processes alone). They then use this co-option to push forward an invalid enthymeme: We have observed (micro)evolution in action; therefore, (macro)evolution must be true.

This disingenuous enthymeme is invalid, for the difference between microevolution and macroevolution is not quantitative but qualitative; it marks a change not in degree but in kind. Just as Lewis argues in his introductory chapter to *The Problem of Pain* (see chapter 2) that there is no logical reason to believe that the fear of wild animals could have evolved into a fear of the unknown, so there is no reason to believe that adaptation *within* species could (given enough time) have yielded evolution *between* species. Nevertheless, Darwinists not only continue to act as if microevolution proves macroevolution but claim that those who reject macroevolution must therefore reject microevolution, a false claim since microevolution can be observed in the way bacteria adapts to antibiotics, necessitating the creation of stronger and stronger forms of penicillin. Darwinists even use scare tactics, claiming that without (macro)evolution, medicine and bacteriology would be compromised—another false claim since such research relies not on macroevolution but on microevolution, the existence of which nobody disputes. Indeed, aside from evolutionary biology itself, science does *not* rest on the unproven theory of macroevolution.

Having exposed the way Darwinists manipulate words like *fact*, *theory*, and *evolution* to disguise the flaws in natural selection, Johnson next exposes the way Darwinists have played fast and loose with the fossil record. Though the last several generations of students have been told that paleontology supports Darwinism, the fossil record actually testifies *against* the theory of natural selection. Noticeably absent from the fossil record are the necessary transitional forms between species; instead the fossils point to an abrupt appearance of species followed by variation *within* species.

Indeed, during the Cambrian explosion (also known as the "biological big bang"), nearly all animal phyla appeared during a brief space of geological time about six hundred million years ago. This is *not* what the Darwinists expected to find when they began their search for fossils that would back up their theory. What they should have found in the fossil record was an evolution *toward* the various phyla; what they found instead were numerous variations *from* the phyla. Modern cars and planes vary quite widely in their shapes, styles, and accouterments, but all cars and planes, no matter their individual specifications, follow the basic model and design set forth by Henry Ford and the Wright Brothers. Contra the theory of evolution, the same is the case for the major animal phyla—they still maintain (with variations) the basic model and design that appeared (abruptly) during the Cambrian explosion. For over a century, the raison d'être of paleontology has been to prove Darwin's theory; ironically, despite its resounding failure, Darwinists *still* invoke the fossil record as proof of macroevolution. Needless to say, the long-sought missing link between ape and man has not been found either, nor has a sound reason been offered for why there have been no new species since man. Since evolution is driven by undirected chance, how could it "know" to stop with us?

Although the distinctly nongradual nature of the fossil record has been one of the best kept secrets of Darwinism, at least one evolutionist did muster the courage to suggest an alternate explanation that would preserve the tenets of naturalism while accounting for the gaps in the fossil record. His name was Stephen Jay Gould, and in the 1970s he, together with Niles Eldredge, posited sudden mutational change (or punctuated equilibrium) as a way to account for the lack of intermediate species—even though by doing so he essentially broke with Darwin's theory of slow descent by modification! The technical word for such sudden mutational leaps is saltationism (from a Latin verb that means "to leap"). Traditionally, Darwinism has criticized all forms of saltationism as violating the "fact" of evolution; they have even used it for decades as a slam-dunk argument against any form of creationism or intelligent design. That an evolutionist like Gould would embrace saltationism as a way to explain the fossil record betrays a desperation on the part of naturalistic science at least to preserve the appearance of Darwinism. Gould may have also realized something that Darwinists rarely admit. The discovery that our universe is only fifteen billion years old dealt a strong, if not fatal blow to Darwinism, for fifteen billion years (less than five billion for our earth) is simply not enough time to accommodate the very slow process of natural selection. Even the neo-Darwinian synthesis, which combines natural selection with mutation, cannot really have taken place over such a short period of time.

In many ways the life of Darwinian evolution has been extended by the discovery of how our DNA replicates and how that system of replication allows for a number of mutations. And yet, ironically, our increased knowledge of DNA marks perhaps the strongest argument for ID—an argument that might very well have convinced Darwin if he were alive today!

Over the last fifty years, scientists have discovered that our cells are vastly more complex than Darwin could ever have imagined. Even a single-celled animal is a veritable storehouse of information. From Watson and Crick's heralded discovery of the double helix structure of DNA to the successful mapping of the human genome, the secrets of life have opened before us. We have discerned not only the structure of DNA but the ingenious way it replicates—a replication system that *does* allow for small mutations that *can* drive (micro)evolution. What is not admitted, however, is that though this replication system can and does facilitate adaptations within species, it could not itself have evolved merely by undirected time and chance. It is simply too complex and does not lend itself to the types of mechanisms that drive natural selection. The proteins that make up our genes are assembled piece by piece in a process that may *seem* to suggest natural selection but that in actuality betrays the existence of intelligent design. For the assembling is done in accordance with a detailed blueprint that is stored in our DNA and that has been there, as far as we can tell, from the beginning of life.

The DNA of all living creatures, from a one-celled amoeba to Einstein, is *front-loaded* with an enormous amount of coded information, and *no mechanism exists that can evolve information*. Indeed, as ID theorists have pointed out, the old idea that the universe is made of matter and energy must be modified. Our discovery of the cell has shown us that the universe is composed of three things: matter, energy, and information. One doggedly naturalistic scientist who was clearly aware that the information-rich nature of DNA precluded its having been blindly assembled by evolution was Francis Crick, codiscoverer of the double helix. That is why he published a book in 1981, *Life Itself*, in which he seriously suggested that aliens might have seeded our planet with DNA. If this is not a veritable admission that our DNA is the product of intelligent design, then I don't know what is! And Crick's admission is no fluke. In the movie *Expelled* (2008), during a debate between Stein and neoatheist and radical Darwinist Richard Dawkins, Stein gets Dawkins to suggest as well that our DNA might have been seeded by extraterrestrials.

## IRREDUCIBLE COMPLEXITY

In the wake of *Darwin on Trial*, a number of top-notch ID theorists have expanded the reach of ID in a number of different directions. Of these, William Dembski has been instrumental in securing for ID a place within the hybrid discipline of philosophy of science. In his truly path-breaking book *The Design Inference*, Dembski provides his readers with nothing less than an ID corollary to the scientific method—one that can guide the empirically driven scientist, as opposed to the assumption-driven naturalist or biblical literalist, in determining whether a given phenomenon was caused by regularity, chance, or design. Dembski's "design filter" is both cautious and conservative, erring always on the side of chance. Only once the scientist has eliminated regularity (something that occurs in accordance with the regular laws of nature) and chance as possible causes should he infer (intelligent) design.

The way Dembski determines design is to look not only for a complex pattern (as one finds in crystals), but "*specified* complexity"—a recognizable design or pattern that has meaning apart from the phenomenon itself. The best way to understand what Dembski means by specified complexity is to consider the methods used by an archaeologist and an anthropologist. If the former digs up a heap of stones in a roughly circular shape, he will not immediately infer that the stones were laid there by a conscious agent. If, however, those stones are carefully arranged in a complex pattern that the archaeologist recognizes as being that of a temple or a human dwelling, he will infer that the stones did not end up there by chance but were put there for a specific purpose. In the case of the latter, if he finds a rock that seems to have a somewhat pointy end, he will likely dismiss it as a natural phenomenon. If however, the rock has been clearly shaped into a tool recognized by the anthropologist (say, a knife), he will conclude that the specified complexity of the rock-knife proves that it was shaped by an intelligent agent.

Indeed, Dembski argues, all of us have a natural understanding of the difference between chance/regularity and specified complexity. If we are taking a walk through South Dakota, and we notice on the side of a cliff the rough image of what appears to be a face, we will most likely dismiss it as the result of natural weathering forces. But if we discern on the side of a second cliff the image of four distinct faces that clearly resemble four presidents whose pictures we have seen (namely, Washington, Jefferson, Lincoln, and Teddy Roosevelt), we will immediately conclude that the second image is not random but designed. The specified complexity of the phenomenon convinces us of this fact beyond a shadow of a doubt. Likewise, if we are walking on a beach and we see wavy lines and patterns on the sand, we will conclude they are caused by the natural forces of wind and tide. But if those lines form a linguistic pattern, we will recognize it as the work of an intelligent agent, *even if we don't ourselves know the language.* I doubt that any person, Darwinist or otherwise, will dispute the four examples I have given, and yet what I have described is exactly parallel to the type of information-rich specified complexity we encounter in our cells and DNA. Well, not really parallel, for the specified complexity of the DNA is vastly more intricate than a hundred Mount Rushmores!

Dembski, though well versed in the sciences, writes primarily as a philosopher, but his findings match perfectly with those of an accomplished biochemist named Michael Behe. In *Darwin's Black Box*, Lehigh professor Behe argues that clear evidence for design can be found within our cells. Behe, referencing Darwin himself, argues that if any biological system can be found that cannot be evolved through a series of slow steps, Darwinism will be disproved. Since evolution is blind—it does not know where it is going—each step in natural selection must possess some type of survival value; otherwise it will not be selected for preservation by the organism. If a chemical or biological system could be identified that could not be formed by a gradual process in which each step possessed survival value, then that system would be "irreducibly complex" and would offer concrete evidence for the existence of some form of intelligence that is not a part of the unconscious, nonpurposeful system of natural selection. Irreducibly complex systems, that is to say, necessitate the preexistence of a controlling intelligence that could front-load the information for the blueprint that assembled the system.

Behe claims to have identified just such a system in the bacterial flagellum, a microscopic, multipart system that works like an outboard motor to propel the organism. The "motor" is composed of a number of intricate parts (including a rotor, a driveshaft, rings, studs, and a universal joint) that must *all* be in place for it to work. Remove even one part, and the flagellum ceases to function. In addition to its remarkable sleekness and efficiency, the bacterial flagellum is irreducibly complex. It cannot have evolved in stages, for until all its pieces are in place, it does not perform any function that would benefit the cell. In his book Behe compares the flagellum to a mousetrap that is composed of five basic parts: the platform, the holding bar, the spring, the catch, and the hammer. Remove even one of these five parts and the mousetrap is useless—it cannot perform its function of catching mice. Like the flagellum, the mousetrap is irreducibly complex.

While Dembski and Behe have carried ID into the realms of philosophy and biochemistry, Jonathan Wells has taken a step back and helped us understand how and why Darwinism has come to exert such a firm grip on the Western mind. In *Icons of Evolution*, Wells, without specifically mentioning ID, deconstructs a number of (false) icons that Darwinists still use to lull the public, especially public school and university students, into unquestioning belief. In *The Case for the Creator*, Lee Strobel, before interviewing Wells, lists four of these icons and attests that his early atheism was bolstered by his adherence to these icons. I mention this specifically as a rationale for why I have devoted an entire chapter to defending a school of thought, intelligent design, that may seem to some irrelevant to the task of the modern apologist. True, one's acceptance or rejection of the theory of evolution is not a determining factor in the truth of the Trinity, the incarnation, the atonement, or the resurrection. Nevertheless, the fact remains that many people in the modern world are, like the young Strobel, kept from faith in Christ by their false belief that "science" has somehow "proven" that God does not exist and that it has rendered obsolete all "medieval" notions of the supernatural interacting with our world.

Let us then consider the four icons that Strobel highlights and that Wells deconstructs. The first is the image of the laboratory, replete with test tubes and Frankenstein-like gadgets, in which Stanley Miller claimed to have produced life out of prebiotic soup. For decades now, Miller's experiment, meant to prove that life could have sprung out of nonliving matter through the intervention of lightning, has been discredited for being false to early earth conditions. Despite this, however, the image of Miller's laboratory persists, etched in the minds of countless modern people.

The second icon is that of Darwin's tree of life, with its graceful evolutionary branches. In biology textbooks across the country, this tree continues to be presented as a picture of reality, on par with the periodic table; yet it has never been proven, and it directly contradicts the fossil record and the evidence of the Cambrian explosion.

The third icon also dates back to the nineteenth century, when a German Darwinist named Ernst Haeckel published a series of drawings of the human embryo in various stages of growth. Haeckel claimed that his drawings supported evolution by documenting that the human fetus, in its earliest stages, proceeds step-by-step through the evolutionary process in its mother's womb. Over a century has passed since Haeckel's drawings were exposed as fraudulent; yet they continue to crop up in textbooks as embryological "proof" of Darwinian evolution.

Finally, the fossil of archaeopteryx, Strobel's/Wells's fourth icon, continues to be touted as the missing link between reptiles and birds, even though most paleontologists have admitted it is not a transitional form but is a bird with some odd features. This admission, however, has not stopped Darwinists from continuing to hold up the archaeopteryx as concrete proof of macroevolution.

Before concluding this chapter, I would like to pause to consider briefly one of the reasons that scientists and other academics who confess a belief in Christ often give for their rejection of ID. ID theorists, they claim, are guilty of falling into a "God of the gaps" fallacy in which

God is simply brought in whenever a natural explanation can't be found. Though I will admit that Christians have been guilty of jumping too quickly to a supernatural (or superstitious) explanation rather than taking the time to seek a natural one, the "God of the gaps" argument is flawed in at least two ways. First, it blinds itself to the fact that Darwinists are often guilty themselves of "evolution of the gaps": just give us more time, and we'll straighten out those intransigent fossils and explain away those annoying irreducibly complex systems. Second, it overlooks the fact that the God of the Bible is defined in part as a God who intervenes. In answer to those who claim that a God who had to keep intervening after the big bang to keep things straight would be a "disorganized" God, I would highlight two major examples in Scripture where God is equally "disorganized": 1) though God implanted a conscience in us, he still intervened to give Moses the Law; 2) though God foreordained the ancestry of Christ, the Bible records numerous divine interventions to preserve that ancestry from being wiped out by war, death, and infertility.

# 23

# ANSWERING THE NEW ATHEISTS

There have been atheists ever since the fall or thereabouts, and there will always be atheists. Only since the Enlightenment, however, has it become socially and intellectually acceptable for someone to declare publicly that he is an unbeliever. Only in the modern Western world did it become possible to embrace that strangest of oxymorons: atheist philosophy.

What *is* philosophy, after all, if it is not a search for ultimate and eternal truth? The Sophists notwithstanding, the role of the premodern philosopher was to discern that which is true from that which is false, that which is permanent from that which is ephemeral. Even earthbound philosophers like Aristotle sought to pierce to the essence of things, to identify the divine blueprint lurking behind the physical form. If there is no God—that is to say, if there is no Unmoved Mover, no Absolute Self-Consciousness, no First Principle, no Transcendent Source of Goodness, Truth, and Beauty—then philosophy is left without a standard against which to measure the very things it studies.

True, in the absence of God, the geologist can study his rocks, the engineer can build his bridges, and the naturalist can pin down his butterflies and seal his beetles in formaldehyde. But what is the philosopher to do? Etymologically, he is a friend (or lover) of wisdom, but there can be no wisdom apart from God, just as there can be no answers to the questions philosophers ask: Who am I? Why am I here? What is my purpose? How do I know I am of value? And even if he puts those questions aside and focuses only on the application of reason and logic, how can he trust his reason if his reason is only the product of blind, mechanical, unconscious forces?

No, the philosopher need not be a theologian, but he cannot do his real work in a godless universe. C. S. Lewis has written that he believes in the sun not only because he sees it, but because by it he sees everything else. In the absence of God, there can be no illumination into the mysteries of Goodness, Truth, and Beauty. There can be only the darkness of the abyss. Indeed, that is exactly what so much of modern philosophy is: a peering into the abyss; an existential despair at the loss of all meaning, all counters, all touchstones. As for those too afraid to peer, naked, into the abyss, there are two alternatives: confine oneself to an arid logical positivism that will accept only empirical data or give oneself over to physical or emotional or intellectual or aesthetic hedonism as a shield from the looming emptiness.

Or if the "atheist philosopher" is unsatisfied with these three options, he can become militant. Rather than passively accept the loss of God and then try to go on with his life as best he can, he takes the offensive and attempts to press his atheism upon the vast majority of his fellow human beings for whom belief in God is as natural as breathing. (Note that I say believing in God rather than obeying him!) If he is a college professor, he will indoctrinate his students by ridiculing theism and theists; if he is a revolutionary, he will create a new state and then banish God from it; if he is a scientist, he will insist that science has disproved God and that the supernatural is henceforth off-limits; if he is a psychiatrist, he will refuse to acknowledge the reality of his patients' belief in God; if he is a social scientist, he will reduce man from a spiritual being to a product of environmental and sociological forces.

If he is a man of letters with a gift for presenting academic ideas in an accessible way, he will write popular books that promise to liberate his readers from the oppressive grip of religion in general and Christianity in particular. Though these militant, if sometimes affable, men of letters have been a fairly constant presence since the Enlightenment (Voltaire, Thomas Paine, T. H. Huxley, H. G. Wells, H. L. Mencken, Bertrand Russell, Carl Sagan), the first decade of the third millennium saw a sudden rise in their number, their influence, and their book sales. The movement, whose unabashed vigor and glee took even post-Christian Europe by surprise, came to be known as the new atheism, and its major authors (Richard Dawkins, Daniel Dennett, Sam Harris, Christopher Hitchens, and Victor Stenger) as the new atheists. In this chapter I shall attempt to refute the atheistic arguments made in the two books that I consider to be the best written and the most representative of the movement as a whole.

## THE ATHEIST DELUSION

In *The God Delusion*, Richard Dawkins offers a critique of religion that merits serious and honest refutation. Dawkins is no simple village atheist to be dismissed and ridiculed. Despite bouts of stridency and bad taste, his critique of God and religion is multifaceted, rhetorically effective, and even, at times, compelling.

Speaking for myself, I prefer a good honest atheist like Dawkins to all those wishy-washy Deists, Unitarians, agnostics, and liberal theologians who want to keep the spirituality and the moral teachings of Jesus while stripping Christianity of its central, supernatural doctrinal claims. At least one can have a real argument with Dawkins. At least he does not claim to believe things that he really does not believe, as the others, I'm afraid, do: I am a Christian (but I reject every doctrine laid forth in the Nicene Creed); I believe in God (but he is an absentee God who does not interact directly with the world); I think Jesus was the most spiritually actualized person who ever lived (but by denying his claims to deity I make him into the worst liar and megalomaniac in history); I believe in ethics and morality (but I don't believe in an eternal standard of morality to which we are all accountable).

Dawkins will not play this game of believing and denying at the same time. Instead he asserts, directly and unapologetically, that nothing exists outside the natural world: God is a delusion; we do not possess an immortal soul; miracles are impossible. Dawkins is not bothered when scientists like Einstein or Stephen Hawking speak of God, for, Dawkins claims, what they mean by God is really a pantheistic reverence for the universe and its ordering mechanisms. If that's what God is, then Dawkins has no problem with him (or better, it). What Dawkins wants to abolish is not awe over the laws of nature but belief in a *personal* God.

Dawkins will have no truck with people like Stephen Jay Gould who want to set up complementary spheres for science and religion (see chapter 11). As far as Dawkins is concerned, religion is false and pernicious and should no longer be tolerated by "enlightened" individuals who have freed themselves from the superstitions of the past and of childhood. (Dawkins, rather arrogantly, has petitioned that atheists refer to themselves as "brights.") According to Dawkins we no longer need God or religion to explain the world or to preserve morality. In the case of the former, Darwinian natural selection has, Dawkins assures us, fully explained the world in which we live; in the case of the latter, well, people don't *really* base their morality on the Bible. On the contrary, religion breeds intolerance, hatred, and war, stands in the way of evolutionary progress, and perpetuates exclusivity, oppression, and scientific ignorance.

Dawkins would further "raise our consciousness" about two things that clearly irk him. First, he warns his readers again and again about the dangers of allowing parents to indoctrinate their children in the teachings of their religion. If he had his way, phrases like "Christian child" or "Jewish child" would be dismissed as being equivalent to such phrases as "Marxist child" or "capitalist child." Though he presents himself as a modern liberal and freethinker, Dawkins is serious about his belief that parents should be forbidden from raising their kids within the "confines" of a religious system. Second, Dawkins insists that natural selection is not a fancy word for chance but that Darwinism offers an alternative to *both* creationism and chance. Dawkins would have us marvel at the simplicity and order of natural selection while dismissing as illusory all evidence of design in nature and ourselves.

If the modern apologist would successfully refute the arguments of *The God Delusion*, he would do best to begin by uncovering one of the most subtle but persistent flaws in Dawkins's book: his ubiquitous use of a rhetorical strategy that is really a logical fallacy. The name of that fallacy is begging the question (it is also known as circular reasoning), and it consists in stating as obvious the very thing that needs to be proved. If I were to argue that "sadistic experiments on animals should be stopped immediately," I would not, merely by stating the quoted phrase, have successfully refuted the practice of medical experiments on animals. Nearly everyone would agree that "sadistic" experiments should be stopped. What I must do, if I wish to prove my point logically, is to provide clear evidence that the experiments *are* sadistic.

In chapter after chapter Dawkins asserts, without providing the tiniest shred of evidence, that atheism and Darwinism are to be equated with intelligence, civilization, logic, critical thought, moral earnestness, and education. Religion, on the other hand, is to be equated with ignorance, primitivism, emotionalism, and stagnation. Those who still cling to God are backward or deluded or indoctrinated, while those who reject him are necessarily enlightened, courageous, and rational. As part of his proof that morality has evolved apart from God, Dawkins quotes protoatheists like T. H. Huxley and H. G. Wells who, despite their liberal credentials, viewed blacks as lesser than whites (not because of the darkness of their skin but because they considered African culture to be backward and ignorant). "See," boasts Dawkins in essence, "we atheists have moved beyond such narrow nineteenth-century prejudices, and we have done so without benefit of clergy." So claims Dawkins and then proceeds to disprove his own claim by illiberally labeling all God-fearing "yokels" as backward, ignorant, and uncivilized.

Although I am a fan of Foxe's *Book of Martyrs*, my Protestant faith does not blind me to the fact that Foxe's work is flawed by the inability of its author to conceive that someone could be both a Catholic and a martyr! Like Foxe, Dawkins is himself incapable of putting together two words: Christian and intelligent. He proclaims triumphantly that most of the intelligent elite of the modern world are atheists, while ignoring completely the genius of Augustine, Aquinas, Dante, Bach, Michelangelo, and Newton. He slyly insinuates that the so-called Christian geniuses of the past had to hold to a pretense of faith to avoid persecution, while conveniently overlooking the fact that many believing scientists and academics today must hide their faith to avoid persecution from their colleagues.

For Dawkins, you see, people can only be indoctrinated with religion, never with atheism. He can conceive of any number of ulterior motives for religious belief, but he never considers that atheism might be a cover for pride, immorality, and the refusal to be held accountable to any authority, whether divine or human. He also overlooks the fact that academics and other intellectuals are often far more gullible than common people. Witness how many elite thinkers believed the lies of the USSR—and continued to believe them until just months before the Berlin wall fell. And Dawkins's unwillingness to deal with inconvenient facts does not stop there. He accepts without question that intellectual and scientific progress will lead naturally to atheism, while simply ignoring the historic resurgence of faith all over the world.

Dawkins is, of course, most persuasive when he moves into the realm of science and Darwinism, an area in which he has special training and on which he has written a number of books. Dawkins is a smart enough writer to understand that he must offer some way of filling the yawning vacuum created by the rejection of God, and he, like Sagan before him, does this through science. I neither exaggerate nor put words in his mouth when I say that science and scientists represent for Dawkins a new religion and a new priesthood. It is science that is best equipped to answer all our questions—at least all the questions that need to be answered.

Dawkins is well aware that the discovery of the big bang and of the finely tuned nature of our universe (see chapter 14) has caused many thinkers to seek a reconciliation between science and religion, but he will have nothing to do with such a reconciliation. Though he admits that the multiverse theory is not a "fact" like evolution, he has faith that something like it will eventually yield a natural explanation for the big bang and the anthropic principle. Needless to say, he *has* to have that faith, for, having dismissed *a priori* the possibility of God's existence, he *must* cling to natural selection and the multiverse. Once again, he begs the question, taking as obvious the very thing that he must prove.

But this time he goes further. With great boldness, he "steals" for his own purposes one of the most powerful apologetic arguments, the appeal to Ockham's razor: all things being equal, the simplest explanation is usually the right one. Rather than accept that the big bang and the finely tuned nature of our universe point to a supernatural Creator, Dawkins recycles the old atheist question, Who created God? For Dawkins the "odds" against a God capable of creating our universe coming into existence are greater than those of the universe coming into being by natural causes; therefore, Ockham's razor favors a natural origin for our universe over a supernatural one. In making this argument, however, Dawkins overlooks what Judeo-Christian doctrine has always taught: God is not a being who came into existence, either by chance or by natural processes, but is an eternal being who has his existence in himself. That God might, in fact, be the great I AM is an idea that Dawkins refuses even to entertain.

And that leads us to what is arguably the central flaw in Dawkins's book: his lack of understanding of, and refusal to take seriously, Christian theology. Dawkins writes like a movie critic who hates all romantic comedies and thus refuses to make any distinction between good and bad films of that genre. To this charge, many of my fellow apologists would add a second: Dawkins has no right to critique religion because he does not have a degree in it. Though I see the merit in this second charge, I do not think it is a fair one. For a Christian apologist to forbid someone from commenting intelligently on something outside his specialty is tantamount to accepting one of the key components of the modernist worldview—that knowledge should always be broken into a number of narrow specialties. I for one reject this Enlightenment prejudice, at least when it comes to the humanities, and I am perfectly willing to allow a nonspecialist like Dawkins to comment on religion.

No, I will not critique Dawkins for his lack of a theology degree. But I *will* critique him for the narrowness of his theological vision. Throughout *The God Delusion*, Dawkins only quotes liberal theologians like John Dominic Crossan, John Shelby Spong, and Bart D. Ehrman who persist in claiming the Gospels are a collection of legends when, as I have shown in chapter 17, they are early, reliable documents based on eyewitness testimony. Dawkins also dismisses the resurrection without considering the growing evidence for its historical reliability (see chapter 18); his *a priori* dismissal of miracles forces him to do so. If we grant that philosophical arguments made by *both* apologists and atheists are ultimately circular—they *begin* with the presumption or rejection of God's existence—then we must turn for our proof or disproof of God to those very claims and actions of Christ that Dawkins refuses to take seriously.

Philosophical arguments for God assure believers that their faith is consistent with reason, but people *come* to faith in Christ because of the *evidence* of Christ's claims and miracles. Unfortunately, Dawkins, having rejected out of hand a personal God, also refuses to acknowledge the possibility that a personal God could reveal himself and be known by humans. Dawkins claims that theological "hairsplitting" over doctrines like the Trinity and incarnation are ludicrous and irrelevant when in fact they represent the heart of Christianity. If God is triune, then "God is love" is not merely a philosophical conundrum but a living, dynamic reality and the foundation of human love, consciousness, and community. If Christ was God incarnate, then God has revealed himself in the most intimate way possible, and the atheist argument that God has given no proof of his existence is silenced.

But once again Dawkins will not even consider that such outdated, superstitious doctrines might be true, a refusal that skews his perspective on both God and man. Thus Dawkins's curt dismissal of original sin and his failure to see that the Cross both proves and reconciles God's perfect holiness and perfect love weakens his argument that the God of the Bible is a cruel, humanity-hating tyrant. Likewise, his refusal to acknowledge the qualitative difference between men and animals or to acknowledge that we possess an immaterial mind apart from our material brain makes his pronouncements on who man is and what he needs both hollow and barren. Dawkins, for all his insight and critical skills, is simply unable to grasp that we are embodied souls—fully physical and fully spiritual. He is equally unable to see two of the most obvious facts about the human race: man is *essentially* religious, and there is a part of him that doesn't belong to nature.

For all the power of his rhetoric, Dawkins's discussion of religion is finally as reductive as the discredited theories of Marx and Freud. Both the sense of awe and reverence out of which religion flows and the loving activity of God within human history are completely lost on Dawkins. He just doesn't get it.

## WHY GOD IS GREAT

In *god is not Great*, Christopher Hitchens, taking up many of the same arguments as Dawkins but from the point of view of a journalist in the field, devotes most of his chapters to detailing the historical atrocities of religion. He documents, with colorful anecdotes and firsthand experience, the past and present tyranny of religious institutions, focusing as much on Islam as on Christianity. With great bravado and a welcome dose of wit, he seconds Dawkins in his attack on the way religion indoctrinates, oppresses, and warps children.

When the reader finishes *god is not Great*, his first instinct is to dissociate himself from all those terrible religious institutions that promote terror and oppression—until he suddenly notices something that Hitchens conveniently overlooks. Hitchens would have us believe that he is diagnosing the sickness of religion when, in fact, what he really diagnoses is what Christianity calls original sin: the belief that all people live in a state of constant rebellion against God. We all possess a sinful nature, and that is a problem not just because it offends a "divine despot" (as Hitchens would have it) but because in rebelling against our Creator, we violate our nature and purpose and cause evil in the world.

A number of apologists have answered the critiques of Hitchens and his fellow new atheists by pointing to the atrocities of the atheistic Nazis and Communists who made the "enlightened" twentieth century the bloodiest century of all. By pointing to these atheist atrocities, apologists do not seek to exonerate past evils done in the name of the church but to show that when atheists like Hitler, Stalin, and Mao gained control, they succumbed to the same human corruption. As Alister McGrath has documented in his fine study *The Twilight of Atheism*, whenever atheists have moved from critics and liberators to wielders of power (as they first did during the French Revolution), they have quickly established their own inquisitions, tribunals, and crusades.

The question, writes Timothy Keller in *The Reason for God*, is not which faith has no blood on its hands (they all do), but whether there is a faith that offers a solution to evil. Only Christianity, argues Keller, offers real hope that fallen man can be transformed, and only Christianity provides a firm, unshakable foundation for the intrinsic worth of every human being. Yes, many slaveholders in the past were Christians, but it was the Christian worldview that supplied the impetus to abolish the slave trade. True, many Christians are racists, but it was the Christian worldview that supplied the impetus for the civil rights movement.

Hitchens tries to get around this apologetic by insisting that Stalin and Mao simply turned communism into a new religion, but in doing so, he inadvertently critiques his critique. Like Dawkins he treats all religions as one, rather than considering that we might have a natural, inbuilt tendency to praise God that manifests itself in good and bad ways. Both seem to forget that the greatest critic of religious hypocrisy was Jesus and that the Old Testament prophets blasted religious leaders who despoiled their flocks. The solution that Jesus offers is not religion and worship per se, but *true* religion and *true* worship. "Even the demons believe—and shudder!" writes James (2:19); just so, the atheistic oppressors of the twentieth century were aware (as we all are) of the divine law that they were obligated to follow—they simply chose not to follow it and then to justify their evil in the name of their new antireligious religion!

Hitchens illustrates better than any preacher the horror and pervasiveness of human depravity; yet he brushes over the implications of that depravity. And because he does so, he ignores completely the great metanarrative of the Bible, by which a holy God seeks to be reconciled to his sinful creatures through the incarnation, the atonement, and the resurrection. God's work in human history is a mystery that neither Dawkins nor Hitchens seeks to explore or understand. Like many of the new atheists, and many liberal theologians as well, Hitchens judges God guilty of evil because he called Abraham to sacrifice his son Isaac. But when God called on Abraham to sacrifice Isaac, he was not abusing his divine power but was testing Abraham's faith in God's covenantal promise to bless his offspring. The Christian understanding of this test is that Abraham trusted (had faith) that God could raise Isaac from the dead (see Hebrews 11:17–19). Also like many new atheists and liberal theologians, Hitchens tries to dismiss the God of the Bible as a narrow, ethnocentric tribal deity. But such a charge ignores the fact that God's covenant with Abraham was meant not only as an ethnocentric blessing for the tribe of Israel but as a means through which to bless "all the families of the earth" (Genesis 12:1–3).

Like Dawkins, Hitchens cements his critique of religion by claiming that religion not only is the major source of evil in the world but is not needed to make men good. With the same unflinching faith as Dawkins's, Hitchens assures us that we can be moral and ethical without religion. But the only reason they can assure us of this is because they *redefine* morality to enshrine tolerance and sexual liberation as absolute goods— and they do this while ignoring the strong links between the breakdown of sexual morality, the spread of AIDS, the poverty of single mothers, and priestly pederasty. Both ignore as well that the liberal causes they believe in are based not upon atheism but upon the vast but diminishing stores of moral capital that the West has built up over its many centuries of belief in the God of the Bible.

Finally, like Dawkins as well, Hitchens is unwilling to entertain serious defenses of Scripture. Indeed, both dismiss the well-attested historical claims of the Bible with a censorious and obscurantist fervor that they would label immoral if they encountered it in a fundamentalist.

# 24

# HOW THE WORLD'S MOST NOTORIOUS ATHEIST CHANGED HIS MIND

The 2004 announcement sent shock waves through the corridors of the academy: famed British philosopher and atheist Antony Flew has renounced his earlier position and now believes in the existence of God! Ironically, I learned of the event not through professional or news channels but from Jay Leno's monologue on the *Tonight Show*. "It appears," joked Leno, "that Flew now believes in God. I wonder, could it have something to do with the fact that he is eighty-one years old!"

What gives Leno's joke its humor is the suggestion that the octogenarian philosopher is shaking in his boots, afraid that his atheism will soon land him in hell. Anyone familiar, however, with Flew's conversion and his current position on the afterlife knows this to be false. During the summer of 2005, while giving a lecture at Oxford on C. S. Lewis, I had the opportunity to attend a public conversation between Flew and Gary Habermas, a first-rate Christian apologist who has been a longtime friend and "sparring partner" of Flew.

During the conversation, Flew made it clear that he does not believe in the afterlife and that, in fact, one of the Christian doctrines that he found the most troubling and untenable was that of hell. Flew's early rejection, first of Christianity and then of the existence of God—he, like onetime atheist C. S. Lewis, was raised in a Christian home—was motivated in great part by his struggle with the problem of pain and his conviction that the existence of hell contradicted the Christian claim that God is good. Although he was aware of Lewis's apologetic writings on hell and the problem of pain, Flew chose not to follow Lewis in his acceptance of Christianity. Indeed, in 1950 he even defended his atheism at the Oxford Socratic Club, a group that provided an open forum for debating the integrity and intellectual soundness of Christianity in a modern, scientific age and that boasted Lewis as its president from 1942–1954.

I belabor the links between Flew and Lewis not only as a way of bringing my book full circle but because one cannot help but think of Lewis's spiritual autobiography, *Surprised by Joy*, while reading Flew's surprising account of his own long road to theism, *There Is a God: How the World's Most Notorious Atheist Changed His Mind*. Though Flew's autobiography lacks the psychological depth and literary flair of Lewis's, both books are equally rigorous in their logical dissection of the philosophical arguments that led them away from and then back toward a belief in God. As such it makes a fitting end to my study of modern apologetics.

## FOLLOWING THE ARGUMENT WHEREVER IT LEADS

From the very beginning of his book, Flew insists that his lifelong goal as a philosopher and as a man of intellectual integrity has been to live out Socrates' exhortation to "follow the argument wherever it leads." For most of his life, those arguments led him away from God. Though, Flew makes it clear, he never accepted the "rules" of logical positivism (rules that reject all arguments, including and especially metaphysical, supernatural claims, which are not based on observable facts), he did long consider the claims of theism, *as claims*, to be problematic.

Flew's first major contribution to philosophical atheism, and arguably his most enduring, came in the form of the paper that he presented to the Oxford Socratic Club and later published in a college journal: "Theology and Falsification." In his paper, Flew asked the following question: "Do the numerous qualifications surrounding theological utterances result in their dying the death by a thousand qualifications?" For example, when a Christian claims that God loves us, he must, to maintain that claim, make almost endless qualifications to accommodate all the evidence to the contrary. And so it went, Flew argued, for all major theological claims.

In *God and Philosophy* (1966) Flew built on his earlier work by propounding a "systematic argument for atheism . . . [contending] that our starting point should be the question of the consistency, applicability, and legitimacy of the very concept of God." By casting into doubt our ability to identify "God" in any real or positive way, Flew sought to dismantle—today we might say deconstruct—theistic arguments that claimed the ability to locate or define a noncorporeal being that inhabits neither time nor space. To bulwark his position further, Flew argued as well that the traditional "design, cosmological, and moral arguments for God's existence [were] invalid . . . [and] that it was impossible validly to infer from a particular religious experience that it had as its object a transcendent divine being."

The third major installment in his atheistic trilogy came in 1976 with *The Presumption of Atheism*. Here Flew continued to hold that the concept of God could not even be adequately explained, much less defended. In the absence of "good grounds" and "sufficient reason" for belief in God, Flew felt the only "reasonable position" was atheism.

By this period in his life, however, Flew was becoming increasingly open to the work of a growing cadre of theistic philosophers—Alvin Plantinga, William P. Alston, George Mavrodes, and Ralph McInerny, among others—who were willing to engage him on his own grounds. Flew had always been open to fair, honest debate and had never stooped to the kind of doctrinaire, triumphalist atheism that one encounters in Richard Dawkins and Christopher Hitchens. He found in the writings and arguments of these young theists an energy and subtlety of thought that he had not encountered before; he even struck up long, rewarding friendships with many of them.

Partly from his interactions with these new theists and partly from his lifelong commitment to follow the evidence, Flew came in time to see that human freedom is not an illusion or a statement without meaning but a reality. He also slowly softened his position on the presumption of atheism, as he came to understand and respect theistic arguments that presumed God's existence as being as logical, primary, and necessary as our belief in the existence of the world or of our own minds.

However, what really spurred on Flew's movement toward theism—and this is what makes his "defection" from atheism a doubly bitter pill for the modern czars of atheism to swallow—was his intense study of modern advances in *science*. None of the arguments that Flew makes in *There Is a God* rest upon divine revelation, and only a few rest on his "renewed study of the classical philosophical arguments" (understood as those of Aristotle rather than those of Augustine or Aquinas!).

No, insists Flew, his pilgrimage has been one "of reason and not of faith": "I now believe that the universe was brought into existence by an infinite Intelligence . . . [and] that this universe's intricate laws manifest what scientists have called the Mind of God . . . [because] this is the world picture, as I see it, that has emerged from modern science." In particular, Flew highlights and spends three chapters detailing how his belief in God rests on three dimensions of our physical world that could not have come about apart from a controlling Intelligence or divine Mind: nature's obeying laws, our being purpose-driven beings, and the fact that nature exists at all.

We live in a complex universe that runs in accordance with unified and stable laws, laws that modern scientists have not invented but discovered. These laws, writes Flew, "pose a problem for atheists because they are a voice of rationality heard through the mechanisms of matter." Likewise, the fact that we are conscious and purposeful beings militates against our having evolved solely out of unconscious, nonpurposeful matter. To the contrary, the fact that our universe and planet are finely tuned to make human life possible (the anthropic principle) suggests that the universe knew we were coming. When one adds to this the discovery that our universe had a beginning (the big bang), one is left with no logical recourse but to infer, if not the God of the Bible, at least the omnipotent, omniscient, omnipresent First Cause of Aristotle.

Flew was aware that the claims he makes in his book would be attacked—and, indeed, they have been attacked—by atheists who accuse him of meddling in scientific affairs for which he lacks specialized training. But Flew remains undaunted. Rather, he turns the challenge back against his critics, berating modern scientists for thinking that their scientific expertise legitimizes them to comment authoritatively and exclusively on the philosophical meaning of the physical data they have observed. To the contrary, it is the job of the philosopher to analyze the physical data to determine what they reveal about the fundamental questions of life.

And besides, demonstrates Flew through a series of carefully selected quotes from the writing of such scientific geniuses as Einstein, Heisenberg, Schrödinger, and Hawking, when the greatest scientists have considered the evidence, it has led them inevitably toward perceiving— not as men of faith but as men of science—"a connection between the laws of nature and the Mind of God." Flew even quotes Charles Darwin himself as attesting to the "extreme difficulty or rather impossibility of conceiving this immense and wonderful universe, including man with his capability of looking far backwards and far into futurity, as the result of blind chance or necessity."

As Flew nears the end of his memoir, he reiterates that none of his philosophical positions rests on revelation and that he himself has never received any form of communication from God. He does, however, grant the possibility of such a communication in the future, a possibility that enables him to conclude *There Is a God* with this final, haunting sentence: "Someday I might hear a Voice that says, 'Can you hear me now?'"

Considering the fact that C. S. Lewis did not proceed directly from atheism to Christianity but spent two interim years as a non-Christian theist, there is certainly reason to hope that Voice spoke to Antony Flew before his death in 2010.

## THE POWER OF TESTIMONY

The author of *There Is a God* writes not as a Christian but as a Deist, and yet his work attests to the apologetic power of a personal testimony. Though it has become bastardized by late-night infomercials for diet programs, acne medications, and Viagra rip-offs, the personal testimony has long functioned as one of the main vehicles for sharing the good news of Jesus Christ. In one way or another, all true testimonies attest to the transformative power of God, to his ability to renew us from within. To quote the best-loved hymn of all time, "Amazing Grace": "I once was lost but now am found / Was blind but now I see."

Christianity has drawn some of its greatest champions from atheists (Lewis, McDowell, Strobel), enemies (Paul), "big sinners" (Augustine), and even felons (Chuck Colson). Indeed, I would bet that everyone reading this book knows at least one person who was *radically* changed by coming to faith in Christ. I myself am friends with a fellow professor who went from being a Catholic-hating, white supremacist in Ireland to a devout Catholic with a warm and loving nature. In the majority of cases, those who experience these miraculous conversions do not morph into robots or prigs or anti-intellectuals, as Dawkins and Hitchens would have us believe, but are filled with a passion to serve others and to grow in their faith.

Contrary to popular opinion, God does not erase the personalities of those he saves or turn them into cookie-cutter Christians. Rather, he *redirects* the talents he has given them so that they might make a new and better use of their gifts. Witness, for example, how Peter's impulsive nature was rechanneled by God's spirit into a missionary zeal that ended with his martyrdom under emperor Nero. As for that other great missionary and martyr Paul, God found an exciting new use for Saul the

Pharisee's extensive knowledge of the Old Testament. Paul likely feared when he converted to Christianity that his years of "seminary" education had been all a waste—that is, until the Spirit set him the task of writing half of the New Testament and of demonstrating how Christ's ministry, death, and resurrection fulfilled the Old Testament Law and prophets.

Just as we cannot see the wind itself but can see its effects, so the invisible God is seen most clearly in the way he restores and renews broken lives. He is alive and still at work in the world.

If I may end with portions of my own testimony, what drew me to Christ was not so much Good Friday as Christmas. Though I was blessed with very good parents, I, like nearly all children, felt at many points in my childhood that my parents did not "understand" me and didn't care to try. As I matured, however, I realized that my parents could never truly understand me unless they could somehow switch places with me, get inside my skin—an observation that is also true for husbands and wives. One of the little epiphanies that turned me toward Christ was the realization that God really *did* understand me—and all people—for he actually became one of us. He didn't just study human anatomy or emotions; he *became* a human being in the fullest sense. Yes, he died for us, but just as important, he lived for us. Indeed, when I carried this insight from Christmas to Good Friday, I became convicted not so much by the pain of the cross, which was intense, as by the rejection, betrayal, and humiliation that God experienced on our behalf. Here at last, I realized with wonder and joy, was a Savior who really knew our pain and agony and despair—who really understood us from the inside!

In tandem with this realization came a second insight into a question that, as a future professor of English, had always troubled me when I read great literature, watched classic films, and pondered my own life. That question was simply this: How do I know, *really* know, that I am of value? All sorts of answers, I knew, could be offered in response to this question: because I am strong or handsome or talented or rich or athletic or a good parent. But all of those things, good as they are, can be taken away from us. A man might base his value on his job, but what if he loses his job? Does he cease to have value? A woman might base her value on having children. But what if she cannot have children, or she does have a child, but the child dies? Has she lost her value? I could rest my own value on my success in the classroom, but what if I lost my job, or lost my voice, or lost my memory? There needed to be a more solid foundation for value, or we were all destined to live our lives on shifting sand.

And then the answer came: the only solid foundation of human value—the only thing that cannot be taken away by accident, disease, or economic downturn—is to know fully and assuredly that our Creator thinks us valuable. And that, I found, was exactly what the Bible promised: "But God shows his love for us in that while we were still sinners [that is, when we were most unlovable], Christ died for us" (Romans 5:8). Only this promise, I decided, could offer a firm basis of value that neither rust nor moth could destroy, nor thief could steal.

As I bring this study of apologetics to a close, I leave those among you who are seekers on the road of faith with a question and a challenge. The question is this: If Christianity *were* true; what would it mean? Let me suggest four answers to this vital question:

1) Then there really *is* a God—not just a divine force but a *real, personal, involved* God who is active in the world and desires as well to be active in our lives.
2) Then God not only has love *within himself* (the Trinity) but desires that we *participate* in that love for eternity.
3) Then history, because God both directs it and entered into it, is *meaningful* and is moving toward a *good end*.
4) Then heaven is *real*—it is not just earth with all the stuff gone—and it promises an *expansion*, not a diminution, of life.

As for the challenge, I leave you with this charge: If you are trembling on the threshold of belief and want to know if you should "take the plunge," then don't take my word for it or the word of any other apologist. If you want to know for certain, then do the following: take up one of the four Gospels, pray this simple prayer ("Christ, if you are real, reveal yourself to me in a way I can understand"), and then read the Gospels from beginning to end. If God is indeed the Creator and Savior of the universe, then he can answer for himself.

May the God of Abraham, Isaac, and Jacob speed you on your way!

# APPENDICES

# TIMELINE

| | |
|---|---|
| 1908 | *Orthodoxy* (G. K. Chesterton) |
| 1925 | *The Everlasting Man* (G. K. Chesterton) |
| 1930 | *Who Moved the Stone?* (Frank Morison) |
| 1940 | *The Problem of Pain* (C. S. Lewis) |
| 1941 | *The Mind of the Maker* (Dorothy Sayers) |
| 1941–1944 | Lewis gives broadcast talks, later published as *Mere Christianity* |
| 1942 | *The Screwtape Letters* (C. S. Lewis) |
| 1943 | *The Abolition of Man* (C. S. Lewis) |
| 1943 | *The New Testament Documents: Are They Reliable?* (F. F. Bruce) |
| 1946 | *The Great Divorce* (C. S. Lewis) |
| 1947 | *Miracles* (C. S. Lewis) |
| 1952 | *Mere Christianity* (C. S. Lewis) |
| 1958 | *Basic Christianity* (John R. W. Stott) |
| 1961 | *A Grief Observed* (C. S. Lewis) |
| 1967 | *Know Why You Believe* (Paul Little) |
| 1968 | *Escape from Reason* (Francis Schaeffer) |
| 1968 | *The God Who Is There* (Francis Schaeffer) |
| 1972 | *Evidence That Demands a Verdict* (Josh McDowell) |
| 1974 | *God, Freedom, and Evil* (Alvin Plantinga) |
| 1977 | *More Than a Carpenter* (Josh McDowell) |
| 1981 | *Eternity in Their Hearts* (Don Richardson) |
| 1982 | *Between Heaven and Hell* (Peter Kreeft) |
| 1984 | *Reasonable Faith* (William Lane Craig) |
| 1985 | *He Is There and He Is Not Silent* (Francis Schaeffer) |
| 1987 | *Scaling the Secular City* (J. P. Moreland) |
| 1988 | *Christian Apologetics* (Norman Geisler) |
| 1991 | *Darwin on Trial* (Phillip E. Johnson) |
| 1994 | *Can Man Live Without God?* (Ravi Zacharias) |
| 1996 | *Darwin's Black Box* (Michael Behe) |

| 1996 | *The Historical Jesus* (Gary Habermas) |
| 1997 | *Jesus and the Victory of God* (N. T. Wright) |
| 1998 | *The Design Inference* (William Dembski) |
| 1998 | *The Case for Christ* (Lee Strobel) |
| 1999 | *How Now Shall We Live?* (Chuck Colson) |
| 2000 | *The Journey of Desire* (John Eldredge) |
| 2001 | *A New Kind of Christian* (Brian McLaren) |
| 2003 | *Blue Like Jazz* (Donald Miller) |
| 2003 | *The Da Vinci Code* (Dan Brown) |
| 2004 | *The Case for the Creator* (Lee Strobel) |
| 2004 | *The Twilight of Atheism* (Alister McGrath) |
| 2006 | *The Language of God* (Francis Collins) |
| 2006 | *Simply Christian* (N. T. Wright) |
| 2006 | *The God Delusion* (Richard Dawkins) |
| 2007 | *god is not Great* (Christopher Hitchens) |
| 2007 | *There Is a God* (Antony Flew) |
| 2007 | *What's So Great about Christianity* (Dinesh D'Souza) |
| 2008 | *The Reason for God* (Timothy Keller) |

# GLOSSARY

**Apologetics:** Apologetics offers a logical defense of the Christian faith. As well as focusing on such central issues as the existence of God, the deity of Christ, the historical accuracy of the Scriptures, the miracles of Jesus, and the resurrection, apologetics also seeks to answer difficult questions that keep people from faith: If God is all-loving and all-powerful, why is the world so filled with pain? How can a loving God condemn people to hell? How can Christians living in a pluralistic world claim that Christ is the only way to God? It also seeks to demonstrate the integrity and consistency of the Christian worldview. Though apologists do not claim we can reason ourselves into Christian faith, they do believe that faith can be a reasoned step rather than a leap into the void. Apologetics, which seeks to provide rational proofs for Christianity, should be distinguished from evangelism, which is the attempt to lead people to a personal decision for Jesus Christ.

**Argument by desire:** An argument for the existence of God made popular by C. S. Lewis. According to this argument, the fact that all people yearn for things that our natural, physical world cannot supply (or even "know" anything about) suggests that there must be a supernatural source that is the origin of the yearning. This argument runs counter to Freud's belief that such spiritual desires have their origins in unconscious, ultimately material forces.

**British School of Apologetics:** I use this somewhat loose term to refer to the apologetic works of **C. S. Lewis**, **G. K. Chesterton**, and **Dorothy Sayers**, all of which have a literary flavor, are Anglo-Catholic in orientation, and appeal to the imagination as well as to the reason. Five other British authors whose work also fits this category are: **George Macdonald** (1824–1905), a Scottish minister who published numerous fantasy and children's stories that are infused with a deep spirituality and a sense of the numinous; **Charles Williams** (1886–1945), an editor for Oxford University Press, an amateur scholar of Dante, Milton, and the Middle Ages, and an author of realistic mystical novels; **J. R. R. Tolkien** (1892–1973), an Oxford professor of Anglo-Saxon and author of the much-loved and critically acclaimed Lord of the Rings trilogy who played an instrumental role in Lewis's conversion; **Owen Barfield** (1898–1997), a philosopher of human consciousness who worked as a solicitor, was influenced by anthroposophy, and played an instrumental role in Lewis's conversion to theism; and **J. B. Phillips** (1906–1982), a minister and Bible translator who helped make the Bible and Christianity accessible to modern man. Lewis, Williams, Tolkien, and Barfield were all members of **the Inklings**, a group that met twice a week for discussion, fellowship, and the reading aloud of works in progress. Though the members were all male, Sayers sat in with the group on a few occasions. See the bibliography for a list of their works that have some bearing on modern apologetics.

**Emergent Church:** An umbrella term used to classify churches that have intentionally reached out to postmoderns. They usually downplay systematic doctrine in favor of a more authentic spirituality and try to emulate Christ by living communally and creatively in a world that has grown increasingly materialistic and mechanistic. **Brian McLaren** is one of the earliest spokesmen for the Emergent Church, though its values have found their way into the writings of **John Eldredge** and **Donald Miller**. More traditional apologists respect the Emergent Church's attempts to reach postmoderns and neo-pagans but have been troubled by its general lack of doctrinal rigidity.

**Heresy:** Any teaching that violates orthodox Christian teaching (see **Orthodoxy** below). Most of the major heresies involve a misunderstanding of the central doctrine of the incarnation. Thus **Arians**, on the one hand, teach that Jesus was a great and God-ordained man but was not himself fully divine, while **Gnostics**, on the other, teach that Jesus was divine but was not fully human (he only "wore" the flesh as a man might wear a shirt). The umbrella of Gnosticism includes the **Docetists** (from the Greek verb "to seem"), who said that Jesus only seemed to be human, and the **Manichees**, who followed an elaborate system by which to liberate spirit from matter. Gnosticism in general taught that the physical world was evil (or even an illusion) and that we should do all we can to sever our ties with the world and our own physical bodies. Gnostics (Greek for "knowers") believe salvation comes not from faith but from secret wisdom. Between (roughly) A.D. 150 and 350, a series of "knower" sects composed **Gnostic Gospels**, purportedly written by one of Jesus' followers, that depict Jesus as a Gnostic sage who speaks in esoteric maxims. It was the threat of heresy that impelled the church fathers to clarify and put in writing the Christian doctrines that were already widely held by the church.

**Historical Jesus:** Since the time of the Enlightenment, numerous attempts have been made by Western theologians of a liberal slant to discover "behind" the divine, miracle-working Jesus of the Gospels a more historically "accurate" Jesus. Fueled by the modern academic "distaste" for the supernatural, the various "quests" for the historical Jesus have presented a number of modern Christs (the Buddha-like sage, the modern cynic, the pacifist, the revolutionary, and so forth) who generally end up resembling the theologians themselves. Much of modern apologetics has centered around defending the historicity of the Gospels and attempting to demonstrate that the "Christ of Faith" is identical with the "Christ of History."

**Intelligent design (ID):** This movement within science and the philosophy of science argues that there is overwhelming evidence within nature that both we and our world were fashioned by a divine designer who transcends our space-time reality. Though often accused of being six-day creationists in disguise, ID theorists generally accept that the universe and our world are billions of years old. They merely contend that Darwinian evolution alone (undirected time and chance working via natural selection) cannot account for the world we see. They see no inconsistency in positing both fixed laws of nature and a God who intervenes in nature. Though ID remains controversial, even among Christians, more and more scientists have been willing to admit that the overwhelming evidence that our universe had a beginning (the big bang) and that it is fine-tuned to an almost infinite degree of precision (the anthropic principle) points strongly to some kind of intelligent Designer. Indeed, so strong is the evidence for the big bang and the anthropic principle that many scientists who are philosophically committed to naturalism have posited (without any proof) a rather outlandish theory that there are an infinite number of universes (the multiple universe or multiverse hypothesis), thus raising the chances for our finely tuned universe to come into being without the aid of a Designer.

**Liberalism:** Liberal theologians (*not* to be confused with liberal politicians or economists) tend to take a nonsupernatural approach to Scripture and to emphasize Jesus the teacher and social reformer over Jesus the incarnate Son of God. For such theologians, the ultimate test of truth is not revelation (the Bible and the creeds of the church) but reason; or to put it another way, doctrines are not God-revealed, eternal truths that the church has preserved but man-made theories put forth by theologians whose cultural baggage and moral tastes are not our own.

**Logical arguments for the existence of God:** Logic either works *inductively* (by accumulating evidence and then working up to a general hypothesis) or *deductively* (working downward from general principles and assumptions to a specific conclusion: All men are mortal; Socrates is a man; therefore, Socrates is mortal). Throughout most of this book, I take an inductive approach; however, several of the classic arguments for the existence of God work deductively from generally accepted premises. The **ontological argument** works downward from a definition of God as that being than which there is none greater to the conclusion that such a being must include existence as one of its attributes. The **cosmological argument** begins with the premise that there must be a First Principle or all will be subject to infinite regress, then theorizes that our contingent status—the fact that we do not possess life within ourselves and that there was a time when we did not exist—demands a first cause (that is, nothing can come out of nothing). The **Kalam or cosmological argument** begins with the premise that whatever begins to exist must have a cause and then theorizes that since the universe came into existence, it must have a cause that is outside time and space and thus is omnipresent and eternal. The **teleological argument** states that the fact that our universe (like a watch) appears to be designed and to have a specific purpose demands the existence of a Designer. Apologists also refer to a **moral argument** for the existence of God; Lewis's discussion of the **Tao** (see entry below) offers one of the most recent statements of this argument.

**Orthodoxy:** The main tenets of Christian orthodoxy, laid forth in the Nicene Creed, are the *incarnation* (the belief that Jesus Christ was fully man and fully God), the *Trinity* (the belief that God is one but exists eternally as three persons—the Father, the Son, and the Holy Spirit), *original sin* (the belief that man is fallen and cannot "earn" his salvation apart from God's grace), *the atonement* (the belief that Christ's death on the cross restored us to a right relationship with God), *the resurrection* (the belief that Jesus rose bodily from the dead), *the second coming* (the belief that Christ will return again), and *the authority of Scripture* (the belief that the Bible is the Word of God and that, like Jesus, it is fully divine and fully human).

**Presuppositionalism:** A form of apologetics strongly linked to Cornelius Van Til and to Reformed Calvinism that insists apologetics be grounded on Scripture as the ultimate source of truth and logic rather than on "neutral" grounds that (regenerate) believers and (unregenerate) nonbelievers share. This school of apologetics is generally contrasted with **evidentialism**, which begins by establishing common ground between believers and nonbelievers. They do so by appealing to reason and the natural law, as well as to our shared spiritual longings. **Classical apologetics** also seeks common ground but takes a more logical approach than evidentialism, which tends to accumulate evidence in a less rigidly systematic manner. Mainstream, popular apologists from Lewis to McDowell to Strobel tend to follow the methods of evidentialism or classicalism. Francis Schaeffer, however, was, at least in part, a presuppositionalist.

**The problem of pain:** Classical theism states that God is both all-powerful (omnipotent) and all-loving; yet the existence of pain, suffering, and evil in our world suggests that God is either not powerful enough to prevent it or not caring enough to eliminate it. That, in a nutshell, is the problem of pain, and it remains, to this day, the strongest argument against the existence of the biblical God and arguably the most common reason why people reject Christianity. A theologian, poet, or apologist who constructs a *theodicy* (formed from the Greek words for "God" and "justice") attempts to exonerate God from the charge that he (rather than our own misuse of free will) is the origin of evil and is therefore an unjust God. The book of Job, *The Divine Comedy*, *Paradise Lost*, and C. S. Lewis's *The Problem of Pain* are all theodicies.

**Tao:** Lewis used this word to refer to the universal, cross-cultural moral code that all people share and that they feel compelled to obey. The Tao serves as the *tertium quid* (Latin for "third thing") that allows us to judge between two actions or instincts. Lewis argues that the source of this moral code must be supernatural and that it could only have been written into our consciences by a divine director. As moral/ethical creatures we know that we ought to follow the Tao but find that we cannot; hence, the need for God to intervene in Christ and bring us back into a right relationship with the Tao and with God himself. Lewis's understanding of the Tao is essentially the same as the traditionally Catholic understanding of *natural law*.

**Theism:** A theist believes in a single God who transcends nature and is perfectly good, but he does not necessarily believe (as Christians do) that God is triune and that Christ was the incarnate Son of God. **Unitarians** are theists who deny the Trinity. **Deists** are also theists, but they posit a God who is uninvolved in history and the basic workings of nature. Theism is to be contrasted with **pantheism**, which teaches that God is immanent in nature and is neither good nor evil, and **dualism**, which teaches that two equally transcendent gods exist—one good, one evil.

**Trilemma:** According to the trilemma made popular by Lewis's *Mere Christianity*, the fact that Christ made claims to be equal with God allows us only three options: either Christ was who he said he was (the Son of God), or he was a deceiver, or he was insane. Since even the greatest critics of Christianity will not accept the latter two options, we must logically embrace the first option—that he was, in fact, who he claimed to be. The thing we cannot say about Christ is what the modern world wants to say— that he was a good moral teacher but not the Son of God. This apologetic argument is also known as the liar, lunatic, Lord argument.

# WHO'S WHO

In keeping with the focus of this book, the names and works that appear here and in the bibliography will reflect orthodox apologists who both defend the traditional creeds of the church and the authority of Scripture and who write for a lay audience. The only exceptions to this are the four major "new atheists" (Richard Dawkins, Christopher Hitchens, Daniel Dennett, and Sam Harris), who appear here and/or in the bibliography/ timeline, and the philosopher-apologist Alvin Plantinga. A list of more academic philosophers/apologists who write in the mode of Plantinga would include William Alston, Kenneth Boa, Paul Davies, Stuart Hackett, John Leslie, George Mavrodes, Ralph McInerny, Alexander Pruss, and Richard Swinburne. A list of prominent liberal theologians and scholars against whom much modern apologetics is directed would include Karen Armstrong, Marcus Borg, John Dominic Crossan, Bart Ehrman, Robert Funk, Elaine Pagels, James Robinson, and John Shelby Spong. A list of influential modern skeptics whose voices come from outside the church would include Joseph Campbell, Antony Flew (*before* his 2004 conversion to theism), Sigmund Freud, Stephen Jay Gould, John Hick, Aldous and Julian Huxley (grandsons of Darwin's bulldog and a founding father of secular humanism, T. H. Huxley), Carl Jung, Karl Marx, Kai Nielsen, Friedrich Nietzsche, Steven Pinker, Michael Ruse, Bertrand Russell, Carl Sagan, Jean-Paul Sartre, George Bernard Shaw, Peter Singer, Victor Stenger, Charles Templeton, H. G. Wells, and A. N. Wilson (until his return to Christian faith in the spring of 2009).

**Michael Behe** (born 1952): This American biochemistry professor at Lehigh University has been the key scientific voice of the intelligent design movement. His major contribution has been to investigate cellular "machines" that are irreducibly complex: that is, they could not have evolved piece by piece by Darwinian natural selection.

**F. F. Bruce** (1910–1990): Born in Scotland, this British professor of Greek, biblical history, and biblical criticism wrote a number of scholarly and popular books defending the authenticity of Scripture against modern higher criticism. Something of a lone voice within the academy during his day, Bruce would have been pleased by the growing number of scholars today who accept the reliability of the biblical record (even if they don't personally believe its claims).

**G. K. Chesterton** (1874–1936): Best known for his Father Brown detective series, this portly and prolific British writer wrote books and essays on every conceivable topic, from politics to literary theory to art to biography to history, and was an accomplished novelist and poet as well. Known as the apostle of common sense, his witty and forceful works of apologetics kept contemporary skeptics on their toes—Chesterton even faced off with George Bernard Shaw in a series of public debates—and played a major role in the conversion of C. S. Lewis. After spending many years as an Anglo-Catholic, Chesterton converted to Catholicism. Chesterton's famous prose style, partly inherited by Lewis, includes such distinctive features as a heavy use of irony to deflate modern arrogance, sudden twists of thought that take the reader by surprise and force him to rethink accepted social norms and opinions, a relentless logic that traces every claim back to its presuppositions, and a love of, if not an obsession with, paradox.

**Francis Collins** (born 1950): This celebrated American geneticist and director of the Human Genome Project is also a committed Christian who has argued forcefully that science and religion need not be antagonistic.

**Chuck Colson** (born 1931): Chief counsel to President Richard Nixon who, while doing prison time after the Watergate scandal, read Lewis's *Mere Christianity* and converted to Christianity. After being set free, he went on to found and run Prison Fellowship and to be a powerful critic of the modern secular humanist worldview.

**William Lane Craig** (born 1949): American professor and writer who is equally adept at philosophy, theology, and biblical criticism. His writings have helped bridge the gap between academic and popular apologetics and to promote an integrated Christian worldview.

**Richard Dawkins** (born 1941): British biologist and defender of Darwinian evolution who has in many ways taken up the mantle of Carl Sagan. His scholarly yet still accessible works of popular science have both defended atheism and strongly criticized intelligent design.

**William Dembski** (born 1960): An American philosopher and one of the leaders of the intelligent design movement, Dembski's controversial design inference and his fearless criticism of Darwinian orthodoxy have caused much controversy not only in the secular world but in Christian universities.

**Dinesh D'Souza** (born 1961): Born in India, D'Souza is best known as a politically conservative writer and speaker; however, his bold apologetic challenge to the new atheists, *What's So Great about Christianity*, catapulted him into the ranks of a foremost apologist.

**Antony Flew** (born 1923–2010): Long regarded as one of the foremost philosophers of atheism, this British professor who heard Lewis debate with atheists at Oxford and who himself taught at Oxford shocked the philosophical world when he announced (in 2004) that he now believes in the existence of God.

**Norman Geisler** (born 1932): American professor of philosophy who has unflaggingly written, spoken, and debated apologetics for half a century. He is also an accomplished theologian and Bible scholar.

**Gary Habermas** (born 1950): This Distinguished Professor of Apologetics and Philosophy at Liberty University (Lynchburg, Virginia) has been a forceful apologist for the historical reliability of the Gospels, the claims of Christ, and the resurrection.

**Christopher Hitchens** (born 1949): English-born American journalist who helped kick off the new atheism with his feisty and controversial *god is not Great*.

**Phillip E. Johnson** (born 1940): Longtime professor of law at UC Berkley, Johnson is the father of the intelligent design movement. Though not formally trained in science, he used his legal skills and knowledge to mount a powerful case against Darwinian theory.

**Timothy Keller** (born 1950): Charismatic pastor of New York's Redeemer Presbyterian Church who may turn out to be one of the most effective apologists of the twenty-first century.

**Peter Kreeft** (born 1938): Long a philosophy professor at Boston College, Kreeft wears well the mantle of such classic apologists as Lewis and Chesterton. A convert from Calvinism to Catholicism, Kreeft's apologetics honors the "mere" Christianity approach of Lewis and appeals to Christians of all denominations. Often employing the method of Socratic dialogue to make his apologetic case, Kreeft is skilled at making difficult philosophical concepts both real and understandable. He has also written seminal studies of Pascal and of Aquinas's *Summa*.

**C. S. Lewis** (1898–1963): Born and raised in Belfast, Northern Ireland, but more commonly identified with Oxford and Cambridge, this Oxbridge English professor is, without dispute, the greatest Christian apologist of the twentieth century. Indeed, it is no exaggeration to say that *every* apologist after him has been influenced in some way by Lewis's work. Though Lewis was a longtime atheist who did not convert to Christianity until he was thirty-two, he spent the next thirty-two years of his life defending the faith in a series of timeless classics. Whether discussing theism, ethics, myth, miracles, hell, the problem of pain, or the claims of Christ, Lewis brought a fresh and invigorating perspective to the discipline of apologetics. Even his fantasy novels for children and his scholarly works are imbued with a Christian worldview.

**Paul E. Little** (1928–1975): An American professor of evangelism who worked for twenty-five years with InterVarsity Christian Fellowship. He played an important role in promoting apologetics on college campuses.

**Josh McDowell** (born 1939): One of the architects of modern American Christian apologetics, McDowell converted from atheism to Christianity during his college years, a result of his determination to investigate (in order to disprove) the claims of Christ. McDowell has long been associated with Campus Crusade for Christ and has been equally effective as a rational apologist, an engaging evangelist on college campuses, and a counselor for teens who desire to live a life of sexual and ethical purity in the midst of a sexualized and relativistic society.

**Alister McGrath** (born 1953): Born (like Lewis) in Belfast, Northern Ireland, McGrath is trained in both science and theology and has shown himself equally adept in the arenas of academic and popular apologetics. He also combines in his writing a broad apologetic vision that can speak both to moderns and postmoderns. Most recently, he has been a strong critic of the new atheism.

**J. P. Moreland** (born 1948): American philosopher and theologian and Distinguished Professor of Philosophy at Biola University—which offers one of the finest apologetics degrees in the world—Moreland has been a powerful critic of the worldview of naturalism.

**Frank Morison** (1881–1950): A British journalist who set out to disprove the Resurrection and ended up believing it instead. Born Albert Henry Ross, he took Morison as a pseudonym.

**Alvin Plantinga** (born 1932): Considered by many to be one of the foremost living philosphers, this American professor of philosophy has been instrumental in making theism respectable once again within the walls of secular academia and, in great part, laying to rest the problem of pain as a default argument against the existence of God. He has been a great inspiration to a growing number of Christian philosophers working within the academy.

**Don Richardson** (born 1935): American missionary whose work with unreached tribal groups in New Guinea first alerted him to a startling phenomenon: the God of the Bible has left himself a witness in even the most remote tribal groups.

**Dorothy Sayers** (1893–1957): Best known for her Lord Peter Wimsey detective series, this British writer shared the wide range of interests evident in the work of Lewis and Chesterton. In addition to her genial and original works of apologetics—which balance a literary playfulness with a firm defense of doctrinal orthodoxy—Sayers translated Dante's *Divine Comedy* and wrote a series of radio plays based on the life of Christ. She was something of a national institution.

**Francis Schaeffer** (1912–1984): An American apologist and evangelist of Reformed background who yet maintained something of a European air. Schaeffer was one of those rare intellectuals who was able to speak to the disillusioned 1960s generation and get them to challenge their prejudiced views of Christianity and the Western tradition. His thorough (if at times simplistic) knowledge of the philosophical roots of modernism is evident in all his work. Together with his wife, Edith, Schaeffer founded a Christian commune in the Swiss Alps (L'Abri) where young people could go to devote themselves to serious meditation, prayer, the study of philosophy, and vigorous dialogue. Schaeffer is also considered one of the architects of the "Religious Right" movement; his work helped galvanize Christians to fight against abortion and other life issues. Long before Pope John Paul II criticized the modern "culture of death," Schaeffer had shown the links between such things as abortion and euthanasia.

**John R. W. Stott** (born 1921): Highly prolific Anglican minister and longtime Rector Emeritus at All Souls Church in London, England. In addition to his apologetics, Stott speaks all over the world and has been instrumental in engaging the modern world with the ethical and philosophical standards laid down by Christianity.

**Lee Strobel** (born 1952): After this longtime American journalist at the *Chicago Tribune* and student of law at Yale converted from atheism to Christianity, he rechanneled his prodigious skills to become the finest living popular apologist. All of his highly regarded "Case for" books are structured around a series of interviews with key believers working in various fields (usually in academia). Strobel has also served as a teaching pastor at Willow Creek Community Church, a megachurch that reaches out to unchurched skeptics and seekers.

**N. T. Wright** (born 1948): This British Anglican minister and professor became the Bishop of Durham in 2003. He is a prolific writer of both scholarly and popular works and has been a major player in defending the historical reliability of the Gospels and the claims of Christ. He is author of a magisterial trilogy: *Christian Origins and the Question of God*.

**Ravi Zacharias** (born 1946): Born in India, Zacharias has worked in Canada, America, and England as an apologist and evangelist. His non-Western background has made him particularly sensitive to the worldview differences between Christianity and Eastern philosophy and religion, and he has been a strong voice in defending the exclusivity of the claims of Christ.

# ANNOTATED BIBLIOGRAPHY

In this bibliography, * denotes essential reading.

## C. S. LEWIS

Those interested in Lewis's apologetics will be happy to know that in 2007 HarperCollins published an inexpensive paperback that includes all seven of Lewis's major apologetic works: *The Complete C. S. Lewis Signature Classics* (HarperCollins also continues to publish each of these books individually):

*Mere Christianity*. Lewis's most popular and forthright apologetic work. It is actually a compilation of three shorter works (*Broadcast Talks*, *Christian Behaviour*, and *Beyond Personality*), most of which were first delivered by Lewis on the radio during the dark days of World War II. Here Lewis sets forth his reasons why the embracing of Christianity need not be a "leap of faith" that has no rational or logical grounds. With great wit and style, Lewis cuts through all the jargon and shoddy thinking that has accumulated around Christianity—both from liberal theologians within the faith and from naturalists and relativists outside of it—and presents the gospel in its original, creedal form. Even the most inveterate atheist cannot help but be enamored of this book. One of the most important works of Christian apologetics ever written, it has directly influenced nearly every other apologist since.

*The Screwtape Letters*. Arguably Lewis's most entertaining and accessible work, it presents itself as a series of letters that Screwtape (a senior devil) sends to his nephew Wormwood (a junior devil) to educate him in the fine art of temptation. Though not as clearly a work of apologetics as *Mere Christianity* or *The Problem of Pain*, it helps modern skeptics grasp both the theological and psychological reality of devils, sin, and temptation.

*The Great Divorce*. The premise of this, my favorite work by Lewis, is that the inhabitants of hell may, if they wish, travel to heaven on holiday. There they are greeted by the souls of the blessed who attempt to convince them, even now, to give up their sin and sorrow and embrace the forgiveness and grace of Christ. A brilliant answer to the perennial question of how a loving God can condemn people to hell, this book shows how damned souls, both theologically and psychologically, choose to live apart from God in hell.

*The Problem of Pain.* In this, his first major work of apologetics, Lewis offers some incisive and thought-provoking answers to this age-old question. Concerned not just with pain but with the origin of evil, Lewis propounds an intriguing thesis that God had to make the world the way he did, with all its potential for pain and sorrow, to ensure the reality of our freedom of will. This book should be read in conjunction with *A Grief Observed*.

*Miracles.* In this difficult but still accessible work, Lewis carries his rational apologetics into the field of miracles. Through a series of arguments, Lewis attempts both to topple modern naturalism and to pave the way for a reasonable faith in the possibility and reality of the supernatural (and the miracles that follow from it).

*A Grief Observed.* Written in the weeks following the death of his wife, this offers a brutally honest wrestling with the problem of pain. Unlike the book of that name—which is logical, systematic, and removed in its approach—this book is emotional, anecdotal, and personal. It chronicles a deep, almost existential despair that slowly resolves itself into a re-found faith.

*The Abolition of Man.* Though more a work of social commentary, this book is vital in terms of Lewis's apologetics because of its incisive critique of the modernist (Enlightenment) worldview and because it introduces the word *Tao* to refer to the universal moral code. It also includes a lengthy appendix in which Lewis offers a cross-cultural list of ethical statements culled from the main philosophical and religious texts of the past to show that the moral impetus behind the Ten Commandments and the Sermon on the Mount is not unique or relative but forms a central core of accepted, *a priori* values (the Tao) that undergird our moral standards and behavior.

Other Lewis works important to Christian apologetics include:

The Chronicles of Narnia (available in numerous editions—singularly, in boxed sets, and in a one-volume paperback edition published by HarperCollins in 2001). Though not meant as works of Christian apologetics, these beloved children's novels help not only to embody the numinous power of Christ but to critique various aspects of modernism's rejection of the Christian worldview. Two other novels by Lewis that have an apologetic edge to them are *Perelandra* (Macmillan, 1978; replays the temptation of Eve on Venus and, by so doing, raises issues relative to the origin of evil and the problem of pain) and *Till We Have Faces* (Harcourt Brace, 1980; retells an ancient pagan myth in such a way that it points forward to the fuller revelation of Christ to come).

"On Obstinacy in Belief," in *The World's Last Night and Other Essays* (HBJ, 1960). A thoughtful essay on the true nature of belief and faith that offers insight into the problem of pain.

*Reflections on the Psalms* (Harvest Books, 1964). Though not a work of apologetics, this book ends with Lewis's great defense of the immortality of the soul, and it includes an excellent chapter on the prophetic meanings in the Psalms.

*Surprised by Joy: The Shape of My Early Life* (Harcourt Brace, 1966). Lewis's spiritual autobiography traces how, in seeking a final object for his early experiences of joy, he found his way into the harbor of orthodox Christianity. As a work of apologetic autobiography tracing how an intellectual came to accept both the simple gospel and the deep profundities of Christian theology, it offers a twentieth-century version of Augustine's *Confessions*.

*The Pilgrim's Regress: An Allegorical Apology for Christianity, Reason, and Romanticism* (Eerdmans, 1981). In the year following his conversion, Lewis also wrote an allegorical account of his journey to faith. Modeled after Bunyan's *Pilgrim's Progress*, it follows Lewis's persona (John) as he travels from the legalistic Puritania to true Christianity. He is led on his journey by an unaccountable sense of joy (or desire) for which he can find no true fulfillment. In seeking the proper source and end of this joy (Christ and heaven), John takes many wrong turns, falling into such philosophical dead ends as hedonism, stoicism, idealism, materialism, and scientism. A very difficult work that expects its readers to have a firm grasp of the many intellectual "isms" of the last century.

*God in the Dock: Essays on Theology and Ethics* (Eerdmans, 1970). Of the many essay collections published during and after Lewis's death, this one is most slanted toward apologetics. It contains a brilliant essay on miracles ("Miracles") and on Jesus as the true myth ("Myth Became Fact"), as well as several more that sound the full depth of the ongoing debate between science and religion, naturalism and supernaturalism. But beware: many of the essays cover the same ground, often in the same words, as *Mere Christianity*, *The Problem of Pain*, and especially *Miracles*.

*The Weight of Glory and Other Addresses* (Macmillan, 1980). The title essay and "Transpositions" offer two of Lewis's fullest reflections on and apologies for the Christian understanding of heaven. The first explains why Christians are not mercenary for seeking heaven; the second fleshes out Lewis's central notion of joy and his antinaturalist, anti-Freudian belief that lower things are reflections of higher things, and not vice versa.

Although this bibliography will keep its focus on primary material, Lewis's status as the major apologist of the twentieth century merits the mention of several secondary sources:

Carnell, Corbin Scott. *Bright Shadow of Reality: C. S. Lewis and the Feeling Intellect*. Eerdmans, 1974. One of the best early books on Lewis and a solid study of his early experiences of joy and how they influenced his apologetic argument by desire.

Holmer, Paul L. *C. S. Lewis: The Shape of His Faith and Thought*. Harper & Row, 1976. One of the finest early assessments of Lewis's work that draws together Lewis the apologist with Lewis the fiction writer, academic, and proponent of classical virtue.

Jacobs, Alan. *The Narnian: The Life and Imagination of C. S. Lewis.* HarperCollins, 2005. Does a wonderful job exploring the apologetic dimensions of Lewis's fiction but unfortunately downplays his rational apologetics. Still, this is the best of the new crop of Lewis biographies.

*Lindsley, Art. *C. S. Lewis's Case for Christ: Insights from Reason, Imagination and Faith.* IVP, 2005. An accessible overview of Lewis's apologetic arguments that is also a practical guide for modern apologists. Lindsley demonstrates that if we combine the many and diverse books written by C. S. Lewis, we can construct a multifaceted apologetic that can speak to a wide array of seekers. Lindsley cleverly bookends each of his chapters with a hypothetical class on the life and writings of C. S. Lewis—a class whose participants include a Christian, an atheist, a New Age universalist, and a woman for whom religion is mostly an emotional experience. We get to eavesdrop on their thoughts on such topics as miracles and morality, rationalism and relativism, the problem of pain, and the relationship between myth and Christianity before moving on to survey what Lewis had to say on these topics.

Markos, Louis. *From Achilles to Christ: Why Christians Should Read the Pagan Classics.* IVP, 2007. In the introduction and conclusion to this book I discuss Lewis's notion of Jesus as the myth made fact and argue that Christianity is the only complete truth.

*Markos, Louis. *Lewis Agonistes: How C. S. Lewis Can Train Us to Wrestle with the Modern and Postmodern World.* Broadman & Holman, 2003. In this book I carry on Lewis's apologetic efforts by using his books and arguments as tools for wrestling with such issues as science, the New Age, the problem of pain, heaven and hell, and deconstruction in the arts.

*Markos, Louis. *The Life and Writings of C. S. Lewis.* In this twelve-lecture series I produced with the Teaching Company in 2000, I offer an overview of Lewis's life and all his major fictional and nonfictional works. The course guide includes a lengthy annotated bibliography.

*Nicholi, Armand. *The Question of God: C. S. Lewis and Sigmund Freud Debate God, Love, Sex, and the Meaning of Life.* Free Press, 2002. Based on a popular class taught by Dr. Nicholi at Harvard, this book brilliantly delivers on its subtitle. It was later followed by a two-part PBS special (*The Question of God*) that alternates back and forth between footage that compares and contrasts the biographies and beliefs of C. S. Lewis and Sigmund Freud and a no-holds-barred roundtable discussion of the issues raised by the works of Lewis and Freud. As might be expected, the participants in the discussion represent every possible stratum of belief and nonbelief. Both book and series (available on DVD from PBS) are highly recommended.

Purtill, Richard C. *C. S. Lewis's Case for the Christian Faith.* Harper & Row,

1981. A standard study of Lewis the apologist; makes a good companion to *Mere Christianity*.

Reppert, Victor. *C. S. Lewis's Dangerous Idea: In Defense of the Argument from Reason*. IVP, 2003. An important overview and defense of Lewis's apologetics.

*Sayer, George. *Jack: A Life of C. S. Lewis*. Crossway Books, 1994 (originally published in 1988 under the title, *Jack: C. S. Lewis and His Times*). Still the best biography by a onetime pupil and longtime friend of C. S. Lewis's that combines personal insight and great respect with critical objectivity and a willingness to find flaws.

Vaus, Will. *Mere Theology: A Guide to the Thought of C. S. Lewis*. IVP, 2004. A very accessible overview of Lewis's thought on a number of issues from Creation and the fall to faith and morality to the person and work of Christ to the Trinity.

Walsh, Chad. *C. S. Lewis: Apostle to the Skeptics*. Macmillan, 1949. One of the earliest assessments of Lewis as apologist.

## G. K. CHESTERTON

*Orthodoxy: The Romance of Faith*. Image Books, 1959. Chesterton's masterpiece that demands multiple readings and that champions both the romance and the reality of a creed-based Christianity. Written before Chesterton's conversion to Catholicism (*The Everlasting Man* was written after), this book seems to have convinced Chesterton himself that the firm doctrinal stance of the Catholic Church was one of its assets.

*The Everlasting Man*. Image Books, 1955. A somewhat more difficult work than *Orthodoxy* that offers what amounts to a Christian outline of history. It begins with a much-needed refutation of that rather silly invention of evolutionary anthropology, the caveman, continues by dividing the pre-Christian world into philosophers and myth-makers and into good pagans (Rome) and bad pagans (Carthage), and concludes by showing how the Church synthesized all that came before it and protected orthodox doctrine from its many enemies. This book played a vital role in the conversion of C. S. Lewis.

*St. Francis of Assisi* (Image Books, 1957) and *Saint Thomas Aquinas: The Dumb Ox* (Image Books, 1956). These two brief but incisive biographies by Chesterton offer a genial Christian humanist perspective that helps readers today understand these two medieval saints (and apologists!) on their own terms.

*What's Wrong with the World*. Ignatius, 1994. Like Lewis's *Abolition of Man*, this is more social commentary than apologetics, but Chesterton's reflections on imperialism, feminism, education, and the state shed light on the often skewed values of modern man.

Lovers of Chesterton will be happy to know that Ignatius Press has published *The Collected Works of G. K. Chesterton* in a number of nicely laid out, inexpensive volumes. Volume 1 includes *Orthodoxy* together with an earlier apologetic work (*Heretics*) that sets the groundwork for *Orthodoxy* as well as the public controversies that led to his writing of *Heretics*. Volume 2 (1986; well worth purchasing) offers the biographies of Saints Francis and Thomas together with *The Everlasting Man*. Volume 3 (1990) offers Chesterton's more specific defenses of the Catholic Church.

## DOROTHY SAYERS

*The Mind of the Maker*. Harper & Row, 1987. One of the most original defenses of the Trinity ever written, this book provides a rare glimpse into the mind of the divine Maker by examining closely the minds of human makers. It also offers unique insight into the nature of free will and the origin of evil.

*The Whimsical Christian*. Macmillan, 1978. This excellent collection of eighteen essays offers selections from all of Sayers's apologetic writings. In such essays as "The Dogma Is the Drama," "What Do We Believe?" and "Creed or Chaos?" Sayers provides a much-needed defense of dogma, showing (à la Chesterton) that orthodoxy is vital and dramatic.

*The Man Born to Be King*. Ignatius, 1990. This is the script for a series of radio plays that Sayers wrote for the BBC on the life of Christ. They offer deep insight into both the divinity and humanity of Christ.

*Divine Comedy: Hell*. London: Penguin, 1950. Sayers's fine translation of Dante's *Divine Comedy* (*Purgatory* followed in 1955, and *Paradise* was published posthumously in 1962, with Barbara Reynolds completing the parts left unfinished at Sayers's death) along with her excellent notes help bring Dante's medieval vision and his Christian orthodoxy to life.

## OTHER BRITISH APOLOGISTS

In the entry "British School of Apologetics" in the glossary, I identified five other British writers who, though not technically apologists, wrote works that complement those of Lewis, Chesterton, and Sayers. Here is a work or two from each of them that readers may wish to consult:

Macdonald, George. *Phantastes*. Eerdmans, 1981. When Lewis read this book, it baptized his imagination with a sense of the holy and the numinous. Like Lewis's Chronicles of Narnia, both this novel and *Lilith* (also published by Eerdmans in 1981) powerfully embody a Christian worldview sure to awaken a spiritual sense in the most confirmed naturalist.

Lewis himself edited *George MacDonald: An Anthology* (Collins, 1983). This collection gives insight into how directly and forcefully Macdonald influenced Lewis's approach to apologetics. Lewis himself once said that he never wrote a book in which he did not quote Macdonald.

Tolkien, J. R. R. "On Fairy-Stories," anthologized in *A Tolkien Miscellany*.

Quality Paperback Book Club, 2002. Originally published as part of *Tree and Leaf*, this extended critical essay offers profound insight into the nature of fantasy. In the epilogue, Tolkien describes Christianity as a true myth, a belief that, when he shared it with Lewis, helped push the doubting Lewis into a full belief in Christ. It also served as a cornerstone of Lewis's apologetics.

Tolkien's Lord of the Rings (available in numerous editions), like Lewis's and Madonald's fiction, embodies a rich Christian worldview, though it carefully steers clear of Christian allegory. His *Silmarillion* (also available in numerous editions) has a clearer Christian structure and offers deep insight into the origin of evil.

Williams, Charles. *The Place of the Lion*. Eerdmans, 1976. Many critics believe this Platonic Christian novel may have influenced the character of Aslan in the Chronicles. Certainly Williams's blend of fantasy and Christian allegory had a profound impact on Lewis, as did his belief that desire can lead us to God. Other Williams novels that may be read in conjunction with Lewis's "fictional apologetics" are *War in Heaven* (Eerdmans, 1991; about a modern-day search for the Holy Grail) and *Many Dimensions* (Eerdmans, 1993; a study of evil).

*Williams, Charles. *The Descent of the Dove: The History of the Holy Spirit in the Church*. Meridian Books, 1956. This fascinating history of the church is best read in conjunction with Chesterton's *The Everlasting Man*. Williams explains from a unique perspective the formation of Christian doctrine and how the church balanced asceticism with an affirmation of images and of the flesh. Like all the British apologists, he is an apologist for the Middle Ages.

Barfield, Owen. *Saving the Appearances*, second edition. Wesleyan University Press, 1988. This book offers in part an apologetic for a more medieval way of viewing ourselves and nature that exerted much influence on Lewis. Barfield was the one who taught Lewis to break down "chronological snobbery" in his writing and in himself.

*Phillips, J. B. *Your God Is Too Small*. Touchstone, 2004. This brief but incisive work of apologetics helps modern readers believe in Christ by distinguishing the real Christ of the Gospels from the meek and mild savior to which he has been reduced.

Here are three additional resources:

Macdonald, Michael H., and Andrew A. Tadie. *G. K. Chesterton and C. S. Lewis: The Riddle of Joy*. Collins, 1989. A fine collection of essays on Chesterton and Lewis that takes both a personal look at the men themselves and a more scholarly look at their fiction and apologetics. It includes Peter Kreeft's "C. S. Lewis's Argument from Desire," a seminal study of what may be Lewis's strongest apologetic. In 1995 Macdonald and Tadie edited, for Eerdmans, another collection of essays with the provocative title, *Permanent Things: Toward the Recovery of a More Human Scale at the End of the Twentieth Century*. In addition to offering more incisive essays on Lewis and Chesterton, it includes considerations of Evelyn Waugh, T. S. Eliot, and Dorothy Sayers.

The story of Lewis's marriage to Joy Davidman Gresham, her subsequent death from cancer, and his grieving process that culminated in *A Grief Observed* is powerfully told in a British made-for-TV movie, *\*Shadowlands* (1985; aka *C. S. Lewis: Through the Shadowlands*), written by William Nicholson, directed by Norman Stone, and starring Joss Ackland and Claire Bloom. In 1993 it was remade into a major film of the same name (the script again was by Nicholson, who had earlier turned his TV script into a play), directed by Richard Attenborough, and starring Anthony Hopkins and Debra Winger. Both versions are well worth seeing, but the TV version is more faithful to Lewis's and Joy's Christian beliefs and, most important of all, incorporates large sections of *A Grief Observed* into the script (most of these are dropped in the film version).

If you are ever in the vicinity of Wheaton College (Wheaton is a suburb of Chicago), make sure to visit the *Marion E. Wade Collection*, home of Lewis's original manuscripts, letters, and papers. The collection specializes not only in Lewis but in Macdonald, Chesterton, Tolkien, Williams, Barfield, and Sayers. It even publishes a very fine journal devoted to the seven writers that is appropriately titled *Seven*.

## BACKGROUND TO MODERN APOLOGETICS

I am indebted to many studies for helping me understand the Enlightenment split that has separated reason from emotion, facts from values, science from religion, and public from private. In addition to Lewis's *Abolition of Man*, the following three books have exerted a strong influence: Alisdair MacIntyre's *After Virtue*, second edition (University of Notre Dame Press, 1984), Mark Noll's *The Scandal of the Evangelical Mind* (Eerdmans, 1994), and Lesslie Newbigin's *Foolishness to the Greeks: The Gospel and Western Culture* (Eerdmans, 1986).

However, the writer who has most profoundly affected my view of the breakdown of reason and faith is Francis Schaeffer.

Apologetics Trilogy: *\*The God Who Is There* (IVP, 1968), *Escape from Reason* (IVP, 1968), and *He Is There and He Is Not Silent* (Tyndale, 1985). In this incisive, if not always accurate, overview of intellectual history, Schaeffer shows how the West has sacrificed its once-unified field of knowledge and made a sharp dichotomy between an objective, mechanistic downstairs reality, in which reason and facts operate but man loses his freedom, and a subjective, mystical upstairs where there is freedom and beauty but no logical categories or binding rational structure.

Schaeffer, Francis. *Genesis in Space and Time*. IVP, 1972. Though the focus here is more on biblical analysis than on apologetics, Schaeffer's defense of the space-time reality of Genesis 1–11 has much to say on the nature of creation and the fall.

Schaeffer, Francis. *A Christian Manifesto*. Crossway, 1981. Though this is more a political call for action than a work of apologetics, its contrast of the Judeo-Christian and secular humanist worldviews is highly relevant to apologetics.

Rookmaaker, H. R. *Modern Art and the Death of a Culture*. IVP, 1970. Written by a disciple of Schaeffer's, this work traces how modern art grew more and more radically abstract and subjective and by so doing lost its previous ability to integrate upstairs and downstairs.

## GENERAL STUDIES OF APOLOGETICS

*Boot, Joe. *Searching for Truth: Discovering the Meaning and Purpose of Life*. Crossway, 2002. A very good all-around apologetics book that condenses what lots of other books have done over the years. It is very readable throughout with good illustrations from everyday life and a few from philosophers and is aimed at the layman who does not have lots of previous knowledge. Boot quotes Lewis extensively and is in his tradition of explaining things to the modern man in a way that he can understand. He also quotes Pascal frequently, a helpful reminder that Pascal was in many ways the first modern apologist.

Colson, Charles (with Nancy Pearcey). *How Now Shall We Live?* Tyndale, 1999. An apologetics book that also looks carefully at competing worldviews. It offers, in particular, a good treatment of the problem of evil. Pearcey began as Colson's protégé but has since moved into her own writing career. Her book *Total Truth: Liberating Christianity from Its Cultural Captivity* (Crossway, 2004) carries on the mixture of apologetics and worldview analysis. Both have been influenced by Lewis and Schaeffer.

Cowan, Steven B. (editor). *Five Views on Apologetics*. Zondervan, 2000. This helpful book written by five different top-notch apologists compares and contrasts different methods of apologetics, in particular presuppositionalism and evidentialism.

*Craig, William Lane. *Reasonable Faith: Christian Truth and Apologetics*, second edition. Crossway, 1994. A standard work by a top-notch apologist that helped throw down the gauntlet before a modern world that had dismissed Christianity as only a matter of faith and emotion. It also helped steer apologists toward fighting not just for Christianity but for the Christian worldview. The first edition of this book appeared in 1984 (Moody Press); a third edition appeared in 2008 (Crossway).

*Craig, William Lane, and Chad Meister (editors). *God Is Great, God Is Good: Why Believing in God Is Reasonable and Responsible*. IVP, 2009. In this masterful collection, Craig and Meister bring together over a dozen cutting-edge apologetic essays that attest powerfully to the massive and growing weight of evidence in favor of theism in general and Christianity in particular. In one way or another, all of the essays respond to the charges laid down by the new atheists (especially Richard Dawkins), but this is by no means a defensive or polemical book. The writers are both genial and unapologetic in their apologies for faith and never sink to the kind of personal attacks, circular reasoning, and special pleading engaged in by the new atheists They set a high bar for reasonable and responsible discourse, and they live up to it. One of the most unique and helpful aspects of the collection is that Craig and Meister have brought under one cover apologists who work in academia but have also written more popular works (Michael Behe, Alister McGrath, J. P. Moreland, Gary Habermas, Jerry Walls, Mark Mittelberg, and John Polkinghorne) and apologists who are less known outside of academia but who should be better known (Paul Copan, Scot McKnight, Paul Moser, Michael Murray, Charles Taliaferro, and Alvin Plantinga).

Geisler, Norman L. *Baker Encyclopedia of Christian Apologetics*. Baker Books, 1999. A standard guide by one of the foremost modern apologists.

Geisler, Norman L. *Christian Apologetics*. Baker, 1988. A standard apologetics textbook that begins by surveying methodologies before mounting its defense.

*Geisler, Norman L., and Chad Meister. (editors). *Reasons for Faith: Making a Case for the Christian Faith*. Crossway, 2007. An excellent collection of essays that not only presents the expected arguments in favor of God and the Incarnate Christ but branches out to consider the claims of growing world religious movements like Mormonism and the Jehovah's Witnesses and to ponder what exactly apologetics *is* and what it should be. It also includes a section on cultural and theological issues within apologetics to which I contributed an essay titled "Aslan in the Public Square."

Geisler, Norman L., and Ravi Zacharias. *Who Made God? And Answers to Over 100 Other Tough Questions of Faith*. Zondervan, 2003. Edited by two excellent apologists, and including the work of several other top-notch apologists (including Lee Strobel), this book not only discusses the expected issues of God, Christ, and the authority of Scripture but looks closely at other religions as well.

*Keller, Timothy. *The Reason for God: Belief in an Age of Skepticism*. Dutton, 2008. Arguably the best apologetics book of the new century, this powerful study synthesizes most of the strongest arguments for Christian faith. Keller devotes the first part of his book to answering the toughest challenges to faith (the problem of pain, the existence of hell, the exclusivity of the claims of Christianity, etc.) and the second half to making his own case for the truth of Christ and the gospel. He boldly answers the critiques of the new atheists and posits Christianity as the world's only hope for achieving peace. This book will challenge Christians, seekers, and atheists alike!

*Kreeft, Peter. *Between Heaven and Hell*. IVP, 1982. This unique and memorable work of apologetics offers a Socratic dialogue between Lewis, Aldous Huxley, and John F. Kennedy—all of whom died on the same day—in which the various merits of orthodox Christianity, pantheism, and humanism are compared and contrasted. A delightful read. Kreeft has also written several Lewis-like meditations on heaven and the desire for heaven, most notably *Heaven: The Heart's Deepest Longing* (Ignatius, 1989).

Kreeft, Peter, and Ronald Tacelli. *Handbook of Christian Apologetics*. IVP, 1994. A very helpful resource for the modern apologist.

*Little, Paul E. *Know Why You Believe*. IVP, 1968. A classic work of apologetics that, along with McDowell's *More Than a Carpenter*, helped bring apologetics to college campuses. In addition to defending the authenticity of the Bible and miracles and answering questions raised by the problem of pain, science, and other religions, it argues both that Christianity is rational and that Christian experience is valid.

McDowell, Josh, and Don Stewart. *Answers to Tough Questions Skeptics Ask about the Christian Faith*. Tyndale, 1986. A helpful apologetics primer that addresses questions related to the Bible, the nature of God and Christ, miracles, and the differences between Christianity and other world religions. In the same year, these two authors published with Tyndale a second apologetics primer titled *Reasons Skeptics Should Consider Christianity*. It addresses further questions related to the Bible and to evolution.

McGrath, Alister E. *Intellectuals Don't Need God and Other Modern Myths: Building Bridges to Faith through Apologetics*. Zondervan, 1993. I think the title pretty much explains what this one is about! What it does not convey, however, is the attempt McGrath makes to show that reason is not the only way to bring people to faith. McGrath has written another fine work that, in many ways, expands on Lewis's argument by desire: *The Unknown God: Searching for Spiritual Fulfillment* (Eerdmans, 1999).

McGrath, Alister E. *Understanding Doctrine*. Zondervan, 1990. Though slanted more toward theology than apologetics, this book gives a needed defense of the centrality of doctrine to Christianity and closes with a close analysis of the doctrines of the Trinity, the incarnation, and the atonement.

*Samples, Kenneth Richard. *Without a Doubt: Answering the 20 Toughest Faith Questions*. Baker, 2004. Samples's twenty tightly organized chapters are broken into three parts that take the reader from general questions about the nature of God and revelation to more specific questions about the nature and role of Jesus Christ to more pragmatic questions about how the Christian faith is to be lived out in the world. Though slanted slightly toward Reformed doctrine, the book nevertheless does a fair job of restating the historic Christian faith, including a good discussion of the Trinity and a helpful expansion of Lewis's trilemma.

Sire, James. *Why Good Arguments Often Fail: Making a More Persuasive Case for Christ*. IVP, 2006. A sort of compendium of Sire's work, this book gives a good overview of logical fallacies, lists the many reasons (many having nothing to do with logic) that people reject a sound presentation of Christianity, and helpfully counsels the would-be apologist to avoid arrogance, aggression, and cleverness. Though ultimately more focused on evangelism than apologetics, this book is worth purchasing for its extensive bibliographical essay. In it Sire surveys the major areas of apologetics—Jesus' claims and his miracles, the existence of God, the problem of pain, the reliability of the Scriptures, and so forth—and discusses the best and most accessible books written in each area.

Sproul, R. C. *Defending Your Faith: An Introduction to Apologetics.* Crossway, 2003. This book doesn't cover much, but what it does cover it does so in depth and with copious explanation. Basically Sproul describes the foundational tenets of logic and several of the classic arguments for the existence of God.

Sproul, R. C. *Reason to Believe.* Lamplighter Books, 1991. A standard work by a fine apologist and preacher.

*Stott, John R. W. *Basic Christianity.* IVP, 1958. Written in the tradition of *Mere Christianity,* this classic and very readable work of apologetics by an Anglican pastor helps the modern reader understand exactly what Christ claimed about himself and how his death and resurrection substantiated those claims. He also explains both the fact and the consequences of our sinful nature and how it necessitated Christ's sacrificial death. In keeping with his pastoral ministry, Stott ends his book by exhorting us to count the cost of discipleship.

*Wright, N. T. *Simply Christian: Why Christianity Makes Sense.* HarperCollins, 2006. Just as C. S. Lewis began his apologetics primer, *Mere Christianity,* by arguing that our intuitive sense of the moral law points toward a supernatural Director of that law, so N. T. Wright, in his similarly titled *Simply Christian,* begins his apologetic work by arguing that our inbred yearnings for justice, spirituality, relationship, and beauty point beyond our world to a Creator. Like Lewis, Wright goes on from there to lay out basic Christian theology and practice without narrowing himself to a single denominational focus, even refusing, à la Lewis, to put forth a single normative understanding of the atonement.

Zacharias, Ravi. *Can Man Live without God?* Thomas Nelson, 1994. Zacharias mounts a spirited and logical defense of Christianity that looks as well at the consequences of belief in or rejection of God.

## ARGUMENTS FOR THE EXISTENCE OF GOD

*Craig, William Lane, and Walter Sinnott-Armstrong. *God? A Debate between a Christian and an Atheist.* Oxford University Press, 2004. Craig, one of the finest living apologists and a good bridge between the popular and academic manifestations of apologetics, faces off with an atheist as they discuss the reasons to believe (and not believe) in God. Well worth reading.

*Flew, Antony (with Roy Abraham Varghese). *There Is a God: How the World's Most Notorious Atheist Changed His Mind.* HarperCollins, 2007. The 2004 announcement sent shock waves through the corridors of the academy: famed British philosopher and atheist Antony Flew has renounced his earlier position and now believes in the existence of God! Flew's book, written with absolute clarity in a direct, measured style that renders arcane philosophical arguments both clear and relevant, documents his journey from atheism to theism. From the very beginning of his book, Flew insists that his lifelong goal as a philosopher and as a man of intellectual integrity has been to live out Socrates' exhortation to "follow the argument wherever it leads." In this book he does just that. The book also includes two appendices that I found particularly helpful: in appendix A, Roy Abraham Varghese critiques the new atheists; in appendix B, N. T. Wright very helpfully sums up his main arguments in defense of the historical accuracy of the Resurrection.

Geisler, Norman, and Frank Turek. *I Don't Have Enough Faith to Be an Atheist.* Crossway, 2004. An accessible and well-put-together book that surveys various types of evidence that all point to the existence of God.

Glynn, Patrick. *God: The Evidence.* Forum, 1997. A good, though fairly general defense of God written by a former atheist.

Habermas, Gary, and J. P. Moreland. *Beyond Death: Exploring the Evidence for Immortality.* Crossway, 1998. Two excellent apologists take up an issue of importance not only to Christians but to nearly all people of faith.

Metaxas, Eric. *Everything You Always Wanted to Know about God (but Were Afraid to Ask).* Waterbrook Press, 2005. If you like your apologetics wrapped up with some clever and incisive New York–style wit, then this is the book for you. A fun read but one that also addresses seriously many of the obstacles to faith. It was followed, perhaps inevitably, by a sequel, *Everything Else You Always Wanted to Know about God* (2007).

Moreland, J. P. *Scaling the Secular City: A Defense of Christianity.* Baker, 1987. A classic work of apologetics that offers a number of proofs of the existence of God. A bit harder than Strobel or McDowell but still more accessible than most academic treatments.

Morris, Thomas V. *The Logic of God Incarnate.* Cornell University Press, 1986. A challenging work but one that is still accessible to nonacademics. It argues for the philosophical integrity of the central claim of Christianity. Morris has also edited a good reader that lies on the border of the academic and the popular: *God and the Philosophers: The Reconciliation of Faith and Reason* (Oxford University Press, 1996).

## THE PROBLEM OF PAIN AND THE RESURRECTION

*Habermas, Gary R., and Michael R. Licona. *The Case for the Resurrection of Jesus.* Kregel, 2004. This book offers an exhaustive defense of the historical reliability of the Resurrection that is as logically sound as it is rhetorically effective. Like two expert lawyers, Habermas and Licona construct an airtight case into which any skeptic would be hard-pressed to poke a hole. Though Habermas and Licona admit that much of their case rests on information found in the New Testament, they make it clear that one need not believe in the inerrancy, or even inspiration, of the Bible to accept the historical validity of their case. The book is richly informed by a wealth of scholarly research—not only from the field of biblical studies but from literature, anthropology, psychology, history, and the sciences—but most of this scholarship is confined to the notes, thus allowing the main narrative of the book to flow effortlessly from argument to argument. Arguably the best and most comprehensive book on the subject.

*Kreeft, Peter. *Making Sense Out of Suffering*. Servant, 1986. One of the finest studies of the problem of pain and a worthy successor to Lewis's book on the subject.

*Morison, Frank. *Who Moved the Stone?* Zondervan, 1958. First published in 1930, this classic work of apologetics was written by an English journalist who set out to disprove the resurrection and ended up believing it himself. The book actually discusses not only the resurrection itself but Jesus' trial and crucifixion. A seminal work in the history of modern apologetics.

*Plantinga, Alvin. *God, Freedom, and Evil*. Harper & Row, 1974. In my book and in this bibliography I have avoided works that are purely academic in nature and that will be mostly inaccessible to lay readers. Still, I feel compelled to include this book by a man who is not only considered one of the foremost living philosophers but who has made great strides in making theism "respectable" again in the secular academy. This brief work, in which Plantinga seeks to solve the problem of pain, is probably his most accessible.

*Strobel, Lee. *The Case for Faith*. Zondervan, 2000. Strobel's follow-up to *The Case for Christ* is just as good as the first. This time he takes up some of the major stumbling blocks that keep people away from faith, including the problem of pain, the exclusivity of the Christian gospel, and the doctrine of hell.

Wright, N. T. *The Resurrection of the Son of God*. Augsburg Fortress Press, 2003. Volume 3 in Wright's *Christian Origins and the Question of God*, this is one of the most original and thoughtful defenses of the resurrection to date. He helpfully sums up the arguments of this very long book in the appendix he contributed to Antony Flew's *There Is a God*.

Yancey, Philip. *Where Is God When It Hurts?* Zondervan, 1990. Though more pastoral than apologetic, this book offers some deep reflections on the problem of pain. The early chapters offer a meditation on physical pain that helps readers understand that pain, inasmuch as it protects our body from degeneration, is a blessing (something Yancey learned from missionary doctor Paul Brand). As always, Yancey brings a fresh perspective to the topic and a unique wrestling with Scripture that helps the reader think again about what the Old Testament prophets, the book of Job, and the Gospels have to teach us about pain.

## THE HISTORICAL RELIABILITY OF THE BIBLE AND THE CLAIMS OF CHRIST

Archer, Gleason L. *Encyclopedia of Bible Difficulties*. Zondervan, 1982. A good source for those who struggle with the apparent contradictions in the Bible.

Bauckham, Richard. *Jesus and the Eyewitnesses: The Gospels as Eyewitness Testimony*. Eerdmans, 2008. One of the most recent scholarly books to argue convincingly that the Gospels are based on eyewitness accounts. This book, and others like it, are proof that the central scholarly consensus is moving away from the Jesus Seminar and toward an acceptance of the essential reliability of the Gospels.

Bloomberg, Craig. *The Historical Reliability of the Gospels*. IVP, 1987. A seminal study of the topic.

Bock, Darrell L. *Breaking the Da Vinci Code*. Thomas Nelson, 2004. A good resource for seeing through the historical inaccuracies of the novel.

Borg, Marcus J., and N. T. Wright. *The Meaning of Jesus: Two Visions*. HarperSanFrancisco, 1989. Borg, a liberal theologian and one of the leaders of the Jesus Seminar, and N. T. Wright, an orthodox Anglican priest, engage in a thrilling debate on the nature of the historical Jesus. Their debate includes such topics as the claims of Christ and his birth, death, and resurrection. A good resource for understanding both sides of the debate, but it does have one flaw: rather than defend a traditional reading of Jesus and the Gospels, Wright, while remaining within the circle of orthodoxy, is too insistent on offering us his own, often idiosyncratic reading of things.

Bowman, Robert M., and J. Komoszewski. *Putting Jesus in His Place: The Case for the Deity of Christ*. Kregel, 2007. Striking a balance between academic scholarship and popular presentation, this book upholds the deity of Christ by arguing that Jesus shared, among other things, the attributes, names, and deeds of God.

Boyd, Gregory A. *Cynic, Sage or Son of God? Recovering the Real Jesus in an Age of Revisionist Replies*. Bridgepoint, 1995. A forceful reply to the Jesus Seminar by a fine and accessible Christian writer.

*Bruce, F. F. *The New Testament Documents: Are They Reliable?* IVP, 1973. One of the classic defenses of the reliability of the New Testament by a noted scholar. Bruce later published *The Defense of the Gospel in the New Testament* (Eerdmans, 1977, revised edition), which considers how the early Christians clung to the gospel as they defended the purity of the faith against pagan, Roman, and Gnostic forces.

*Edwards, James R. *Is Jesus the Only Savior?* Eerdmans, 2005. Edwards has written just the right book to speak to those in the Church who find it hard, if not impossible, to reconcile their faith in One who claimed to be the only-begotten Son of God with their (often unconscious) cultural commitment to relativism, pluralism, and multiculturalism. He has also written a book that will speak to skeptics and seekers who are drawn to Christ but who feel that they cannot, in this day and age, embrace a Savior (or at least a church) who claims to be the exclusive mediator between God and man. Edwards is particularly adept at laying bare the antisupernatural assumptions that have fueled the last three searches for the "historical" Jesus.

*Geisler, Norman L., and Thomas Howe. *When Critics Ask: A Popular Handbook on Bible Difficulties*. Baker Books, 1992. If you are tired of hearing people claim that the Bible is "full of contradictions" or have started believing this tired cliché yourself, then this is a book you must read. It gives answers to over eight hundred supposed contradictions and, in so doing, defends the accuracy and reliability of the Bible.

Habermas, Gary. *The Historical Jesus*. College Press, 1996. A fine defense of the historicity of the Jesus of the Gospels that is both well-documented and scholarly. Readers of this book may also wish to consult his *The Verdict of History* (Thomas Nelson, 1988).

Hanegraff, Hank, and Paul L. Maier. *The Da Vinci Code: Fact or Fiction?* Tyndale, 2004. A good resource. Hanegraff is known informally as the "Bible answer man" and edits an excellent apologetics magazine, *Christian Research Journal* (CRJ).

Hurtado, Larry. *Lord Jesus Christ: Devotion to Jesus in Earliest Christianity*. Eerdmans, 2005. A carefully researched, scholarly work that argues that the earliest Christians looked upon Jesus as divine. Offers an important rebuttal to the Jesus Seminar and to other liberal theologians who see belief in the deity of Christ as a later, mythic accretion.

Johnson, Luke Timothy. *The Real Jesus*. HarperSanFrancisco, 1996. Though written by a fine academic scholar, this excellent defense of the historical Jesus of faith is accessible to the lay reader.

Markos, Louis. "An Open Letter to Lovers of *The Da Vinci Code*." *Saint Austin Review* 7, no. 6 (November/December 2007): 27–30. This essay expands on the argument I make in the second half of Chapter 20—namely, that *The Da Vinci Code* appeals to three deep, inner desires that are better answered and fulfilled by Christianity than by Gnosticism.

McDowell, Josh. *The Da Vinci Code: A Quest for Answers*. Green Key Books, 2006. A brief but well-documented response to the wild claims of the novel by an apologist who is still going strong!

*McDowell, Josh. *More Than a Carpenter*. Tyndale, 1977. This brief work of popular apologetics is a classic in its field—there are more than ten million copies in print—and inspired countless imitations. Another brief book along the same lines was written by the longtime leader of Campus Crusade for Christ (an organization strongly identified with McDowell),

Bill Bright: *A Man without Equal: Jesus, the Man Who Changed the World*. New Life 2000, 1992.

*McDowell, Josh. *The New Evidence That Demands a Verdict: Fully Updated to Answer the Questions Challenging Christians Today*. Thomas Nelson, 1999. This is the most updated incarnation of McDowell's classic two-volume study, *Evidence That Demands a Verdict* (first published in the 1970s). Though not an exciting read in terms of style and transition, this study lays out in outline format the massive evidence in favor of the historical accuracy of Scripture and of Christ's having fulfilled the Old Testament prophecies of the Messiah. A very good resource to have on your shelf.

*Strobel, Lee. *The Case for Christ*. Zondervan, 1998. Strobel's first major success, this is a must-read that revolutionized the world of apologetics and gave it a fresh and appealing face. Strobel's book is broken into three major divisions that take up the historical reliability of the Gospels, the claims of Jesus to be the Son of God, and the evidence for the Resurrection. This third part has also been published separately as *The Case for Easter*.

Strobel, Lee, and Garry Poole. *Exploring the Da Vinci Code*. Zondervan, 2006. A brief book that explores the issues raised by the novel. Like all Strobel's books, it contains excellent interviews with experts in the field.

Wilkins, Michael, and J. P. Moreland. (editors). *Jesus under Fire: Modern Scholarship Reinvents the Historical Jesus*. Zondervan, 1995, This book collects the mounting scholarly evidence in favor of the historicity of the Gospels and of Christ.

Wright, N. T. *Jesus and the Victory of God*. Augsburg Fortress Press, 1997. Volume 2 in Wright's *Christian Origins and the Question of God*, this offers Wright's carefully researched and well-presented defense of the historical Jesus.

Wright, N. T. *Who Was Jesus?* Eerdmans, 1992. A brief and accessible book in which Wright defends the historicity of the Gospel accounts from such critics as A. N. Wilson and John Shelby Spong. Wright does a particularly fine job of explaining the new worldview ushered in by the Resurrection, of defending the Gospels as reliable biographies, and of demonstrating that Jesus' claims to deity did not contradict the true Old Testament understanding of monotheism.

## CHRISTIANITY AND SCIENCE

*Allen, Lad (director). *Unlocking the Mystery of Life: The Scientific Case for Intelligent Design* (DVD, 2002). This excellent documentary, produced by Illustra Media, presents some of the strongest scientific evidence for intelligent design. It is well worth viewing. Illustra Media made a second documentary also worth viewing titled *The Privileged Planet*, which boasts narration by actor John Rhys-Davies. The two can be purchased together from amazon.com.

*Behe, Michael J. *Darwin's Black Box: The Biochemical Challenge to Evolution.* The Free Press, 1996. If Johnson's *Darwin on Trial* sparked off intelligent design, Behe's book gave it its first great scientific classic. Behe argues on the basis of irreducible complexity that the slow gradual changes of Darwinian natural selection cannot account for the existence of complex biological "machines" like the bacterial flagellum.

*Collins, Francis. *The Language of God: A Scientist Presents Evidence for Belief.* Free Press, 2006. What makes Collins's book unique—almost sui generis—is that, in keeping with its provocative subtitle, it weaves together, almost seamlessly, scientific speculation and Christian apologetics. And it does so via the medium of Collins himself, whose intensely readable book is really an extended testimony of how a former atheist became a Christian and was led by God to use his prodigious gifts for research to head the Human Genome Project. As an apologist for the faith and a mediator between science and religion Collins succeeds brilliantly, but his reluctance to question in any way the reigning orthodoxies of Darwinian evolution limits the potential impact of his book. Although eager to see the hand of God in the big bang and the anthropic principle, Collins quickly loses his eagerness when the focus shifts from physics and cosmology to biology and chemistry. Still, this is a must-read for those interested in the interaction between science and religious belief.

*Dembski, William A. *The Design Inference: Eliminating Chance through Small Probabilities.* Cambridge University Press, 1998. Along with Johnson's *Darwin on Trial* and Behe's *Darwin's Black Box*, this book marks the third foundational text of the intelligent design movement. In it, Dembski first lays out his design inference, a "filter" that allows researchers to determine whether a given structure or phenomenon is random or designed. His *The Design Revolution: Asking the Toughest Questions about Intelligent Design* (IVP) followed in 2004. It too merits an asterisk.

Dembski, William A. *Intelligent Design: The Bridge between Science and Religion.* IVP, 1999. Another seminal work by Dembski that includes a look at how God's "divine finger" is recognizable in Scripture and in miracles.

Dembski, William A., and James M. Kushiner (editors). *Signs of Intelligence: Understanding Intelligent Design.* Brazos Press, 2001. An excellent reader that features a number of well-written essays.

*Frankowski, Nathan (director). *Expelled: No Intelligence Allowed* (DVD, 2008). In this playful but very pointed documentary, Ben Stein exposes the strong-arm tactics used by the scientific establishment—and their accomplices in the media and other watchdog groups—to crush and/or humiliate the work of intelligent design theorists. Three things make Stein's documentary unique: 1) he himself is not a Christian, and about half the people he interviews to substantiate Darwinian censorship within the scientific community are not Christians, thus expelling the false stereotype that all people who disagree with Darwinism are "fundamentalists"; 2) Stein, who is Jewish, reveals the strong influence that Darwinism had on Hitler and the Holocaust, as well as on twentieth-century eugenics; 3) Stein engages in a face-to-face debate with Richard Dawkins (author of *The God Delusion*), during which Dawkins actually suggests that our DNA was seeded by aliens—a startling admission that the complexity of our DNA suggests the need for some form of intelligent design (in this case, "natural" rather than supernatural intelligence).

*Heeren, Fred. *Show Me God: What the Message from Space Is Telling Us about God*. Searchlight Publications, 1995. I think this book offers the best overview of the many scientific discoveries that led up to the almost universally accepted theory of the big bang. Readers should be warned that Heeren has a very quirky sense of humor that will delight some and distract others, and he has a slight tendency to go beyond the scientific facts at times. Still, this is a book that is both highly entertaining and carefully researched and presented. It also includes an appendix that surveys fifty key scientists who were both orthodox believers and path-breakers in the development of science. The appendix itself is worth the price of the book.

Hunter, Cornelius G. *Science's Blind Spot: The Unseen Religion of Scientific Naturalism*. Brazos Press, 2007. Though he is not part of the "inner circle" of intelligent design, Hunter raises issues in this book that complement the work of Johnson, Behe, and Dembski. His main task is to expose the philosophical and theological worldview that underlies scientific naturalism. His is a voice that needs to be heard in the debate.

*Johnson, Phillip E. *Darwin on Trial*, revised edition. IVP, 1993. This is the book that really kicked off the intelligent design movement; if you only have time to read one book on the subject, this is the one to read. Johnson exposes both the numerous weaknesses in Darwinism and the near irrationality of those who continue to defend it in the face of the mounting evidence against it. By questioning orthodoxies essential to modernism, Johnson has ruffled many academic feathers and has even provoked the ire of many of his fellow believers. Johnson has written many other books on the subject, all of which have value. I would strongly suggest *The Wedge of Truth: Splitting the Foundations of Naturalism* (IVP, 2000) for its incisive analysis of the widespread influence of naturalism.

Miller, Kenneth R. *Finding Darwin's God: A Scientist's Search for Common Ground between God and Evolution*. HarperCollins, 1999. If you are interested in theistic evolution (which allows God direct play in the big bang but leaves almost all the rest to natural selection and other evolutionary forces), this is probably the best book available. It is strongly dismissive of intelligent design and stays firmly within the Darwinian "camp," but it does thankfully try to live up to its subtitle. For a collection of essays by Christians who are quite open about their faith but still cleave closely to Darwin, see *Perspectives on an Evolving Creation*, edited by Keith B. Miller (Eerdmans, 2003). Finally, if you are interested in reading a debate between theistic evolution, young earth creationism, and old earth creationism (essentially intelligent design), consult *Three Views on Creation and Evolution*, J. P. Moreland and John Mark Reynolds (editors) (Zondervan, 1999).

Polkinghorne, John. *Belief in God in an Age of Science*. Yale University Press, 1998. With high credentials as both a theoretical physicist and a theologian, Polkinghorne is a great voice for moderation in the science/religion debate, a voice that has gained much respect in the secular world and in academia. In terms of his views, I would put him somewhere between Kenneth R. Miller and Francis Collins.

Poythress, Vern S. *Redeeming Science: A God-centered Approach*. Crossway, 2006. Written more directly to believers and taking a firmer Reformed stance than most of the other books listed in this bibliography, Poythress offers a slightly different approach to intelligent design and the harmonization of science and faith.

Ross, Hugh. *The Creator and the Cosmos: How the Latest Scientific Discoveries of the Century Reveal God*. NavPress, 1993. Ross, an astrophysicist, has written a number of books about how modern science not only points toward the God of the Bible but also helps us understand things about the nature of the Creator. This one is probably his best; it is written in lay terms and offers an exciting overview of the links between science and faith.

Stannard, Russell (editor). *God for the 21st Century*. Templeton Foundation Press, 2000. A helpful reader on the interrelationship between science and religion. What is nice about this collection is that all of the essays are very brief, allowing us to hear from fifty different key thinkers.

*Strobel, Lee. *The Case for a Creator*. Zondervan, 2004. In the space of a single book, Strobel covers with sufficient depth all the main arguments for the existence of an eternal, personal Creator that have been granted to us by advances in physics, cosmology, astronomy, biology, biochemistry, and a host of other sciences. He also factors in his own personal odyssey toward faith, confessing that his early acceptance of atheism was spurred primarily by his belief that Darwinian evolution had been decisively proven and was an incontestable fact. This is the best and most readable book available on the subject of how modern science has offered more proofs in favor of God's existence than against it.

Wells, Jonathan. *Icons of Evolution: Why Much of What We Teach about Evolution Is Wrong*. Regnery, 2002. A major study within the intelligent design movement that helps expose the icons (or, better, idols) that have made Darwinism a part of the modern mind.

Wells, Jonathan. *The Politically Incorrect Guide to Darwinism and Intelligent Design*. Regnery, 2006. Despite the silly series title, this offers an excellent review of the major arguments put forth by intelligent design that is written by one of its main defenders. It is very accessible and makes for both a fun and informative read.

Woodward, Thomas. *Doubts about Darwin*. Baker Books, 2003. The definitive history of the intelligent design movement. It was followed in 2006 by *Darwin Strikes Back*, a sequel that not only continues the history but documents the increasingly paranoid responses of Darwinists and the great lengths to which they will go to crush intelligent design.

## NEW ATHEISM AND OTHER RELIGIONS

*Bock, Darrell L., and Mitch Glaser (editors). *To the Jew First: The Case for Jewish Evangelism in Scripture and History*. Kregel, 2008. This collection of essays written both by Gentile Christians and Jewish believers in Jesus (Messianic Jews) issues a powerful and biblically convincing wake-up call to a church that has, in great part, abdicated its responsibility to evangelize the Jews. The essays, all of which balance eschatological urgency with sensitivity to post-Holocaust realities and top-notch scholarship with a high degree of lucidity, present a compelling case for abandoning supersessionism (the belief that Israel has been completely "replaced" by the church) and for returning to the practice and theology of the early apostles, as evidenced in Acts and Romans: "to the Jews first and also to the Greek." A must-read for anyone interested in Jewish-Gentile relations.

*Dawkins, Richard. *The God Delusion*. Houghton Mifflin, 2006. Arguably the key book of the new atheists, written by a popularizer of science (in the Carl Sagan mode) whose earlier *The Selfish Gene* (Oxford University Press, 1976) and *The Blind Watchmaker* (Longman, 1986) inspired similar controversy.

Dennett, Daniel C. *Breaking the Spell: Religion as a Natural Phenomenon*. Viking, 2006. Closer to Dawkins than Harris and Hitchens in his defense of Darwin, Dennett would have his readers treat religion solely in accordance with naturalist methodologies.

*D'Souza, Dinesh. *What's So Great about Christianity*. Regnery, 2007. A spirited, wide-ranging critique of the new atheism that takes up not only science but history, philosophy, morality, evil and suffering, and other religions. D'Souza brings to the more standard apologetic arguments a wider sociopolitical focus that makes his book particularly timely and exciting to read. Though he may at times attribute just a few too many things to Christianity, his bold and confident defense of the church is much needed in a time like our own, when the church continues to receive unfair and historically inaccurate criticism from the academy and the media. Pluses of D'Souza's book are his fresh and intriguing look at the legacy of Kant and Pascal, his exploding of Enlightenment myths about the supposed war of science and religion, and his well-documented argument that atheism, not Christianity, has been responsible for the greatest number of murders in history.

Harris, Sam. *The End of Faith: Religion, Terror and the Future of Reason*. Norton, 2004. One of the new atheists, he is closer to Hitchens than to

Dawkins in approach but more political than either. He followed this book with *Letter to a Christian Nation* (Knopf, 2006).

Hitchens, Christopher. *god is not Great: How Religion Poisons Everything*. Twelve Books, 2007. Hitchens's case against Christianity hails out of the world of journalism rather than science (as does Dawkins's *The God Delusion*) and sees more danger than delusion in it.

McDowell, Josh, and Don Stewart. *Handbook of Today's Religions*, revised edition. Thomas Nelson, 1996. A good resource for contrasting Christianity with other religions.

*McGrath, Alister. *The Twilight of Atheism: The Rise and Fall of Disbelief in the Modern World*. Galilee (Doubleday), 2006. First published in 2004, this book offers a powerful response to the new atheism, even though it came out before Hitchens's *god is not Great* and Dawkins's *The God Delusion*. It argues that atheism (not Christianity) is on its way out and that religion and faith are seeing (and will continue to see) a resurgence around the world. McGrath very helpfully and convincingly shows that the modern embrace of atheism that began with the French Revolution and climaxed in communism has caused great misery. In 2007 McGrath published a book titled *The Dawkins Delusion*.

Newbigin, Lesslie. *The Gospel in a Pluralist Society*. Eerdmans, 1989. Though not a specifically apologetic work, this book, written by a missionary in India, has profoundly influenced apologists (such as Alister McGrath, James Edwards, and Timothy Keller) who struggle to answer critics who accuse Christianity of being antipluralistic, if not downright imperialistic. Part of my analysis, in chapter 19, of the blind men and the elephant goes back to this book.

Rainer, Thom S. *The Unexpected Journey: Conversations with People Who Turned from Other Beliefs to Jesus*. Zondervan, 2005. Though this book is more descriptive and pastoral than apologetic, its well-written interviews with people who have converted to Christianity from other belief systems (both formal religions like Islam, Judaism, and Hinduism, and less traditional "faiths" like New Age astrology and Satanism) help draw out the distinctiveness of faith in Christ.

*Richardson, Don. *Eternity in Their Hearts: Startling Evidence of Belief in the One True God in Hundreds of Cultures throughout the World*, revised edition. Regal Books, 1984. The claim made in this book's long subtitle may sound far-fetched, but Richardson backs it up through his own missionary experience and that of many others. A moving and engrossing work, it offers an entirely new perspective on the way God has worked (and continues to work) through "primitive" tribal groups whose religion may seem at first to be nothing but superstition. In *Peace Child* (newly released in 2007 by YWAM Publications), Richardson focuses on a single New Guinea tribe with which he worked directly and that he felt lacked the ability to understand the Christian gospel—that is, until he witnessed one of their ancient rituals that miraculously pointed to the gospel message.

*Zacharias, Ravi (editor). *Beyond Opinion: Living the Faith That We Defend.* Thomas Nelson, 2007. This unique collection of essays helps its readers not only to distinguish the claims of Christianity from those of postmodernism, Islam, Eastern religions, and science but also to wrestle with the challenges posed to faith by culture and philosophy, doubt and persecution, idolatry and self-deception. It lives up to its subtitle by providing apologetic arguments that have actually been tried and found effective.

Zacharias, Ravi. *The End of Reason: A Response to the New Atheists.* Zondervan, 2008. A passionate and much-needed response to the new atheists (Sam Harris, in particular) from one of the finest living apologists.

Zacharias, Ravi. *Jesus Among Other Gods: The Absolute Claims of the Christian Message.* W Publishing Group, 2000. Zacharias contrasts the claims of Christ with those of the founders of several Eastern religions. A helpful, if "politically incorrect" book that argues forcefully for the uniqueness of Christ and Christianity.

## CHRISTIANITY AND POSTMODERNISM

In many ways postmodern apologetics is an oxymoron, for postmodernism—most exemplified in the Emergent Church movement—tends to downplay reason and logic in favor of emotion, intuition, and mystery. Technically speaking, none of the books listed below are apologetic works, but when taken together they give a good overview of the varied voices of postmodern Christianity and its attempt to engage postmodernism with the gospel. Of the six authors listed below, McLaren is the least orthodox (something that has troubled many Christian apologists, myself included), while Driscoll is the most orthodox. Choung, Eldredge, Miller, and Seay all lie somewhere in between. Another branch of "postmodern apologetics" may be found in the more politically nuanced (even partisan) writings of Tony Campolo, Ron Sider, and Jim Wallis. Rick Warren and Joel Osteen have appealed to the modern/postmodern yearning for purpose and self-help, while Bill Hybels, Rick Richardson, and Garry Poole have shown a powerful ability to reach out to unchurched seekers who want spirituality but are turned off by religion. Most of these writers have been influenced by the work of Lesslie Newbigin and Dallas Willard.

Choung, James. *True Story: A Christianity Worth Believing In.* IVP, 2008. In this very readable book—which belongs more under the rubric of evangelism than apologetics—Choung, a popular Korean-American speaker who directs the San Diego division of InterVarsity Christian Fellowship, lays out a simple (but not simplistic) method for presenting the gospel to modern and postmodern skeptics who resist Christianity because they find it exclusivist, narrow-minded, and irrelevant. Choung uses a series of four circles to describe 1) our world as God originally designed it, 2) the broken world that now exists in the shadow of the Fall, 3) the inner restoration that Christ accomplished through the atonement, and 4) the need for Spirit-filled believers to help build the kingdom by spreading that inner restoration to the world. In true postmodern fashion, most of Choung's book is written in the form of a story about a young man seeking a fuller vision for the gospel.

Driscoll, Mark. *Radical Reformission: Reaching Out without Selling Out.* Zondervan, 2004. Though more a work of evangelism and church formation than apologetics, this energetic and passionate book attempts to find ways to reach the postmodern, if not neo-pagan world that will avoid the extremes of liberalism and fundamentalism, relativism and judgmentalism. It accepts many of the ideals of the Emergent Church while fighting for a stricter adherence to doctrine.

*Eldredge, John. *Epic: Discover the Story God Is Telling.* Thomas Nelson, 2005. This is not a book but a live DVD recording of Eldredge delivering a fascinating lecture in which he retells the sacred narrative of the Bible by comparing it to such works of epic fantasy as Lord of the Rings, The Chronicles of Narnia, the Harry Potter series, and Milton's *Paradise Lost.* To listen to this DVD is to get on the inside of the postmodern yearning for story. Eldredge's lecture has also been published in book form under the same title.

Eldredge, John. *The Journey of Desire: Searching for the Life We've Only Dreamed Of.* Thomas Nelson, 2000. In this and several other books, Eldredge has taken Lewis's argument by desire and run with it. His focus on our inner yearnings for meaning, adventure, and romance has appealed strongly to young postmoderns who seek a more authentic spirituality.

McLaren, Brian. *A New Kind of Christian.* Jossey-Bass, 2001. One of the seminal works in the Emergent Church movement that seeks an apologetic and evangelical approach that relies less on systematic doctrine than on conversation and spirituality. Although this is his "cutting-edge" book, his *Finding Faith: A Self-Discovery Guide for Your Spiritual Quest* (Zondervan, 1999) is a bit more relevant to apologetics.

Miller, Donald. *Blue Like Jazz: Nonreligious Thoughts on Christian Spirituality.* Thomas Nelson, 2003. Though not exactly a work of apologetics, this modern classic that countless twenty-somethings have taken to their hearts finds endlessly clever ways to make the creeds of Christianity relevant to a postmodern age. In many ways Miller follows in the footsteps of Brian McLaren in his attempt to appeal to a new generation who feel confined by an overfocus on doctrine to the exclusion of spiritual experience. *Blue Like Jazz* is often compared to Anne Lamott's *Traveling Mercies.*

Seay, Chris. *The Gospel According to Tony Soprano: An Unauthorized Look into the Soul of TV's Top Mob Boss and His Family.* Thatcher/Putnam, 2002. Seay is the pastor of a postmodern church in Houston, Texas, that like many such churches, not only integrates the visual arts into its services but is adept at making connections to popular culture. This book is representative of the attempt made by postmodern apologists and evangelists to forge links between Christianity and popular culture. *The Gospel Reloaded: Exploring Spirituality and Faith in the Matrix* (cowritten with Greg Garrett) followed in 2003. Seay has also overseen a new translation of the Bible (The Voice) designed specifically to appeal to postmoderns.

## WEB SITES

**www.apologetics.com**

"Apologetics.com exists," says the Web site, "to remove intellectual impediments to Christian faith, thereby enhancing believers' confidence in, and weakening skeptics' objections to, the gospel message." And the Web site lives up to its mission, offering numerous essays and videos on a wide range of apologetic topics.

**www.apologetics.org**

Sponsored by the C. S. Lewis Society and Trinity College of Florida, this Web site is particularly strong on intelligent design.

**http://www.leestrobel.com/**

Lee Strobel's Web site allows visitors to watch for free dozens of videos related to apologetics. A nicely laid-out and easy-to-navigate site.

**www.reasons.org**

According to its founder, Hugh Ross (PhD in astronomy), "The mission of Reasons to Believe is to show that science and faith are, and always will be, allies, not enemies. . . . It is our conviction that since the same God who 'authored' the universe also inspired the writings of the Bible, a consistent message will come through both channels." Though not "technically" an intelligent design theorist, Ross shares their conviction that belief in biblical inerrancy does not necessitate a belief in a young earth or universe.

**www.wheaton.edu/wadecenter**

This is the Web site for the Marion E. Wade Center, housed at Wheaton College. It offers information on and resources for C. S. Lewis, Owen Barfield, G. K. Chesterton, George Macdonald, Dorothy L. Sayers, J. R. R. Tolkien, and Charles Williams.